Samuel Rowles Pattison

The rise and progress of religious life in England

Samuel Rowles Pattison

The rise and progress of religious life in England

ISBN/EAN: 9783337718350

Printed in Europe, USA, Canada, Australia, Japan

Cover: Foto ©Lupo / pixelio.de

More available books at **www.hansebooks.com**

THE RISE AND PROGRESS

OF

RELIGIOUS LIFE IN ENGLAND.

BY

SAMUEL ROWLES PATTISON.

"Among whom ye shine as lights in the world, holding forth the Word of Life."—Philipp. ii. 15, 16.

LONDON:
JACKSON, WALFORD, AND HODDER,
27, PATERNOSTER ROW.

MDCCCLXIV.

"BEYOND THE NARROW SPHERE WITHIN WHICH THE POWER AND ACTIONS OF MAN ARE RESTRAINED, IT IS GOD WHO REIGNS AND ACTS."

GUIZOT.

PREFACE.

Mr. Gladstone says that revealed religion derives its strength "from the fact that it not merely presents to us a body of abstract truths, but carries with it the *executory powers* neccessary to procure their acceptance,—the vital influences without which we cannot receive, digest, and assimilate these truths."* The true history of our religion must, therefore, consist in tracing the working of these powers, and influences, in successive generations of good men. By excluding from this narrative, so far as is practicable, the consideration of all collateral history, it is not intended to deny that secular public events have an

* "The State in its Relations with the Church," p. 292.

influence on the progress of the Kingdom of Christ. But the specific task which I have proposed to myself is, to discover and follow the single line of evangelical doctrine and practice. Doubtless, when larger fields of view shall open upon us, and fuller powers of vision, brighter faculties, and larger hearts shall be given to us, we shall perceive how the whole web of worldly affairs, so tangled in appearance now, has been pervaded by the one beautiful design of Divine mercy.

The Papal Church is constructing a biographical history of enormous dimensions. It is framed on the basis of the Romish calendar, and consists of an exhaustive life of every canonized Saint. All the famous libraries of the world have been laid under contribution in order to its accomplishment. For nearly two hundred years, a succession of learned men have given their lives to the task as a religious duty. The Bollandists, the most diligent and devoted compilers, have given a name to the colossal undertaking. It is still progressing; its steps are measured by decades, and its least utterances are folios. The fresh-looking volume published in 1863 is the continuator of a series of which the first members already bear the venerable hue of past ages.

My aim is vastly more restricted than this, and may well be expressed by the Latin proverb, "*Melius est petere fontes, quam sectari rivulos.*"

ANALYTICAL CONTENTS.

A.D.

CHAPTER I.

Introduction.

CHAPTER II.

The First Planting.

Cimmerian Epoch, 5.
Christianity from the East, 8.
219. Romano-British period, 9.
314. British Bishops, 9.
Pelagius, 9.
Alban, 10.
400. Irish Saints, Patrick, 11.
544. St. David, St. Asaph, 12.
562. Columba, Iona, 12.

A.D.

CHAPTER III.

The Second Planting.

597. Augustine the Monk, 14.
British Church, 15.
Anglo-Saxon Church, 16.
St. Oswald, 16.
Bede, 16.
Anglo-Saxon Bible, 17.
Cædmon, 17.
669. Theodorus, 18.
694. Wilfred, 18.
Kilian, 19.
705. Aldhelm, Offa, 19.
Ælfric, 19.
718. Boniface, 20.
735. Alcuin, 20.
Alfred, 24.
994. Education, 24.

A.D.

Slavery, 25.
Identity of Principles, 27.

CHAPTER IV.

The Normans.

1066. Effects of Conquest, 29.
1092. Anselm, 31.
Character of Church, 32.
Darkest Ages, 33.
1190. Traces of Scriptures, 34.
Ecclesiastical Buildings, 35.
Mediæval Preaching, 35.
Chapels — Haddon-Hall, 36.
St. Bernard, 38.
Hidden Evangelism, 38.
Roman Breviary, 39.
Crusades, 39.
Religious Excitement, 40.
Pre-reformation signs, 40.
Pre-reformation protests, 42.
1158. Obscure Reformers, 42.
Mayors' Chronicles, 42.
Italian and other Reformers, 43.
1087. Berengarius, 43.
Heresy, so called, 44.
1253. Hugh Greathead, 45.
British Monachism, 45.
Convent Life, 47.

A.D.

CHAPTER V.

The Wycliffites.

Bradwardine at Merton, 49.
Richard Fitz Ralph, 50.
Signs of the Dawn, 51.
1362. Piers Plowman, 52.
1370. Wycliffe, 56.
First Tracts, 56.
Chaucer and Gower, 58.
1384. Wycliffe's Missionaries, 59.
Wycliffe's Inner Life, 59.
His Influence, 60.
1399. Queen Anne, 63.

CHAPTER VI.

The Lollards.

1389. Lollardism and Lay Preaching, 65.
1391. Swinderby, Brute, 67.
William Thorpe, 68.
1401. Statute against heresy, 70.
1409. John Badby, 70.
Sir John Oldcastle, 71.
1416. Conventicles, 73.
University of Oxford, 74.
Ploughman's prayer, 75.
Complaint of clergy, 76.
1414. John Claydon, 77.
Spread of the Truth, 77.
1422. Lollards in Scotland, 80.
Ultimate Triumphs, 82.

A.D.		A.D.	
	CHAPTER. VII.		Scripture readers, 108.
			Cambridge and Oxford Students, 112.
	The Course of the Movement.		Becon, 113.
	Mysticism, 84.		The Christian Brotherhood, 113.
	Dramatic Representations, 86.	1526.	Young Men, 113.
	Printed Books, 87.		Garrett and his Friends, 115.
	Character of the Movement, 88.	1531.	Bilney, 117.
1422.	Progress in various places, 89.		Latimer, 119.
	Characteristics, 90.	1538.	Publication of Bible, 120.
	Half-hearted Reformers, 93.		Its reception, 121.
	Tract Literature, 93.	1548.	Rogers's Concordance, 123.
	Model in Scripture, 94.		*Fisher, of Rochester, 124.
			Dean Colet, 125.

CHAPTER VIII.

Reigns of Henry Seventh and Henry Eighth.

CHAPTER IX.

Edward Sixth.

A.D.		A.D.	
1530.	Tracy's Testament, 96.	1548.	Demand for Preachers, 127.
	Witnesses to the Truth, 97.		Itinerant Ministers, 128.
	Practical Treatises, 98.		Hooper and Latimer, 128.
1527.	Tyndale, 98.		Hancock, 129.
	Benet, 102.		Richard Taverner, 130.
1529.	John Tewkesbury, 103.		Dramatic Representations, 131.
	Bainham and Bayfield, 104.		Miles Coverdale, 131.
	Harding and Wife, 104.		Dr. W. Turner, 131.
	Colchester Brethren, 105.		Southern Europe, 132.
	Provinces and Registries, 107.		Protestant Teachers, 133.
	Buckinghamshire, 107.		Protestant Emigration, 134.
			The Young King, 134.

xii ANALYTICAL CONTENTS.

A. D.
Sir John Cheke, 135.
Studies of the Higher Classes, 136.
Lady Jane Grey, 137.

CHAPTER X.

The Reign of Queen Mary.

John Bradford, 141.
1555. Private Assemblies, 144.
Thomas Rose, 146.
George Marsh, 148.
1557. Eagles, of Suffolk, 152.
Lawrence and others, 153.
Ridley, 154.
Smithfield Tragedies, 155.
Laurence Saunders, 157.
Perpetuity of Truth, 158.

CHAPTER XI.

The Elizabethan Age.

Religious Language, 160.
Secondary Influences, 160.
Shakspeare, 161.
Lord Bacon and Coke, 163.
Sidney's Family, 166.
Sacred Poetry, 167.
Lecturers, 169.
Coverdale, 170.
Rise of Religious Parties, 171.

A. D.
1583. Origin of Nonconformity, 171.
1590. Rise of Puritanism, 175.
Independency, 175.
Phases of Nonconformity, 176.
Separatists and Baptists, 176.
Prophesyings, 178.
1599. Education, 180.
Outbreak of Nonconformity, 180.
Penry and his Friends, 181.
Hooker and Travers, 185.
Municipal Ordinances, 186.
Religious Troubles, 188.
1592. Gatherings of the godly, 188.
Paleario, 189.
Return of Foreign Refugees, 190.

CHAPTER XII.

James First, Charles First.

Editions of Scriptures, 192.
Influence on Literature, 193.
1600. Cambridge Home Mission, 193.
Missions on Mendip-hills, 193.

A.D.
Lord Bacon's testimony, 194.
1613. Purchas, 195.
Mr. Herring, 195.
1620. Baptists at Bristol, 196.
Dr. Harris, 197.
Shakspeare's contemporaries, 197.
Rise of preachers, 199.
Baxter's family, 200.
Sibbes, 201.
Milton's opinions, 201.
Progress of Nonconformity, 202.
John Canne, 203.
John Carter, 204.
Lady Bowes, 205.
1627. Lectures, 205.
Herbert, 205.
Missionary workers, 207.
Woodward, 207.
John Eliot, the Apostle of Indians, 207.
Home missionary spirit, 208.
Rothwell, 209.
Tendency of court, 211.
Lady Apsley, 212.
Usher's preaching, 212.
Early Puritans, 213.
Lady Falkland, 214.
1633. Henry Jessey, 215.
Pilgrim Fathers, 217.
Smart, of Durham, 217.
Character of the age, 219.

A.D.
CHAPTER XIII.
The Commonwealth.
Increase of personal religion, 220.
Dr. Owen, 221.
1643. Westminster Assembly, 223.
Cromwell's Soldiers, 224.
Mrs. Hutchinson, 225.
1650. Cromwell's Letters, 226.
His Inner Life, 227.
1653. Establishment of Religion by Ordinance, 234.
George Fox, 236.
Religious experiences, 237.
Selden and Usher, 239.
Hanserd Knollys, 242.
Kiffin, 243.
Dr. Gouge, 244.
Philip Henry, 244.
Mr. Blackerby, 245.
Experiences, 247.
John Rogers,
Usher,
Puritan Literature, 246.
The "Friends," 247.
Establishment of Dissent, 251.

CHAPTER XIV.
The Reigns of Charles Second, James Second, and William Third.
1660. Effects of the Restoration, 253.

xiv ANALYTICAL CONTENTS.

A.D.

1661. Savoy Conference, 254.
Course of Legislation, 254.
Howe, 255.
Bartholomew Act, 258.
Farewell Sermons, 259.
Pursuits of the Ejected, 260.
1662. Hughes, Alleine, 271, 273.
The Henry Family, 269.
Flavel, 267.
Bunyan, 274.
1665. The Plague, 261.
1666. Fire of London, 262.
Baxter's Works, 262.
Mrs. Baxter, 266.
Merchants' Lecture, 257.
1676. Cockermouth, 277.
1692. Ralph Thoresby, 277.
Howe and Spilsbury, 278.
Gouge of St. Sepulchre's, 278.
Wadsworth, of Cambridge, 279.
1695. Young Men's Associations, 279.
1680. Earl of Rochester, 280.
Decay of Piety, 281.
Intercourse with Holland, 282.
Flavel and Alleine, 283.
1682. Guthrie and Traill, 283, 284.
1697. Dr. Horneck, 285.
Matthew Henry, 286.
Decline in standards, 286.

A.D.

CHAPTER XV.

The Eighteenth Century,— First Part.

Contempt for Religion, 291.
Reformation Societies, 291, 292.
Progress of Decay, 293.
1706. Dr. Watts, 295.
1722. Samuel Harvey, 298.
Mr. Barker, 300.
Defoe, 300.
1711. Address for New Churches, 302.
Dr. Doddridge, 303.
Col. Gardiner, 306.
1729. The Wesleys, 308.
The Societies, 311.
Thomas Hanby, 315.
1735. Howel Harris, 316.
Whitefield, 312.
1743. Scottish Revival, 317.
Adam of Winteringham, 318.
The Countess of Huntingdon, 319.
Berridge, 324.
1740. John Nelson, 326.
1741. Deacon and Taylor, 327.
1746. Jonathan Edwards, 328.

CHAPTER XVI.

The Eighteenth Century,— Second Part.

Extent of Prior Decay, 329.
1760. Robert Hall Senior, 330.
1757. Abraham Maddock, 331.
1751. Society for Promoting Christian Knowledge, 333.
1754. Henry Venn, 333.
1775. Edwards the Engineer, 334.
Attempts at alliance, 335.
1767. Revival at University, 335.
The Apostle of Sussex, 336.
Lord Dartmouth, 337.
The Hills, 338.
Toplady, 339.
Ireland, 340.
Religious periodicals, 341.
1764. Cowper, 342.
London Churches, 345.
Booth, 347.
Jones, 347.
Picture of Leicester, 348.
1777. Burder, 348.
1784. Baptist Missions, 349.
1799. Bacon the sculptor, 351.
Wilberforce and his friends, 352.
Simeon, Milner, 35
Wilson, 357.
Romanist Piety, 357.
Signs of the Future, 361.

CHAPTER XVII.

Conclusion, 362.

THE RISE AND PROGRESS

OF

RELIGIOUS LIFE IN ENGLAND.

CHAPTER I.

INTRODUCTION.

CHRISTIANITY on earth is essentially historical. We ourselves are ever comparing that which it is now, with that which it seemed to us to be at the commencement of our career: we read the annals of our country, and find that it has an historical development there; we investigate the unfolding of Western civilization, and discover it as the moving power there; we extend our view to the whole ancient world, and find it to be the greatest fact left to us by the entire past. Inseparably linked to chronology, it gives interest to all time; we are taught to carry our contemplation concerning its course backward amid the unknown successions of primeval things, and forward to the ultimate arrangements which shall stand in perpetual relation to its completion. Its connexion with *place* may be but of fleeting interest, but not so its associations with *time*, for it is the true and only key to the dynasties of all things.

Its history, therefore, is not like that of a sect or school of arts or sciences or philosophy, but it stands unique amidst the forces and facts of the world, availing itself of all the laws of thought and sympathy, yet superior in its origin and supreme in its action.

We cannot account for its prevalence in this country on the ground of its congruity with the desires of mankind, or of its intrinsic power as an institution. It is not a mere product of civilization, or consequence of the social compact; nor did it arise from Latin or barbarian peculiarities of race. It does not owe its success to the Church as a worldly corporation, for when the latter was most powerful the former was in its weakest condition; nor to the state, else the Italian republics would have possessed it in perfection. Its lineage is higher than all these, for its kingdom is not of this world.

"God, who at sundry times and in divers manners spake unto the fathers in time past by the prophets, hath in these last days spoken unto us by His Son:" "that in the dispensation of the fulness of times, he might gather together in one all things in Christ."

But inasmuch as its essence is the personal obedient reception of Divine revelation, its annals can consist of little more than a succession of biographies of individuals who influenced each other by the laws of association, themselves still more influenced by the force derived from a common source of life and truth and love. This renders its delineation difficult, for spirituality ever shuns the light when left to its own free choice; and we know, that of the work of the Holy Spirit, "we hear the sound thereof, but cannot tell whence it cometh or whither it goeth."

The persons, too, who have ever formed the bulk of its votaries, have been unknown to fame, and unskilled in letters.

A cause so potent as to give ultimate shape to all history must, however, have left some waymarks along the highways and byways of Time. To trace these, and try to connect them, by the aid of the very imperfect materials available, may yield us some present instruction. To do it perfectly, will be one of the grateful occupations of heaven.

In England the progress of piety has been a pursuit under difficulties. The truth had to be discerned and selected whilst in fellowship with error; it had to be eliminated in the face of opposition; it had to be won with courage and held with constancy, in spite of successive failures apparently total: and this, too, after many great combatants on its side had sunk in discouragement, though not in despair. After heroic exertions made for many years without either public fame or immediate fruit, it pleased God ultimately to crown the long course of warfare with glorious triumph.

The very failures were consoling; for, unlike the denial of political liberty, the prevention of religious freedom in society, could never hinder its prevalence in the heart of the combatant. Though the victory *were* deferred, yet the individual always won. Even in outward bondage he enjoyed all the immunities of inward emancipation.

The history of religion has been usually depicted in Rembrandt-like style,—all darkness in one part of the field, and all light in another; but Guido's picture of the dawn is a better symbol of the historical reality, for there we see light from the eastern heavens shedding down and becoming diffused over the lower landscape, until the dark shadows lingering over tower and town slowly disperse, and glorious day comes on.

> " O Spirit of the Lord! prepare
>   All the round earth her God to meet;
> Breathe thou abroad like morning air,
>   Till hearts of stone begin to beat.
>
> " Baptize the nations far and nigh;
>   The triumphs of thy Cross record;
> The name of Jesus glorify,
>   Till every kindred call Him Lord."

CHAPTER II.

The First Planting.

A.D. TO A.D. 500.

IN search of a commencement, we must pass over the primordial period of European life, whose scattered flint implements are sole witnesses of the most ancient dwellers: the age of stone monuments, too, characterized by cromlechs and cairn-burials, yields us no response; nor do any of the generations anterior to the Roman invasion echo back a reply grounded on Divine oracles. No relic has come down to us, from those remote distances, to indicate the nature of the religious hopes of the original settlers, or early colonists, of Atlantic Europe. Further researches into the cave-resorts, grave-pits, and battle-fields of our remote forefathers (if such investigation should ever disinter aught save axes and arrow-heads) may bring to light proofs of the prevalence of suffering and of sin, and indications of some recourse to the supernatural. We need not these, however, to assure us of the inevitable wretchedness occasioned by outliving all knowledge of the true God. The records of Holy Scripture prove the rapidity and certainty of human declension, consequent on the abandonment of Divine teaching and the repudiation of Divine guidance. Man, like the prodigal, takes his portion, goes into the far country, and speedily becomes little better than the beasts that perish, save in the fertility of his resources for offence, or in some scanty recognition of higher life, manifested more in superstition than in obedience.

An attempt has been made, or rather renewed, of late years, to deduce from the history of society a *natural law* of progress, and to show that the march of improvement has been an evolution of nature, effected, not by means of, but in spite of, Christianity; and that the latter has greatly contributed to the irregularities and retardations of the natural stream of human advancement.* It is no part of the present undertaking to venture out into the province of the secondary influences of Christianity; but, in dealing with the history of religion, it is impossible for any candid student not to perceive that the whole present civilization of the world is just what Christianity has made it, in spite of obstacles, and that it is by no means the result of inherent social law. The slightest comparison of Christian with Pagan communities, either ancient or modern, will prove the error of those who attribute the advancement of the world to anything save revelation. The closer the comparison is carried on, the more manifest will it become, that conformity to the revealed will of God is the measure of true civilization and human happiness. In resorting to the sources and tracing the course of spiritual life, we are drinking at the

* By the late Mr. Buckle, in his "History of Civilization."

very fountains of social science as it regards man's highest interests.

In the westward march of the wanderers who originally peopled our shores, the degeneracy of their condition had augmented at every step, until, on their arrival here, the last traditions of patriarchal knowledge had died out, and they had become reduced to unmitigated barbarism. They had willingly left, and now totally lost, the light from heaven. They knew not of the special events taking place beyond the Mediterranean, whereby God was preparing for the advent of Him who should be a "light to lighten the Gentiles;" nor of the approach of that auspicious hour, of which it should ever after be sung—

> "This is the month, and this the happy morn,
> Wherein the Son of Heaven's Eternal King,
> Of wedded Maid and Virgin Mother born,
> Our great redemption from above did bring."

The nearest approach to this knowledge, was the indication, which by the observance of the rite of sacrifice they gave, of the need of a propitiation in their approach to God. This appears to be of the essence of all human religions; and as the tradition of a Redeemer lies at the basis of all sacrificial observance, so Christ, though unknown to the worshippers, is the true groundwork of all historical religion. "Of Him, through Him, to Him, are all things!" But our barbarous progenitors knew not the dignity or end of the rites they used, they had lost hope even in religion, and no one had yet come to say to them,—"Whom therefore ye ignorantly worship, Him declare I unto you."

The first Christianity of this country was communicated by an impulse of that wave which, beginning its flow at Jerusalem on the death of the proto-martyr Stephen, passed over Asia Minor, by Macedonia, into Greece; thence to Italy, Africa, Spain, and Gaul; everywhere fertilizing as it flowed. It came to us coloured with some few corruptions which had been thrown into its pure waters in their westward course, but still free from the baneful mixtures which Rome afterwards added to the noble current. The earliest historical relations of British Christianity,—rejecting the hypotheses which would assign its origin to Apostolic preaching,—or to the influence of Claudia, celebrated by the verse of Martial, and possibly the same as is referred to in the Epistle to Timothy,—or to Bran, the father of the patriotic British king Caractacus,—appear to have been with ecclesiastical Gaul, of which Lyons and Vienne were the chief cities.*
From this circumstance, our historians have fondly deduced the pedigree of British Christian doctrine and discipline from Antioch, rather than from Rome; and this conclusion is supported by Neander and by Lappenberg, as well as by our own writers.†

---

* Several of the public museums of France and Germany (for instance, those of Lyons and Mayence) contain a series of inscriptions and antiquities of the Romano-Gauloise epoch, showing the transition from heathenism to Christianity, especially in epitaphs. I am not aware that the collections of Romano-British antiquities contain any distinctively Christian art-relics, though doubtless many such have existed.

† Neander, "Church History," vol. i., p. 30; Lappenberg, vol. i., p. 48; Soames' "Anglo-Saxon Church," p. 41.

There is very little direct evidence on a subject so trivial in the estimation of the Latin writers, as the introduction of the "new superstition" into a part of the world so remote as Britain.

Tertullian's testimony, in the year 219, is, "In whom but in Christ have all nations believed? Parthians, Medes, Elamites, and the inhabitants of Mesopotamia, &c.,—all the borders of Spain, the various nations of Gaul, and those parts of Britain inaccessible to the Roman arms,—are now subdued to Christ."* Eusebius, in the beginning of the fourth century, states that some missionaries of the Gospel had "passed over the ocean to those which are called the British Isles."† Chrysostom and Jerome, both writing in the fourth century, and Theodoret in the fifth, severally affirm that Britain and its people had received the glad tidings of salvation.

The profession of Christianity in Britain, which thus commenced towards the close of the second century, is also attested, first, by the fact that the Diocletian persecution, A.D. 303, extended to these remote parts; next, by the circumstance that three British bishops were present at the Council of Arles, in Provence, A.D. 314; at Sardica in 347; and at Rimini in 359. Its vitality and activity are proved by the existence within its borders of fierce doctrinal disputes, which originated in the teaching of Morgan, usually known as Pelagius. The efforts of the latter were directed to the vain task of reducing into systematic logical consistency, tenets concerning liberty and grace. The existence and extensive prevalence of controversy on this subject shows that even at this period

* Adv. Judæos, vii.   † Evang. Demonst., iii. 7.

the scope of Scripture and the nature of our subjectiveness to its deliverances, were well known. There were many persons who, amidst the din of this and other controversies, effected an escape from the strife of polemics, into the safe hiding-place of communion with God.

We may safely conclude that the faith of the Romano-British believer, who preferred death to apostasy, was of the right New-Testament sort; but we have to draw on imagination only, when we seek to complete the picture, by surrounding the primitive brotherhood with all "the things which accompany salvation." Such, however, is the true nature of the life of God in the soul, that we may well rest satisfied with the conviction, that the measure of it allotted to the soldiers of the Cross at that time, arming them for the higher combats of faith, was also found to yield in daily life the peaceable fruits of righteousness.

Among the 48,000 Roman soldiers who for thirty-three years constituted the Italian force here, succeeded by a number for very many years only one-third less, there were, doubtless, many disciples of our Lord.

The story of the youthful martyr Alban, is true in its leading facts; it is only one of a class of occurrences, the details of which are lost in the obscurities of time, but to be recovered and reinstated in true historic sequence amidst the restitutions of eternity. Such events must have happened ere Christianity could be established in the face of Roman law. The latter required sacrifice to the gods, the former rested on the fact of the one sacrifice "once for all offered." The assertors of the one must die rather than conform to the other, because conformity involved the absolute denial of their faith.

The power of the Divine life, the identity at all times of evangelical truth and obedience, are manifested in the lives of St. Patrick and the missionary teachers who, from Great Britain, carried the Gospel in this age into regions beyond the pale of the Roman empire. In truth, a missionary spirit is essential to Christianity. The religion of the Bible is so truly cosmopolitan, that it cannot disavow its duty of overleaping the barriers of nationality and race. If it had been content to be local, it would have encountered no opposition; the Pantheon would have been open to a statue of the King of the Jews : but its votaries could not ignore the obligation, inherent in its profession, to proclaim throughout the world its doctrines and its facts, in order that others might believe and be saved. This circumstance rendered it inevitably antagonistic to all other forms of faith and worship : hence was it that the demons of persecution trooped from all quarters, in hostile attitude, towards the novel intruders.

It was about the year 400 that St. Patrick, then a bondman in Ireland, but who had been trained in the knowledge of Christian doctrine by his mother, became imbued with its power and true meaning. His experience, as quoted by D'Aubigné from Archbishop Usher, is deeply interesting. He says — "The love of God increased more and more in me, with faith and the fear of His name. The Spirit urged me to such a degree, that I poured forth as many as a hundred prayers in one day.

And even during the night, in the forests, and in the mountains, where I kept my flock, the rain, and snow and frost, and sufferings which I endured, excited me to seek after God. At that time I felt not the indifference which I now feel : the Spirit fermented in my heart."*

The ministry of St. David, and of St. Asaph, in Wales, which closed about A.D. 544,—of Columba at Iona, from 563 to 596, though somewhat in advance of this epoch, yet belong to it, as they all derived their impulses from Romano-British Christianity.

Columba was born at Gartan, a wild place in the highlands of Donegal, in Ireland, in the year 521 ; he became a pupil of Finnian, then a priest, went to Scotland, and settled in Iona in the year 562, and died in 597. He was, says Dr. Lindsay Alexander, "an eminently pious man ; a man exercising a continual faith in God, feeling that, unworthy as he was, it was only through the merit of Christ he could be accepted of God, and seeking the favour and approbation of God as the richest reward he could obtain. He was much given to prayer, both social and private."†

The earliest strata of our history, like the most ancient layers of our rocks, present but few traces of former life; but in the one, as in the other, the traces we do find instantly attest identity of Divine operation. The faith of the martyr, the perseverance of the believer, the spirituality of the life,—in a word, the *Christology*, of the obscure specimens furnished by these old records, are all

---

* D'Aubigné, Rep., vol. v. p. 25, from Patrick Conf.
† Iona.

products similar to those with which we are familiar now, and which we have been taught to expect by the examples of holy writ. There has been no revolution in the constitution or government of the kingdom of Christ.

The trump of the archangel will call up strange forms from the grassy graves of our remote forefathers; they will come from cromlech and cairn, from the soil of buried cities, from the margins o the silent Roman roads, but their utterances will be the same.

> "They, with united breath,
> Ascribe their conquest to the Lamb!
> Their triumph to his death."

It is a grand idea of St. Augustine, to designate the whole church of all time, "The City of God,"—the building made without hands, which grows up through all the centuries, to stand when time shall be no more. At present we live in its narrow streets, we cannot command a view of the whole; but when our stand-point is in heaven, we shall be able to trace its vast circumference and progressive architecture.

CHAPTER III.

The Second Planting.

On the arrival of the Pagan Saxons, the religion of the Britons became a mark for political proscription. It was, with its luckless professors, driven into the remote districts of Wales, Cornwall, and Strathclyde, where it soon subsisted in lingering weakness, rather as a creed than as a power.

The poor Britons have been reproached with not having endeavoured to convert their oppressors to the true faith;* but their position as a conquered people, fugitive and enslaved, fully accounts for their subsequent obscurity. Their private efforts and fruitless struggles have found no place in historic annals.

The second planting of Christianity in this island (much more corrupted than at the first) occurred in the year 597. It was accomplished by the mission of Augustine the monk, who, with his followers, came from Pope Gregory on that express errand.

The well-known story of the beautiful Anglian slave-boys in the market-place of Rome; the mission originated by the Pontiff; the ceremonial at landing in the Isle of

* Blunt, "Hist. Reformation."

Thanet; the preaching before Ethelbert; the foregone conclusion of his Queen; the adoption of the new creed by the mass of Kentish men; the baptizing of 10,000 on one Christmas-day, the re-diffusion of Christianity nominally, after this fashion, throughout the island, are well known to all readers of our ordinary histories.

The feeble light, however, of the persecuted Christianity of the native people was never quite extinguished. Their faith was not only alive, but was sufficiently vigorous to struggle for its own usages and formulas, in opposition to those brought by the Italian missionaries. For many years, efforts for the retention of their own liturgy and calendar were made by the representatives of the Romano-British Church.

These remonstrants are usually regarded as the predecessors of those who, in subsequent ages, protested against the usurpations of Rome. But the strife was respecting ritual only, and the growing power of the Papacy prevailed. Both parties held the main truths of the evangelical system as a creed; but it was in both cases overlaid with so great a burthen of human inventions, that its action, and even its true character, were lost. The pure doctrine finds no place in the monkish annals which constitute our only materials for the history of the period. Some slender hopes may be founded on the fact that Gregory sent to King Ethelbert, (together with the wretched relics and vestments on the glories of which the chroniclers love to dwell) one copy of the Bible, two Psalters, two copies of the Gospels, lives of the Apostles and Martyrs, and an exposition of the Gospels and Epistles.

Doubtless, like the diamond, these gems gave out some light in the dark.

The Anglo-Saxon Church, which subsisted for nearly five centuries, was a church protected by the government, richly endowed, possessed of all the learning and mental power of the realm. Yet, as an institution, it was a disastrous failure. It did not secure or promote the diffusion of gospel truth. Amidst the mass of Anglo-Saxon literature still preserved to us, it is impossible to deny that there are tokens of vital piety in fragments few and far between. As a whole, however, it is characterized by the prevalence of trivial superstitions. Pretended miracles, puerile tales, trumpery ritualisms, usurp the place of Christ's pure and holy word. The pages of Venerable Bede, who wrote in the eighth century, show that already the simplicity of the truth "as it is in Jesus" had been set aside for the dogma of many mediators between God and man, and that the missionary commission, given at first to the whole race of believers, had been usurped by the priesthood exclusively. Personal religion was not unknown, but other things had far greater renown.

Bede tells us of St. Oswald, King of Northumberland, interpreting to the people the preaching of Aidan. Bede himself translated, as it is said, the whole Psalter and a great part of the Bible into English.

The following verses form part of a hymn attributed to Bede. Whoever was the writer, he was not unacquainted with the communion of the heart with God.

"A hymn of glory let us sing;
New hymns throughout the world shall ring:
By a new way none ever trod,
Christ mounteth to the throne of God.

* * * * * * *

May our affections thither tend,
And thither constantly ascend,
When, seated on the Father's throne,
Thee reigning in the heavens we own!

Be thou our present joy, O Lord;
Thou wilt be ever our reward;
And as the countless ages flee,
May all our glory be in Thee!" *

The notices of personal character which we obtain from a perusal of Anglo-Saxon literature, just suffice to assure us that the doctrine of salvation by the work of Christ was not unknown. It was, doubtless, influential in constituting the hope and happiness of many a soul otherwise benighted and forlorn. But it does not shine forth as the staple of their religious life; evangelism was not the characteristic of the age.

Indeed, the Saxons had not, at any time, the whole Bible translated into their language. We find the laity asking for it, and the clerics labouring to give it; but the work was never completely done. Whilst it was admitted that the Scriptures should be the rule of life, they used them too much as if they were a mere storehouse of marvels, as in the remarkable paraphrase of Cædmon. Faintly in this rugged, beautiful poem are the

---

* "Voice of Christian Life in Song," p. 141.

traces of the Saviour's own work of atonement recognized, and yet the whole is intended to magnify his name.

> "O let us resolve,
> Throughout this world,
> That we the Saviour
> Seek to obey:
> Fervently, through God's grace,
> Remember the inspiration of the Spirit,
> How the blessed there
> Sit on high,
> Even with the heaven-bright
> Son of God." *

Theodorus, who was consecrated Archbishop of Canterbury in 669, on his first visitation, amongst many directions concerning trivial things, is said to have preached the pure Gospel: he directed that every father should teach his child the Creed and the Lord's Prayer in the vulgar tongue. †

We turn with fond but vain desire to these scanty records for fuller information. The glimmering taper is not sufficient to illuminate the palace of truth, but it enables us to make out some of its foundations.

The best feature of the Anglo-Saxon Church was its missionary spirit. In the year 694, Wilfred, Abbot of Ripon, organized a mission to Friesland, which, under the leadership of Willibrod, became successful in planting the Gospel along the coasts of the German Ocean opposite to us, and whence our Saxon forefathers had emigrated. Winfred, a native of Crediton in Devonshire, became the

---

* Thorpe's "Cædmon," 305.

† Dr. Hook, "Lives of the Archbishops of Canterbury," vol. i., p. 150.

apostle of Germany. Though a strict adherent of the Papacy, yet he evinced zeal for the honour of Christ, for the conversion of souls, the spirituality of worship, and the advancement of pure religion. In 680, Kilian with twelve companions went to Franconia on the like errand.

The bishops published homilies on Scripture topics, several of which are still extant, to be read by the clergy to their flocks. The Gospels were translated from the Latin more than once. Many manuscripts of these translations still exist among the rarer treasures in our libraries.

In the year 705, "when Aldhelm became Bishop of Sherborne, he went to Canterbury to be consecrated by his old friend Berthwold. At this time, ships arrived at Dover with merchandise; and, amongst other works, a copy of the Old and New Testament was there, which he bought and placed in the church at Sherborne."* It is pleasant, too, to read of the same Aldhelm, disguised as a minstrel, stationing himself on the bridge over the river Ivel, attracting a crowd by his sweet music and song, and then, having secured their attention, turning his theme from the deeds of heroes to the glad tidings of the Gospel.

In the year 780, King Offa gave a great Bible to the church at Worcester. Alfred translated portions of the Psalter, and wrote devout reflections, in his version of Boethius, for the spiritual instruction of the people.

The canon of Ælfric to Wulfinus, a bishop in 970, enacts that — "On Sundays and festivals, the priest ought to explain to the people the sense of the Gospel in

* Maitland, "Dark Ages."

English, and, by the Lord's Prayer and the Apostles' Creed, to excite men to religion."

It would have been gratifying to have given a distinguished place in the noble army of martyrs to Boniface, the Devonshire monk or missionary of 718, who carried the knowledge of Christianity to the Germanic tribes, and met his death in the year 755, whilst attempting to win them to the cause of the Church. But the extant records of his writings show that he had no higher motive or ambition than to extend the dominions of his sovereign the Pope.

Alcuin, the most learned man of the eighth century, and a native of York, where he was born about the year 735, belongs more to France than England; for his chief works were written either during his residence at the Court of Charlemagne, or in his retirement at the Abbey of Tours, where he died in 804. He was unquestionably a man of deep personal piety, of devout habit, and of large Scriptural knowledge. But his voluminous writings seldom display the progress of his own inner life. For sixteen years he superintended, at York, the college in which he had been trained. It is refreshing to think of the young man opening his literary career by a Scriptural defence of the worship of Christ, and of the old man closing it by a revision of the Latin text of the Bible.

Alcuin, in his instructions to Christian missionaries, requires them to teach the doctrine that our Saviour came into the world for the salvation of the human race; but he accompanies it with the direction that the pagans should be previously informed for what sins they would have to suffer everlasting punishments, and for what good deeds they will enjoy unceasing glory with Christ.*

The same writer urges on his correspondents the paramount duty of studying the Scriptures. To one he says, "Write the Gospel in your heart;" to another, "I wish the four Gospels, instead of the twelve Æneids, filled your breast;" "Read diligently, I beseech you, the Gospels of Christ." Still more explicitly he writes—"Study Christ as foretold in the books of the prophets, and as exhibited in the Gospels; and when you find Him, do not lose Him, but introduce him into the home of thy heart, and make Him the ruler of thy life. Love Him as thy Redeemer and thy Governor, and as the Dispenser of all thy comforts. Keep His commandments, because in them is eternal life."† The dedication of his Notes on Genesis to his friend Sigulf acquaints us with his mental activity, and serves to show that the scholars of that day were no mean students of Holy Scripture. It is as follows:—
"As thou, my dearest brother, hast so long been my inseparable and faithful companion, and as I know with what ardour thou studiest the Holy Scriptures, I have collected and dedicated to thee a few questions upon the Book of Genesis, which I remember thou hast at different times proposed to me. I have done this that thou mayst always have at hand a means of refreshing thy memory, which often loses that which it should retain, if we do not preserve those things we desire to remember, in writing. This is especially the case with us, whose thoughts are

---

* Turner's "Anglo-Saxons," vol. iii., p. 487.
† Ibid., p. 498.

distracted by temporal business, and who are frequently exhausted by the fatigue of long journeys. As we cannot encumber ourselves with ponderous volumes, we must provide ourselves with abridgments, that the precious pearl of wisdom may be lightened, and the weary traveller possess something wherewith he may refresh himself without fatiguing his hand with too heavy a burthen. There are, however, in this book, many difficult questions, which at present I am neither willing nor able to solve, and concerning which thou hast not desired information. Those which are here treated of are chiefly historical, and for which a simple answer will suffice: the others, on the contrary, require more profound investigation, and a more copious explanation." The object of the work is to point out the connexion between the narratives of Genesis and the doctrines of redemption and life of Christ. In his homage to the Divine Saviour, he allows his fancy to run riot in search of types and analogies; but the scope of his teaching is usually correct and valuable.

One of the capitularies of Charlemagne (probably indited by Alcuin) is, "Let preaching always be performed in such a manner that the common people may be able to understand it thoroughly." * One of Alcuin's letters to Charlemagne relates to the mode of the atonement, and is a reply to the inquiries and suggestions of a subtle Greek on this vital subject. The Anglo-Saxon gladly recognized and taught the universal scope of the offer of salvation made in revelation. His works abound

* Guizot, "History of Civilization," Lecture 21.

in proofs of his ample knowledge of the springs of human action, but they are somewhat deficient in the full appreciation of higher things.

The vitiated atmosphere of earth sadly distorts the images of heavenly things seen through its medium. We must wait for the clear vision of the future ere we can know as we are known; but still it remains true that the effect of the religion of Christ, on the personal standing and character of every one who receives it, is real and decisive for eternity.

In the dissensions which arose between the advocates of the newly-established form of Christianity imported from Rome and the partisans of the ancient British faith, we first discern the workings of the good and evil of the mediæval church institutions. On the one side there lies the grand dominant idea of the Papal Church;—that of a society united in spiritual bonds, independent of all nationalities, and of time itself, rising in its unity triumphant over differences of race, manners, language, and political government; accepting one symbol; bowing before one general council; submitting to the rule of one officer as God's sole vicegerent and interpreter; promoted by agents whose passports insure universal introduction. On the other, we see in the suppression of the right of private judgment, abundant proof that this much-vaunted unity was external only; that, in fact, it extinguished the true unity which our Lord bequeathed to his followers, for the sake of a hollow territorial uniformity. When the Primacy, with congenial taste, accroached to itself political power, it immediately turned it into an engine of oppression against those whom, but for political considerations, it would most have cherished. The temporal views of the Papacy were fatal to true religious union.

The proverbs of King Alfred show that he held in high regard the person and work of Christ, towards whom he enjoins love and reverence, for "He is Lord of life." His translation of portions of Scripture, Extracts from St. Augustine, and other works, exhibit remarkable discernment. From his introduction to his translation of Gregory's "Pastoral Care," we learn that personally, and almost alone, he promoted the diffusion of Scriptural knowledge in the mother-tongue of his people. He aimed at filling the pulpits throughout the land with earnest ministers who should be able to preach intelligibly. He wished to create a nation of readers and a literature founded on the Bible. His Will shows that though not free from some superstitions then inwoven with the form of religion, yet he possessed, and chiefly valued its substance. We cannot recover all the lost sentences of the religious journal which we are told that he kept, but we know that it indicated communion with God by the one Mediator and a humble reliance on heavenly aid.

Theodolph's capitular, in 994, enjoins the priests to be prepared to teach the people *by preaching to them the Scriptures*. No priest can excuse himself from teaching, "for every one of you has a tongue by which he can reclaim some."

True it is, that in the presence of the superstitious perversions of Scripture then prevalent, Divine truth could exert only a precarious influence; but doubtless, notwithstanding this, many of the teachers and the taught, as they conned over the story of the life of Christ, experienced the surprise of a heavenly light, darting into the dark chambers of their minds, converting them into temples of the Most High.

One of the capitulars passed in the reign of Æthelred, A.D. 994, directs that each of the Christian laity should pray at least twice a day. In the same year we find a law of the Witenagemote directing that "Christians be not sold out of the land; also that they shall not be condemned to death for trifling offences."

One proof of the influence of personal religion at this period is afforded by the practice of bestowing freedom on slaves from religious motives. This became more and more prevalent down to the days of King Harold. Sometimes there was more of superstition than religion in the motive of the emancipation; but in many instances it is expressed to be grounded on the love of Christ, and I know not why we should doubt that the sacrifice arose from an individual reception of the Gospel of salvation. The parties went to the altar of some well-known church, called on the priests to witness the act, proclaimed it to the assembly, and had it registered in the church copy of the Gospels as the most sacred and enduring of records. It is not too much to believe also, that, in some cases, the light and love which induced this action on the part of the master reached as well to the heart of the grateful slave; so that the latter became likewise free by a surer title, and in an infinitely higher sense.

The advancement of Anglo-Saxon Christianity as an

ecclesiastical system was accompanied by its degeneracy as an exponent of the truth. The tenets relating to the invocation of saints and the worship of relics, which at first appeared as sentimental excrescences, became of greater relative importance as years rolled on, and ultimately superseded Gospel truth itself. Meanwhile, there were still some who concerned themselves more with the kernel than the husk or its accessories. The existence of a controversy on the old topic of free-will and God's decrees, proves that men's minds were not altogether engrossed in ritual observances. The followers of Alcuin held to the line of truth embraced by Augustine, whilst others expressed the relentless logic of more extreme views.

The popular literature which characterizes the later period of Anglo-Saxon Christianity is not calculated to afford any high idea of the knowledge or taste of the learned. It consists of lives of the saints, which were written and dispersed in great numbers, but in which fiction prevails to an extent which renders it now impossible to separate the fact from the fable. The same legends were also pictorially represented on the church walls. The genuine seeker after Divine truth was embarrassed and confused by these misleading guides.

It is extremely difficult to obtain materials for our work from the older annalists. The history of external things may be recovered from the waymarks left along the track of time; but internal things, the successive consciousness of successive generations, can never be fully recalled.

From such slender stores we gladly escape into the

lawful charities of a wide induction, using the well-chosen words of an American writer:—

"During all these ages of corruption, however, the Spiritual Church existed, represented in the persons of devout men, who walked with God amid the night of error, sufferers from the evil of their times, unable to explain or to break away from them, but seeking in their monastic cells, or in the walks of ordinary life, that purification and peace which are received only by faith; and the ecclesiastical historian finds grateful relief, as he gropes through the dark ages, in being able continually to point to these scattered lights, which, like the lamps in Roman tombs, gleamed faintly but perennially amid the moral death of the visible Church." *

The objective history of redemption will ultimately be the most interesting of all tales. The work of God in this land will form no inconsiderable chapter in that great history. It gleams out occasionally in the pages of ordinary chronicles, but it has been evolved by a series of causes principally operating out of our view; working out results, not in accordance with men's anticipations, but in spite of them.

One feature characterizes the subject which, at first sight, appears to deprive it of interest; namely, the absolute identity of vital religion wherever and whenever found. We discern the same enlightened apprehension, the same enlivened heart, whether the grace of God has produced them in the barbarous Celt or the refined Englishman—whether in the gloom of the

* Dr. Stevens, "History of Methodism," chap. i.

eighth or the light of the eighteenth century. But the grand succession of human events through and in which true Christianity is displayed to us, renders its career one of continual diversity.

All unknown to the majority of our countrymen, there was at this time spreading under the shadows of the Maritime Alps, and along the rich plains of Provence, the evangelism which, under the name of the Albigensian heresy, was afterwards so ruthlessly stamped out, partly by the aid of English soldiery.

CHAPTER IV.

The Normans.

DOUBTLESS, all the political movements of human society are connected with the advancement of Christ's kingdom; though we cannot, at present, always see the connexion. This kind of knowledge properly belongs to the future condition of our being, when we shall be unembarrassed by the limitations which now clog our powers and obstruct our view.

The Norman Conquest left unaltered the state of things spiritual. Whatever there was of true piety in Britain, was still a rare and hidden product.

The invaders were in good odour with Rome before their descent on England. In accordance with the fashion of the times, the Duke of Normandy had sought and obtained the Pope's sanction for his great enterprise. It was begun and continued in the sacred name of God; a perversion, alas! too common on the pages of history to excite any remark.

The Norman ecclesiastics, whilst deeming themselves accountable to Rome alone for their faith and practice, yet held of the local nationalities the land attached to their benefices. In this respect they were amenable to law. They struggled to get rid of this subjection, and to have it acknowledged that they held the temporals as well as the spirituals from the Pope. This was the source of the quarrel about investitures, which constitutes so large a portion of the so-called history of the Church in this dreary period. The claims of the Gospel and of man's spiritual necessities, were never once considered or referred to, in the contest which culminated in the murder of Becket at Canterbury. True it is that the encroachments of Rome led to a reaction towards national freedom; but this was grounded on motives of patriotism only. A few fine outbursts of manly protest against the claims of the Papacy were uttered now, and remembered in coming years.

Nor is the inquiry more inviting with regard to the inner life of this period. Men of vast intellectual capacity there were; men who had an intelligent, lofty perception of spiritual truth; but in their teaching they ignored alike the simplicity of the Gospel and the inductions of common sense. They elaborated an eclectic system of scholastic notions concerning all things; a system quite unconnected with, or rather setting aside, the actual woes and wants of humanity. Altogether unlike was it to the provision made by Him who "knew what was in man." Never can the sentiment of Cowper be more aptly quoted than with reference to the fine-spun logomachy of the schoolmen:

"Oh, how unlike the complex works of man,
Heaven's easy, artless, unencumber'd plan!"

And yet Anselm, archbishop of Canterbury in 1093,

was a Christian of no common order, of large heart and mind, profoundly learned, acute and pious. His works are lasting monuments of genius applied to some of the highest problems of humanity. His teaching on the atonement is a masterly exposition of the judicial aspects of that infinitely great transaction. He failed, however, to give or to restore to the common people the knowledge of Christ, although they would have received it with gladness and gratitude. In the works of Anselm, the intricate sentences and subtle reasoning conceal an unwavering faith in Christ as a Divine Saviour: his teaching, though deformed by the ugly scaffolding of formal logic, is nevertheless based upon the Scriptural foundation of man's guilt and Christ's satisfaction, man's need and God's aid. Humble, and at times almost desponding, yet his firm grasp of the power and love of Jesus makes him a joyful conqueror in the conflicts of the inner life. His biographer Eadmer says, "Christ was never absent from his lips." He crowned his long life of various effort by composing a treatise on the concord between grace and free-will, and expired whilst, at his request, his attendants were reading to him the dying sayings of our Lord.

We may well sympathize with the sentiments of Mr. Stoughton, expressed in his Lecture to Young Men in 1862, whilst speaking of Anselm,—that he would not for the world resign the reverence and love he felt for him, and Bernard, and Augustine, and Cyprian, and Chrysostom. "None of them were so much disciples and advocates of a church system, as they were believers in a personal redeeming Christ. Whoever looks below the surface of such men's characters will find the same elements of spiritual life,—faith, purity, obedience, self-denial, love. Could they now meet us and enter into conversation, we should find some difficulty in understanding them at first. Their speech and ours would need some sort of translation; but getting below metaphysical theology, and forms of worship, and ecclesiastical discipline, and certain personal predilections, when each came to speak to the other of God, as a personal and ever-present Father,—of Christ, as the Son of God, the Brother and Redeemer of man,—of the Spirit, as the soul's sanctifier, and the Divine presence in the church,—heart would answer to heart, and men divided by ages, and by other things broader than ages, would be drawn into a circle of blessed sympathy, and would clasp hands and kneel down together before the one cross and the one throne. We should all join in the *Te Deum Laudamus.*" *

Public affairs connected with religion at this epoch furnish us with no materials for the history of personal piety. In resorting to contemporary annals, we soon find that "the Church," in their language, means something very different from the institution designated by this name in the New Testament.

In the latter we find it used to denote a society of persons believing in the Divine mission and person of our blessed Lord. † In mediæval phraseology, it means the

---

* Exeter Hall Lectures, 1862, p. 123.

† "The most radical and fundamental idea of the Church is, that it is the company or society of those who are called by God

clergy alone as an order. In its character of a secular corporation the Church was deservedly popular. It was less exacting in its government than were the feudal landowners: its honours were open to all. Its temporal position required that it should possess right to allegiance and the power of coercion. Its dangerous nature arose from this double aspect,—the addition of the terrors of the sword to the terrors of conscience. These twofold powers, aided by its unbroken succession, rendered it the most potent combination for government ever exhibited to the world. Had not man's urgency for personal salvation led him to the study of the Bible, and by its lessons ultimately to break through the barriers of the Church, the whole civilized world must have become permanently subjected to hierarchical government.

The claim of infallibility made on its part, was allowed, not only by barbarous or effeminate people, but by the strong-minded leaders of the age. Man's right and duty of private judgment was surrendered; absolutism spread over the nations like the fatal flow of poisonous waters from a mine. The Church claimed the right of coercion; its punishments were awarded, not against sin, but against free thought and free speech.

Christianity, being faith in the revelation concerning Christ, and obedience to Him; it would at first sight appear to be simply impossible to pervert these into faith in *man*, and implicit obedience to him; yet, such is

to a knowledge of supernatural truth, and an acquaintance with the way of salvation."-- Principal CUNNINGHAM, "Historical Theology," Introd.

the skill of Satan, that this was actually accomplished. It thence results that, for the subject of our present inquiry, the history of the so-called Church is practically useless.

A few conclusions may be drawn from facts incidentally recorded.

In the reign of Rufus, Godfrey, abbot of Malmesbury, stripped of their coverings twelve copies of the Gospels, in order to contribute the price of these costly wrappings towards the purchase of Normandy. In the year 1190, William de Longchamp, bishop of Ely, pawned thirteen copies of the Gospels to raise 160 marks towards the ransom of Richard Coeur-de-Lion, including one copy of great value said to have belonged to King Edgar. The fond reverence indicated by their adornments was paid, we fear, not to the precious truth enshrined, but to the piece of ecclesiastical furniture which was thus decorated.

Had the Anglo-Saxons, instead of sumptuously adorning the book for their sacristy, multiplied its pages for the perusal of the people, how different had been the history of the world!

When disappointed of the object of our search in princely courts or monastic cells, shall we find it in the home of the Franklin or the hut of the slave? No encouraging response comes back from the dark caverns, —no voices of the day!

It is not *impossible* that a beam of transmitted light, struggling through the dust of ritual, may have struck on the conscience of some solitary one and guided to the

Saviour. Truly a forlorn hope, and yet all that we can express.

For about two hundred years after the Conquest, for six average generations of English life, all opinion is hushed,—not a finger is raised,—there is one common prostration. Great activity prevailed in the "Church," total torpor in the kingdom of Christ, save where some undercurrent carried forward the waters of life without the music or sparkle of their daylight flow.

This age is also characterized by that which, at first sight, would appear to be directly connected with our subject,—namely, the erection of costly edifices for the worship of God. These noble structures were raised by the offerings of piety for purposes of Christian service. Beautiful are the Romanesque buildings of the Norman epoch, beautiful the transition tracery of the Early English; gracefully diverging from the stiff patterns of Greece and Rome, and yet reminding of both,—plastic yet solid, poetical in detail, solemn in mass. In proportion as they are now adequately restored to us by the conscientious travail of the architect, it becomes apparent that they were never intended, and can never be applied, for the services of a simple Scriptural worship. The voice of the preacher, the ear of the listener, the eye of both, are all bereft of their offices. There is no congruity whatever between these dark, solemn temples, and the religion whose denomination they bear. Daily, for a thousand years, in some of their lofty naves has there reverberated the echoes of sentences in honour of the Redeemer, but, during the greater portion of the time in a sealed language, and during all the time in an obscure method. The stately ceremonial, the imposing procession, the swelling organ, and ringing voice, have been repeated until the very atmosphere is full of memories; but never, for ages, was the free, glorious Gospel proclaimed, so that all in the temple could hear "all the words of this life;" never, to the apprehension of the multitude, did the music of God's own message of forgiveness for Christ's sake reverberate through their "long-drawn aisles and fretted vaults."

Doubtless, at all times there have been some faithful, persevering ones, who have penetrated the sevenfold envelopes of mediæval ceremonial, and seized the kernel of truth within; but there is no instance recorded, of any powerful work for God originated through the medium of the dim revelations of doctrine enfolded in the Romish ritual.

The chapels attached to the few Plantagenet mansions now left—*e. g.*, Haddon Hall—are so much smaller than the dining-room, that they could never have contained even the half of the denizens of the castle. They are evidently adapted only to the performance of the offices of the Church, and of individual devotions at a few shrines there set up. Very rarely in the dark ages do we read of pious clerks or missionary chaplains; very rarely do we find traces of godly faith in the deep bays of the drawing-room, or arbours of the pleasaunce. Some witnesses for the truth there were, who held with marvellous and marvelling faith to the creed of Romanism, and yet lived in humble confidence in Jesus as the only

Saviour. They died and left no sign, nor had they any following.

Popular writers have been much in the habit of darkening the sombre aspect presented by the faint spirituality of the Middle Ages. It is unjust to decry it altogether. The scarcity of Holy Scripture, the paucity of Gospel teaching, the absence of Gospel sympathies, the obscurity in which the doctrine of justification was involved;— these cannot be denied. But the eclipse was never total. Here and there a pilgrim may be discerned with his face Zionward, "striving to enter in." The men were better than their ritual; the pulpit, which in later times has, it is said, been corrected by liturgies, was then in advance of them. The sermons of mediæval preachers abound in large quotations from Scripture,—not always well applied, but always treated as absolute authority. They thus testify for preachers and hearers that the facts of Holy Writ were common knowledge. Undoubtedly, there is in these compositions more of superstition than of sense, more of allegory than plain speaking; but, amidst all their defects, there were sentences which enabled men to discern the blessed truths of the Gospel of salvation.

The honour of God is not promoted by representing Romanism, either before the Reformation or since, as a condition of unmitigated religious perversion and ignorance. Gross darkness and extensive corruption prevailed, but yet there was to be found "faith on the earth." Wherever found and whenever, the latter asserts its own substantial identity. The truth-bearers are always in strict alliance with each other, though they neither know of nor desire the union. No Babel can ever confound that language. St. Bernard strikes the key-note for the whole choir when he sings:—

> " O Jesus! Thy sweet memory
>   Can fill the heart with ecstasy;
> But passing all things sweet that be,
>   Thine actual presence, Lord!
> Never was sung a sweeter word,
> Nor fuller music e'er was heard,
> Nor deeper aught the heart hath stirr'd,
>   Than Jesus, Son of God.
> What hope, O Jesus, thou canst render
> To those who other hopes surrender!—
> To those who seek thee, oh, how tender!
>   But what to those who find!
> When thou dost in our hearts appear,
> Truth shines with glorious light and clear;
> The world's joys seem the drop they are,
>   And love burns bright within." *

We dare not conclude, that of the multitude of worshippers successively entering the portals of mediæval churches, each giving a passionate glance at the crucifix, and kneeling before the altar of the patron saint, there were absolutely none who found their way to the Saviour. We do trace in the dim records unmistakable proofs that there were a few, at least, who regarded with faith "The Lamb of God which taketh away the sin of the world;" we will not give up the hope that there are many jewels yet to be recovered from the dust of the

* "Jesu dulcis." Translated in "Voice of Christian Life in Song," p. 163.

crowded sepulchres, around the ancient fanes throughout our beloved country.

> "As evening's pale and solitary star
> But brightens while the darkness gathers round,
> So faith, unmoved amidst surrounding storms,
> Is fairest seen in darkness most profound."

The Roman Breviary displays a symbolical connexion between the appointed order of daily service and the facts of our Lord's life on earth. Each service is associated with one of those mysterious acts and sufferings which constitute the historical groundwork of our faith in the atonement. This arrangement, which must have appeared to some persons to be utterly without significance because purely artificial, yet has to others been a source of grateful sympathy and a means of spiritual refreshment. So thousands of minds have been excited to lofty thought or fervent devotion by the utterance of the grand invitatory services at Matins, the urgent ejaculatory prayers at Prime, the Scripture lessons and collect at Vespers, and the hymn at Compline. But biography shows that in the great majority of instances these services have been an unprofitable weariness, whilst to the mass of the people they have been mere dumb show.

The Crusades, which for two hundred years occasioned so much excitement and action, and which have left so many traces of their influence in arts and arms, appear to have had no effect whatever on spiritual life. Beyond the fact that some of the few warrior pilgrims who returned, founded chantries or larger ecclesiastical establishments, we have no record whereby to connect them with the religious history of our country. The originals of the crossed and mailed figures on altar-tombs, girt with sword, were, we fear, animated by feelings altogether different from the spirit of the true champions of the Cross. It is not until after this page of history is closed that we perceive the dawn of free religious thought in England. Defective alike in object and method, we look in vain through the annals of the Holy Wars for any trace of personal spiritual life. We may imagine it to have existed and been nourished by the higher associations of the enterprise, but we have no record which opens to us this aspect of the strange phenomenon then exhibited in Christendom.

The eleventh century was throughout Europe a period of great ecclesiastical and religious excitement. The power of the Papacy had no sooner become consolidated and fully organized, than it was rebelled against by individuals and communities all over the so-called Christian world. The doctrines of the Church had no sooner been thoroughly eclipsed by the inventions of men, than the seekers for the hidden forbidden truth appeared in all countries. The early doctrinal reformers are said to have sprung from the East under the name of Paulicians, and to have travelled through Bulgaria and Hungary into Lombardy, and thence into Italy, the South of France, Germany, and even England. It was rather the desire for better things, the yearning for purer Divine light, that characterized this movement, than any single feature common to all the manifold varieties into which it spread.

We learn its purport only by the lurid light of the fires which flamed in its wake from land to land.

A very cursory glance at the history of mediæval controversies will serve to convince us of the vast seething and surging of opinion on religious subjects during the dark ages. Many persons amidst the turbulence of these disputes found their way to the peace which Christ ever gives to his true followers; and most of them served to exemplify the truth of the Master's saying, "If they have persecuted me, they will also persecute you."

Indeed, there were never wanting men who in the bosom of the Church protested against its misdeeds. The records of heresy must here furnish us with testimonies for the proof. The events suggested by the following enumeration extending through about two centuries, show that there was a continuous agitation for more or less of evangelical conformity, for the sacred right of private judgment, and for the honour of Scripture.

A.D.

1000. Wilgard of Ravenna and his followers put to death. The first capital punishment for heresy in Italy.

„ Leutard of Chalons imprisoned.

1017. A dozen persons burnt at Orleans for heresy.

1030. Gandolfo, a missionary heretic, at Arras.

1034. Heretics burnt at Milan

1046. Hangings and burnings in Germany and France

1079. Berenger, bishop of Angers.

1130. Peter de Bruys burnt at St. Gilles.

1135. Arnold of Brescia.

A.D.
1147. Henry the monk died in prison.
1160. Peter Waldo of Lyons.
1183. Waldenses excommunicated.
,,   Whitehorsts and other sects of reforming friars.
1209. Disciples of Amaury of Chalons burnt.
1229. War of extermination against Albigenses ended.
1234. Heretics persecuted at Oldenburg and throughout northern Germany.
,,   Paterini burnt at Rome.
1260. Sect of "Apostles" begun at Parma.
1270. Dolcino burnt at Vercelli.

The proud boast of the great Romanist writer, that the doctrine of the Papal Church could stand the test of universal consentaneousness in time and space, is dissipated by the most cursory glance into ecclesiastical history.*

Such instances serve to show us how much more has occurred in the transactions of time than our historical records reveal. The picture-gallery of the past is so scantily and irregularly lighted, that we see but the shadowy outlines of things; only here and there is a subject disclosed to us with all its figures and accessories complete. In the Chronicles of the Mayors and Sheriffs of London, in the possession of the Corporation, we read about this time of a transaction which just serves to make darkness visible :—"A.D. 1247. In this year, on the Translation of Saint Edward the King and Con-

* Vincent de Lerins, "Quod semper, quod ubique, quod ab omnibus."

fessor, a portion of the blood of our Lord Jesus Christ was brought to London, being sent by the Patriarch of Jerusalem to his lordship the King, and was deposited at Westminster." *

Grim visions do we get, about the year 1158, of luckless Italian reformers, a band of thirty, under two leaders, who, driven from the valleys of the Lower Alps, sought refuge here. Unlike the England of modern days, our soil then rejected these forlorn ones. On account of their heresies, they were, "by the king and the prelates, all burnt in the forehead, and driven out of the realm; and afterwards, as Illyricus writeth, were slain by the Pope."†

Another band, of Germans, met with a similar reception, and a fate still more painful. The old Saxon penalty of outlawry was enforced against them. They were judicially declared friendless, and consigned to the elements: the sentence was obeyed; these foreign brethren of our blessed Lord perished of cold and hunger and exposure, in the depth of a northern winter, in the very centre of Old England, within sight of noble feudal castles, hospitable granges, and religious establishments.

Matthew of Westminster says that, in the year 1087, Berengarius had many followers in England; Possevin states that Baldwin, archbishop of Canterbury, wrote, in the year 1180, a treatise "Contra Reliquias Berengarii." The Council held at Chichester in 1289 condemned the fraternity of "Apostles." It is not, of course, to be inferred that all who opposed the ruling belief and discipline

* Chronicles translated by Riley, 1863.
† Foxe, vol. ii., p. 198.

were true followers of Christ; but the existence of such continuous wide-spread dissent is a proof that many persons were individually seeking for light and truth; and we may safely infer that in such a pursuit, followed with perseverance, guided by Scripture, hallowed by prayer, many persons found for themselves the prohibited treasure.

In the year 1210, whilst England was under the Papal interdict for the contumacy of King John in not accepting the Pope's nomination of Stephen Langton as archbishop of Canterbury, (the same prelate who was then a diligent Bible student and teacher, and afterwards the patriotic compiler and upholder of Magna Charta,) we first read of heresy in the sense of evangelical opposition to the dominant system. It was introduced from the South of France, where it was at this time born and soon afterwards most cruelly strangled. An old chronicler, with meagre detail and confused spelling, informs us that "in this year certain *Ambigensis* (Albigenses) were burnt in London."

It is painful to find that in this terrible manner the truth is to be transmitted down through the ages. What must be the intrinsic value of a belief, the difficulties of which, in its contact with society, required and repaid such sacrifices!

The punishment of heresy during the middle ages effected a double injury. It sought to extinguish both truth and freedom. The power of the sword in matters of religion was apparently countenanced by Hebrew precedent, and was certainly authorized by the code of Justinian.* It is sometimes stated that it was a morbid introduction brought on by perverted Christianity; but this is not correct. To the latter belongs the disgrace of having adopted and used it; but the evil notion of religious constraint by Government is founded on errors in jurisprudence previously common in the Pagan world.

Hugh Greathead, bishop of Lincoln, who died in 1253, was a celebrated Greek scholar, and a man of true piety as well as of rare accomplishments. He recommends that all priests who cannot preach should resign; and that if they are unwilling to do so, they should weekly explain the Gospel to the people. He promoted translations of the Scriptures, and advocated numerous independent works of this kind, in order that accuracy and perspicuity might be attained. He was not only a good and great, but a bold man, preaching before the Pope in a strain of holy indignation against the arrogance, impiety, and incompetence of the clergy. His powerful precepts and example led many a forlorn one to the fountain of life.

If we turn from the province of active life to that of the contemplative, and visit the cloister, we find but feeble traces of evangelical power.

Monachism was introduced into England as early as the fifth century, if not before. Columba was a monk, as was Bede. During the ages characterized by the ruthless invasions of the Northmen, the religious establishments were the asylums of piety and civilization; often destroyed, but again renewed, with all their corruptions and defects, the only witnesses for God and heaven in

* Code, Book First.

those times of trouble. The monasteries of Ireland, especially, became schools renowned throughout Europe for the promotion of religion and science, whence Christianity and the seeds of civilization were transported to other countries.*

The monastic system received its first systematic reform from Cuthbert in 747, its second from Dunstan in 965, its third from Lanfranc in 1075, its deathblow, in these islands, from our Legislature in 1539.

For upwards of eight hundred years, in many of the most beautiful valleys of the kingdom, daily and nightly orisons arose from companies of religious recluses; the music of the convent bell floated over woods and pastures green, its call to heavenly things; the broad gates of the abbey were opened with equal hospitality to the cavalcade of princes as to the meanest beggar. Much of temporal benefit was done, many defects of mediæval society compensated. Good men, thoughtful men, earnest practical men, occasionally arose and became influential. In all parts of the country we find traces of their labours and monuments of their skill.

History is silent as to the manifestation of that special powerful spiritual life which it was the professed object of these institutions to promote. If they had been successful in this, it would have changed the character of their own and following ages; but we are compelled to state, that as an attempt to advance the reign of God in the soul, and of Christ in the Church, it was a total failure, and became a source of evil instead of good. It dis-

* Neander, "Memorials of Christian Life," p. 416.

countenanced the truth concerning the atonement of Christ, which is the only solution and solace of the difficulties which press humanity.

Monasticism as an institution never became thoroughly acclimated in England, either in its contemplative eastern, or its more active western phase. The great monks of our country were missionaries only: such were Patrick, Columba, Boniface, and Lillebrod. We have no fathers and founders of the system amongst our great names.

Two beautiful pictures, the one of the temporal, the other of the spiritual aspect of convent-life, are to be found in modern literature, besides the lofty eulogiums of Montalembert.

The first is furnished by Mr. Froude:—"Ever at the sacred gates sat Mercy, pouring out relief from a never-failing store to the poor and the suffering; ever within the sacred aisles the voices of holy men were pealing heavenwards, in intercession for the sins of mankind; and influences so blessed were thought to exhale around those mysterious precincts, that the outcasts of society— the debtor, the felon, and the outlaw—gathered around the walls, as the sick men sought the shadow of the apostle, and lay there sheltered from the avenging hand till their sins were washed off from their souls. Through the storms of war and conquest, the abbeys of the middle ages floated, like the ark upon the waves of the flood, inviolate in the midst of violence, through the awful reverence which surrounded them."*

The other is by Dr. Hook, who admits, however, the

* Froude, vol. ii., p. 406.

limited extent to which his language applies :—" The monastery was, however, more especially the city of refuge to those who sought deliverance not so much from the vengeance of Norman law, as from the tyranny of sin, the power of Satan, the love of the world, the fear of eternal death. Here their eyes and hearts were directed to the cross of Christ, and they were taught to rely on Him crucified. They were told of the blood of Christ, which could cleanse the most aggravated sin, and of the Spirit of Christ, who can sanctify the most polluted nature."*

The religious life of the cloister appears to have been singularly unsuccessful in producing any local or general social religious effect. No purely evangelical succession or school sprang up from monasticism in this country. Doubtless, there were men who by the force of personal piety made gospel truth the tradition of their convent home, but no such exhibition was sufficiently illustrious or permanent in England to raise it into Church history.

* "Lives of the Archbishops," vol. ii., p. 18.

CHAPTER V.

The Wycliffites.

Religion has in all ages vindicated its Divine origin by manifesting independence of human institutions. The elaborate machinery of the Papal Church obstructed it; the worldly policy of European States polluted it; yet, like the hidden current of lava, it always flowed on beneath the crust of visible things. Just as the most dreary wastes in the world yield some vegetation to interest and reward the naturalist, so the Christian may rejoice in the belief that the most barren wastes of history have had their living spiritual plants; the latter may dwell hidden in clefts and caves, but are of the Lord's planting, and destined to bear flowers of amaranth in paradise above.

The Gospel was well expounded and well defended in Merton College, Oxford, by Thomas Bradwardine, called "the profound doctor," who became Divinity Professor, and afterwards Chaplain to King Edward the Third, and who, for a very brief space, was Archbishop of Canterbury. His teaching on the vital question of justification by faith in the atonement of Christ, is quite clear, and was maintained with ability. In this respect he was the doctrinal precursor of the more illustrious man of the same college who laid the foundation of the future English Church, John de Wycliffe. Both were Augustinians, deriving their cast of thought from the writings of the great Bishop of Hippo; but, better even than this, both were thorough practical Christians.

Merton College, as it now exists, is one of the few places in England where we can trace an unbroken connexion of association, between the present and the remote past. Bradwardine and Wycliffe both trod the same cloistered passages we now see there, *then* marvellous in freshness of elaborate architecture, *now* dark and worn by the action of five centuries.

In 1356, when London was ringing with the tidings of the victory of Poictiers and the exploits of the Black Prince, one of the favourite ecclesiastics of Edward the Third was preaching there the doctrines of grace. This was Richard Fitz-Ralph, who was made, first, Dean of Lichfield; then, in 1333, Chancellor of Oxford; and, afterwards, Archbishop of Armagh. He died in 1360, having, as he confessed, been led from Aristotle to Christ. We have only a fragment of one of his prayers left to us, but it is decisive as to the ground of his hope of salvation:—"Holiest and sweetest Jesus! to thee be praise, and glory, and thanksgiving! Thou, who hast said, 'I am the way, the truth, and the life!'—way without a turning, truth without a shadow, life without an end!—Thou hast shown me the way, taught me the truth, promised me the life!"

So has it ever been. The ancient promise has been fulfilled in the happy experience of God's children, in spite of surrounding darkness and peril. They have rejoiced in the fulfilment of the prediction—"For the Lord shall comfort Zion : He will comfort all her waste places ; and He will make her wilderness like Eden, and her desert like the garden of the Lord ; joy and gladness shall be found therein, thanksgiving, and the voice of melody."*

Intellectual and social activity had now somewhat suddenly recovered from the collapse of the Conquest. Society was astir, from the throne of the prelate to the hut of the bondman. In some minds the new zeal took the form of protest against the fiscal or political exactions of the Papacy, or against the vices of the monastic order, or the ignorance of the secular clergy ; but, we hope not a few, sought and obtained new life in Christ Jesus. Dr. Hamilton characterizes this period with his usual felicity of language :—"Sometimes in February, or early in March, there comes through all the land a prophecy of spring. The atmosphere is strangely mild; primroses peep through, and the redbreast grows bold and warbles a regular roundelay. But the wind shifts, the snows return, and the whole precocious summer, buds, blossoms, music, and all, are buried in the frosty sepulchre. Such an anticipatory flush of spiritual life passed over Europe towards the close of the fourteenth century. Tauler in Germany, Conrad of Waldhausen, and Matthias of Janow, and, a little later, Huss and

* Isaiah li. 3.

Jerome of Prague, Marsilius of Padua, our own William Occam, the University of Paris, all spoke out against Papal usurpation, or gave utterance to sentiments so free, so scriptural, so spirit-rousing, that it seemed as if the Heavenly Bridegroom were saying to His Church, 'Rise up and come away: for, lo, the winter is past, the rain is over and gone; the flowers appear on the earth, the time of the singing of birds is come, and the voice of the turtle is heard in our land.' And, doubtless, the spirit of God was in the movement. It was 'a little reviving' towards the close of the long mediæval winter; but the Council of Constance followed, with the burning of heretics, and of the Book which had made them heretics; and another century was to pass before that general resurrection of buried truth, and that grand outburst of life and freedom, which we call the Reformation." From the nature of the case, we are best acquainted with the *political* aspect of the great protest which now universally began to be made against the ecclesiastical system. Hallam says, "The greater part of the literature of the middle ages, at least from the twelfth century, may be considered as artillery directed against the clergy, I do not say against the *Church*, which might imply a doctrinal opposition by no means universal."*

We may obtain a full insight into the religious activity of the period from the remarkable series of allegories written, probably in 1362, by Langland, a monk of Malvern, called "Piers Plowman's Vision." This contains a spirited survey of the then ecclesiastical world,

* "History of Literature," vol. i., p. 138.

accompanied by indications of a desire for a healthy theology and for Church reform. It will probably surprise many persons to find, that in those days, the writer presumed his readers, of all classes, to possess perfect familiarity with the letter of Scripture. Little account is made of the intercession of saints, or even of the Virgin; right apprehensions are shown of the saving work of Christ, and of the renewing efficacy of the Holy Spirit, the force of the law as a rule of life, and the inefficacy of nominalism of any kind.

We may fain hope, from the popularity of this lively, clever production, that there was then considerable sympathy not only with the opposition to Roman supremacy, but with saving truth, even amongst those who, like Piers, despised the "Lolleres," classing them with vagrants and vagabonds. One of their names of reproach, "Biblemen," doubtless marks the popular estimate of a Lollard.

The early multiplication of plain non-illuminated copies of the MSS. of this work, many of which are still preserved, proves that it was the book of all who could read, or get it read to them. The leading idea is produced over and over again in other publications in succeeding years, showing the hold which it obtained on the popular mind.

The mingled light and darkness of mediæval days, (occasionally affording enough of the former to lead an earnest soul to Christ,) is characteristically displayed in the monk's address to Mother Church.

"Thanne I courbed on my knees,
And cried hire [her] of grace ;

And preid hire piteously
Prey for my sinnes,
And also kenne [make me to know] kyndly
On Christ to bi-leve,
That I might werchen *his* wille
That wrought *me* to man.
Teche me no tresor [Tell me no fable],
But tell me this ilke [same],
How I may save my soule!—
Thou that seint are y-holden" [accounted]. *

Two other passages may be paraphrased in some of the obscure parts.

"There are none sooner saved,
Nor of truer faith,
Than ploughmen and hinds,
And labourers common.
Shoemakers and shepherds,
And other ignorant folk,
Pierce with a paternoster
The palace of heaven.
They pass purgatory penance-less,
When going from hence,
Into bliss of paradise;
For their simple faith,
Though imperfectly, they knew,
And obscurely they lived."

And so—

"Theology has held me
Tenscore times:

* "Vision," p. 17.

"The more I muse therein,
The mistier it seemeth;
And the deeper I dive,
The darker I find it.
Forsooth, it's no science
To cultivate subtilly;
Hateful it would be
Without love, which is its law.
Ye that seek Saint James [of Compostella]
And saints of Rome,
Seek Saint Truth;
He may save you all."

Another instance may be quoted, showing the struggle between man's notions and God's. Baptismal regeneration is taught, and yet contrary conclusions expressed in the conviction of the writer.

"In much perplexity I cogitated,
And with myself disputed,
Whether I were chosen or not chosen.
I thought on Holy Churche,
That upheld me at the font
For one of God's chosen.
But Christ bade us all
Come if we would,
Turks and schismatics."

And again—

"For moore belongeth to the lyttel bairn,
Ere he the lawe knowe,
Than the nempnynge of a name,
And he never the wiser."

Wycliffe was, however, the real regenerating instrument of the middle and lower classes in England: other agencies had been at work, but it was his translation of the Scriptures, his plain popular summaries of the Christian doctrines and precepts, his numerous sermons, and his vigorous evangelizing efforts, which first called up the spirit of the English commonalty. He distinctly conceived, and diligently executed to the extent of his opportunities and influence, the work of carrying the glad tidings of the Gospel throughout the land. He is the precursor (by, alas, how long an interval!) of those noble home missionary efforts which, under various names, are now promoting the spiritual welfare of our country.

In Wycliffe's Sermons we read—"The Gospel relates how Jesus went about in the places of the country both great and small, as in cities and castles or small towns, and this to teach us to profit generally unto men, and not to forbear to preach to a people because they are few, and our name may not in consequence be great. For we should labour for God, and from Him hope for our reward. There is no doubt that Christ went into small uplandish towns, as to Bethpage and Cana in Galilee; for Christ went to those places where he wished to do good. And he laboured not thus for gain, for he was not smitten either with pride or with covetousness." *

So precious were the fragments of Gospel light, that written books containing them were actually entailed. At the end of one of the MSS. of the "Pore Caitiff," in the British Museum (MSS. Harl. 2335) is the following

* Vaughan's Wycliffe, vol. ii., p. 23.

note :—" This book was made of the goods (*i. e.*, at the charges) of John Gamalin for a common profit (*i. e.*, for a public benefit), that the person that hath power to commit it have the use thereof for the time of his life, praying for the soul of the same John. And he that hath this aforesaid use of commission, when he occupieth it not, leave he it for a time to some other person. Also that the person to whom it was committed for the term of life, under the foresaid condition, deliver it to another the term of his life. And so be it delivered and committed from person to person, man or woman, as long as the book endureth."

The " Pore Caitiff " served its generation. It was the type of the religious tracts of modern days. It was indited in the fashion then prevalent; but contains the everlasting truth, beyond all controversy, and above all price.

Seldom do we see the sower actually at work in the fields; but the results of his labour are visible in the landscape on every hand. By the time the yellow grain waves over the field, the hand that sowed it is, perhaps, gone for ever. So, in the days of the Plantagenets, the observer in the field of English history becomes sensible of the presence of a new party in the community, which has come without heralds or clamour. We have heard faint murmurs of evangelism before now, in the sighs of the mystic, the postulates of the scholar, or the confessions of some ill-understood prisoner. But now, under the eaves of princely portico or peasant's hovel, the good seed having been cast into the ground, the blessing comes. Men slept and rose, night and day, and it grew, they knew not how.

There were not wanting, in the Establishment, persons who clearly saw the defects of the dominant system. From the synodal constitutions of Simon Langham, bishop of Ely, in 1364, we may extract the following :—" Let all shepherds of souls and parish priests, when they have finished the divine offices in the church, devote themselves with all diligence to prayer, and the reading of the Holy Scriptures ; that by the knowledge of the Scriptures they may, as belongs to their office, be prepared to satisfy every man demanding a reason concerning hope or faith. And let them always direct their attention to the doctrines and precepts of the Bible (like the staves passing through the rings of the ark), so that devotion may be nourished and increased by constant study, as its daily food."

Chaucer had a just appreciation of the scope of Christian teaching, and it may reasonably be concluded that he wrote (in 1389) from observation of living instances of parish priests who were guiding others to the Saviour they themselves had found.

> " A better priest I trowe that no wher now is.
> He waited after no pompe ne reverence,
> Ne maked him no spiced conscience,
> But Cristes lore, and his apostles twelve,
> He taught ; but first he folwed it himselve."

So his contemporary, Gower, in his poetical works, discloses salvation by faith in the work of Christ alone. *

---

* "Confessio Amantis," book v.

The life of Wycliffe is that of a man of great natural parts and shrewdness, eminently practical and wise; rising, by his abilities and attainments, to the highest seats of learning, and yet preserving in full force the freshness of personal piety. He became Master of Balliol College in 1361; next, Warden of Canterbury Hall in 1365; began to publish his independent views on the doctrine and practices of the Church; espoused the anti-Papal side in politics; was ejected from his wardenship in 1370, after an unsuccessful appeal to the Pope; became parson of Lutterworth, took his doctor's degree in 1372, sent out Gospel itinerants; was denounced by the Pope in 1377; appeared at St. Paul's in triumph over his enemies in 1378; died in peace in 1384.

He was not only a herald of salvation himself, but the restorer of Scriptural methods as well as doctrines. He abandoned and condemned the metaphysical style of the schoolmen with the authority of a master in the art, and addressed himself with the simple weapons of Scripture, directly to the plain common sense and affections of the people. More than three hundred of his preparations for the pulpit are among the MS. treasures of the British Museum. By their simple perspicuity and Gospel plainness, they show that he had seized hold of God's great engine for spiritual work. His expository method, styled "postillating," led the way to the most instructive kind of pulpit teaching.

The progress of his inner life was unusual. First came a strong patriotic conviction of the political evil and degradation wrought by the Papacy; next, an equally powerful impression of the doctrinal errors of the Romish Church; lastly, a thoroughly evangelical conception of the need and nature of the truth concerning the work of Christ. Under the influence of the first, he stirred up the zeal of England's statesmen, and raised a country party; guided by the second, he waged war without quarter against the religious orders of the Church; prompted by the third, he translated the Bible into the vulgar tongue, and sent forth itinerant missionaries, two by two, throughout England, to preach the newly-recovered saving truth. This is the real foundation of the English Reformation. The seed thus sown in faith by the wayside, though submerged by local and even national floods of persecution, yet preserved its divine vitality, and ultimately sprang up and everywhere bore fruit. The testimony of the heroic Huss to the effect of Wycliffe's writings, doubtless, well characterizes them :—" I am drawn to them by the manner in which they strive to lead all men back to Christ."

The multiplication, in portions, of Wycliffe's translation of the Scriptures, and the effect of the preaching of his russet-clad emissaries, excited a feeling throughout the country towards evangelical truth which has never since wholly disappeared.

"The Sacred Book,
In dusty sequestration wrapped too long,
Assumes the accents of our native tongue;
And he who guides the plough, or wields the crook,
With understanding spirit now may look
Upon her records, listen to her song,
And sift her laws." *

* Wordsworth.

The growth of homely English piety was for many years to be obstructed, stunted, and trodden down. But it vindicated the divinity of its vital principle, and became the essential characteristic of society. It energized successive generations of believing men, who, through evil report and good report, laboured to promote the Redeemer's cause in this kingdom.

"Wycliffe," says Dr. Reinhold Pauli, "most completely departed from that which his contemporaries understood by the Church; for in their eyes it was only an institution composed of the higher and lower clergy, as well as of his sworn opponents, the monks, and to which the laity belonged merely in respect to the outer limits that had been drawn around it by the hierarchy. According, however, to his conception of the Church, it consisted of all true believers, who had access to the Divine mercy independently of any human intervention; while hypocrites and godless persons, even though they ranked among the highest prelates, did not belong to it. This is the same idea of the priesthood, which so essentially contributed to the development of the Reformation in Germany."*

The readiness with which the reformer obtained his evangelists, as well as the welcome with which they were everywhere received, proves that all things were ready;—the harvest for the reapers, and the reapers for it. In 1384, the citizens of London encountered the opposition of the clergy, and overcame it, in their choice of a Wycliffite mayor, John of Northampton.

* "Pictures of Old England," translated by Otté, p. 271.

The pages of Foxe abound in testimony that from this time, evangelical religion, as a protest against ritualism, became a subsisting, continuing manifestation among the commonalty of England. Henceforward we may trace its progress. The first views we get of inner Evangelical life amidst the lowlier classes of our land, display a people surprised and grateful at the reception of God's free mercy, and then prepared to do battle to the death in defence of so dear a treasure.

In the British Channel the pebble-banks advance in a direction contrary to the surface-run of the tides, being influenced by some powerful under-current: so was it with the doctrines of Wycliffe. All the tides of human society ran in an opposite direction, and yet evangelical truth grew and advanced beneath and in spite of them. We find traces of its influence in the south of Europe, notwithstanding the imperfect methods of intercommunication in those days. In the year 1497, Savonarola, the ardent patriotic reformer of Italy, was excommunicated. In the deliberations of the Florentine Council upon his fate, after he had been condemned by the ecclesiastical court, the proposal for his imprisonment for life was combated by the argument, that, though imprisoned, he might still write, and his writings be as obnoxious as those of "that pestilent fellow Wycliffe." The Florentine merchants in London entered into the dispute, and formed parties, *pro* and *con.*, in the great controversy, raised by Wycliffe in England, and Savonarola in Italy.

A hard task, however, was that of the solitary men of

God in early mediæval times : they had no Christian literature to feed upon, save some crumbs of the bread of life; no friends to aid them; no public to sympathize with them; obloquy and misrepresentation, pains and penalties awaited them; darkness all around, and in the horizon no streaks of the dawn. Yet how many there were, who, under these adverse circumstances, lived to God and for God; breathing the atmosphere of a Divine life; quietly waiting, in the confidence that when their allotted race should have been run, God would realize, in the Church and in the world, the majestic purposes and high hopes of their hearts! Truly this was "the patience of the saints."

We would fain know something more than we do, of that "good Queen Anne" who lies buried beneath a canopied tomb in Westminster Abbey. She was not only a lover of the Scriptures, and a promoter of evangelical truth, but her sojourn in England, from the festival of Christmas 1381 to her death in that of Whitsuntide 1394, was conducive to the communication of Wycliffe's views to her fatherland of Bohemia, and thus became an important link in the succession of spiritual life in Western Europe. It is interesting to conceive of personal religion flourishing in her youthful nature, amidst the exciting revelries and disorders of her young husband's court. She had to preside at tournaments, and to share in the costly spectacles in which Richard the Second, the spoilt son of the Black Prince, took chief delight. The tumults of his reign must have rendered her queenly happiness precarious from the first. The love of the English people for the gentle accomplished young foreigner who delighted to study the four Gospels in the new translation of Wycliffe, whose character and conduct cheered the last years of the great reformer, and whose memory became a household word after her brief career of life, was based upon her outspoken sympathy with the free message of God's grace to mankind.

Wycliffe's translation was finished the year before Queen Anne came to England. Its homely sentences are still intelligible to us; no wonder that we regard them as possessing peculiar interest. As copyists plied their vocation to supply a demand unknown before, they were unconsciously ministering to the power of an endless life.

Notwithstanding the comparative abundance of copies of Wycliffe's translation yet extant, they are held in high esteem. In July, 1863, a beautiful MS. of the precious volume was sold by auction in London by Sotheby and Wilkinson for £350.

CHAPTER VI.

The Lollards.

THE quick spreading of the Wycliffite teaching, and the nature of the methods by which it was carried on, are well shown in the preamble of an Act of Parliament passed three years before the death of the venerable reformer, in the fifth year of the reign of Richard the Second (1382), which is as follows :—

"Item, forasmuch as it is openly known that there be divers evil persons within this realm, going from county to county, and from town to town, in certain habits under dissimulation of great holiness, and without the licence of the ordinaries of the place, or other sufficient authority, *preaching daily not only in church and churchyards, but also in markets, fairs, and other open places, where a great congregation of people is,* divers sermons, containing heresies and notorious errors, to the great emblemishing of the Christian faith, and destruction of the law, and of the estate of Holy Church —" The act provides a penalty, and is in conformity with a prior proclamation to the same effect issued the same year. It is satisfactory to reflect on the vigorous efforts in favour of the truth, indicated by this violent opposition on the part of the ecclesiastical powers which then virtually ruled the State.

One of the tenets of Lollardism condemned at Leicester in 1389 is, that "every layman may preach and teach the Gospel everywhere;" affording a most decisive proof of the genuine earnest character of the revival movement. In time of urgent need all ordinary barriers are overleaped by religious zeal.

The poor Lollard was impelled and sustained by faith in God's word alone. He knew not of the great cloud of witnesses who had trodden the same path before him, nor dreamt of those who should follow him still more numerously, in succeeding ages. He was ignorant of history, and traditions were all against him. He stood alone, save that God was with him, and that he knew right well. If it is true concerning human affections, that "One touch of nature makes the whole world kin," so is it with the divine: one touch of grace unites the whole brotherhood in heaven and on earth. But this blessed association was unknown to the obscure heroes of the early Reformation. They wrought simply and severely for God, and unto Him.

> "Faith makes man's heart,
>   That dark, low, ruin'd thing,
> By its rare art,
>   A palace for a king,
> Higher than proud Babel's tower by many a storey:
> By faith Christ dwells in us, the hope of glory."
>
> F. TATE.

It has been stated by no mean authority, that Lollardism died entirely out, Wycliffe's labour perished, and the whole pre-Reformation movement became extinct.* This is true only of its political action against Rome, and is not true of its evangelical effects, for the fire was burning unobserved; and, afterwards, when public events necessitated or encouraged a manifestation of personal religious conviction, the foundations laid in Lollardism formed the solid base of the whole structure of English Protestantism.

Wycliffe's teaching became, indeed, immediately fruitful; but the pages of history contain but few distinct memorials of its progress.

In 1391, William Swinderby, a priest of the diocese of Lincoln, encountered trouble, condemnation, and disgrace for the profession of evangelical doctrines. He submitted to the demands of his ecclesiastical superiors, and, in a qualified way, recanted certain of his opinions; but he still held to those which prove the genuineness of his faith in the Atonement. His appeal to the Parliament is an eloquent, stirring address, full of Scriptural arguments. It opens with the noble prayer: "Jesu, that art both God and man, help Thy people that love Thy law, and make known, through Thy grace, Thy teaching to all Christian men!" He quaintly says, "This land is full of ghostly cowards, in ghostly battle few dare stand." Doubtless, there were many who hid their convictions, and were disciples, though in secret.

At the same time, Walter Brute, an educated yeoman of the diocese of Hereford, was finding his way to the enjoyment of spiritual peace through Him who has said

* Froude, vol. ii.

that He is "the way, the truth, and the life." The cottages and hamlets of his neighbourhood witnessed the evangelic exertions of this predecessor of the lay preachers. His elaborate manifesto of belief, given by Foxe, reflects the confused condition of theology in those times of transition; but there is also displayed the pure light which directed him to "the Lamb of God who taketh away the sin of the world."

The most notable of the immediate successors of Wycliffe was Master William Thorpe, whose history, recorded by his own hand, was freely circulated in MS., and ultimately printed by Tyndale. This document affords internal evidence that he had many friends and sympathisers. His examination or trial took place on the 3rd of July, 1407.* On his part he displayed ample accurate Scripture knowledge, combined with manly, sound sense, ready wit, and deep piety. He held fully the whole scheme of evangelical doctrine. For twenty years he had diligently taught it as an itinerant. He speaks of many men and women of his acquaintance who "stand in the truth, and are in the way of salvation." We are thus introduced into the secrets of old Lollardism. It was not a political creed, or even social reformation, but something far higher and better in its nature.

The conclusion of Thorpe's account shows the workings of his inner life. "And so then I was led forth and brought into a foul unhonest prison, where I came never before. But, thanked be God, when all men were gone forth then from me, and had barred fast the door after

* "State Trials," folio ed., vol. i.

them, by and by after, I, therein by myself, busied me to think on God, and to thank him for His goodness. And I was then greatly comforted in all my wits, not only for that I was then delivered for a time from the sight, from the hearing, from the presence, from the scorning, and from the menacing of mine enemies; but much more I rejoiced in the Lord, because that through His grace He kept me so, both among the flattering specially, and among the menacing of mine adversaries, that without heaviness and anguish of conscience I passed away from them. For as a tree laid upon another tree, athwart or across wise, so was the archbishop and his three clerks always contrary to me, and I to them. Now, good God! for Thine holy name, and to the praising of Thy most blessed name, make us one together, if it be Thy will (by authority of Thy Word, that is true perfect love), and else not. And that it may thus be, all that this writing read or hear pray heartily to the Lord God, that He for His great goodness, that cannot be with tongue expressed, grant to us, and to all other which in the same wise, and for the same cause specially, or for any other cause, be at distance, to be knit and made one in true faith, in stedfast hope, and in perfect charity. Amen."*

Of him may be said, in the beautiful words of Lord Macaulay, "While the multitude below saw only the flat, sterile desert in which they had so long wandered, bounded on every side by a near horizon, or diversified only by some deceitful mirage, he was gazing from a far higher stand, on a far lovelier country, following with his eye

* "State Trials," vol. i.

the long course of fertilizing rivers, through ample pastures, and under the bridges of great capitals, measuring the distances of marts and barns, and portioning out all those wealthy regions from Dan to Beersheba."*

Henceforth we have to plunge into the actual shock of the battle between light and darkness, in search of the votaries of truth. The history of religion is not a tale of peace, but of terrible war. Evil in its most hateful form is manifested in strenuous opposition to the good. We are shocked and distressed at the dreadful character of the scenes, in some of which the Tempter has apparently triumphed. The "agony and bloody sweat" of the Man of Sorrows was symbolical of the baptism wherewith His Church was prepared for final, but long-delayed, triumph.

No sooner do we open the annals of persecution, than we are struck with the fortitude and patience of the sufferers. A cheerful tone pervades their confessions. They learnt to direct upwards to heaven the energy of affection which might not expand on earth. We find in their sayings, no morbid reflections on their sad destiny, no bitter accusations against their enemies, but, on the contrary, exulting joy in God their Saviour, and firm hope in the future. They "endured as seeing Him who is invisible," and comforted one another with thoughts kindled at the same source as Luther's Hymn:

> "This prison where thou art,
> Thy God will break it soon,
> And flood with light thy heart,
> In His own blessed noon."

* "Essays," p. 413.

For traces of the higher life in man we must often search amidst the lower forms of man's social condition, and there find them under terrible outward disadvantage.

The fearful statute "De Heretico Comburendo," 2 Hen. IV., c. 15, (1401,) tells us by what means the truth, which it arrogantly aimed to burn out of the land, was being promulgated. It states, that "divers false and perverse people of a new sect . . . . usurping the office of preaching, do perversely and maliciously, in divers places within the said realm, under the colour of dissembled holiness, preach and teach these days openly and privily divers new doctrines and wicked heretical and erroneous opinions, contrary to the same faith and blessed determinations of the Holy Church; and of such sect and wicked doctrine and opinions *they make unlawful conventicles and confederacies, they hold and exercise schools, and make and write books;* they do wickedly instruct and inform people."

This terrible engine of cruelty was not allowed to become rusty. The second sufferer under its enactments was an artisan of Worcester, John Badby.

Early in the morning of the 15th of March, 1409, the city of London was in an unusual ferment. An august tribunal was assembled in conclave at St. Paul's. The Duke of York, the Earl of Westmoreland, the Chancellor Beaufort, the archbishops, and numerous other dignitaries of church and state, were there. The occasion of the gathering was merely that Badby had expressed himself to be of opinion contrary to the dominant creed on the subject of the real presence, and held the doctrines of Wycliffe. He was the first of the working class in England prosecuted for heresy, the predecessor and type of a great number of the same class who afterwards dared to suffer and die in testimony of their personal religious convictions of evangelical truth. After his condemnation in the early morning, a brief respite was allowed him until noon; the king's writ obtained, the terrible preparations in Smithfield made, and then at mid-day, in the presence of Prince Hal (who vainly attempted to snatch him from the actual fire by promises of worldly advantage if he would recant), in the face of a crowd of the best and wisest people of the realm, this devoted man was "done to death," calling upon the Lord.

Henceforth there was no cessation of activity for the Gospel on the one hand, and against it on the other. The laws indicate that the truth was being promulgated under fearful difficulties by the time-honoured methods common among faithful men from the first.

The most illustrious in rank of the Lollards, and one of the bravest of English martyrs, was Sir John Oldcastle, Lord Cobham. This nobleman was a mirror of knighthood. Born in the palmy days of chivalry, trained in courts and camps, living whilst the tournament was a fashion of the times, he became obnoxious to the frightful charge of heresy, and after trial, imprisonment, escape, and betrayal, was ultimately cruelly put to death at St. Giles's Cross. His whole demeanour was worthy of the heroic age. On learning that he had been accused, he manfully wrote, signed, and sealed a declaration of his belief, and took the document straight to the King. Henry the Fifth, though free and brave in his youth, became the servile tool of bigoted Italian priests in his maturer age. He refused to receive the paper from his brave old companion in arms. Then the good knight demanded to be tried by his peers, after the old custom :—

"Than desired he in the Kinges presens, that an hundred knightes and esquiers might be suffered to come in upon hys purgacyon, which he knewe wolde clere him of all heresyes. Moreouer, he offered hymself, after the lawe of armes, to fight for life or death with any man lyuing, Christen or Heythen, in the quarrel of his faith, the King and the lordes of his councill excepted. Fynally, with all gentlenesse he protested before all that were present, that he wold refuse no manner of correction that shuld after the lawes of God be ministered unto him; but that he wold at all times with all mekeness obey it."* The subsequent examination of the brave knight shows that he was skilled in the Scriptures, quite sound in the faith, and that he experienced the personal enjoyment of peace with God, through our Lord Jesus Christ, in whom he had affectionate and reverential faith. He had openly embraced evangelical views, and had employed itinerant preachers to promulgate them, after the example of Wycliffe.

When brought from the Tower to the Hall of the Dominicans, within Ludgate, before the archbishop, bishops, doctors, officials, and priests, he says, in answer to the urgent entreaties for his recantation and con-

* "State Trials," vol. i., p. 39.

fession,—"'Nay, forsooth will I not, for I never yet trespassed against you, and therefore will not do it.' And with that he kneeled down on the pavement, holding up his hands towards heaven, and said, 'I shrive me here unto Thee, my eternal living God, that in my frail youth I offended Thee, O Lord, most grievously! Many men have I hurt in my anger, and done many other horrible sins; good Lord, I ask Thee mercy.' And therewith weepingly he stood up again, and said with a mighty voice, 'Lo, good people! lo; for the breaking of God's law and His great commandments they never yet cursed me, but for their own laws and traditions most cruelly do they handle both me and other men; and therefore both they and their laws, by the promise of God, shall be utterly destroyed.' With a stout heart, at the end of his trial he spoke to his judges before the multitude with cheerful countenance. 'Though ye judge my body, which is but a wretched thing, yet I am certain and sure that ye can do no harm to my soul, no more than could Satan to the soul of Job. He that created that, will of His infinite mercy and promise save it. I have therein no manner of doubt. And as concerning these articles before rehearsed, I will stand to them even to the very death, by the grace of my eternal God.'"* Sentiments and language echoed one hundred years afterwards, by the great German reformer at the Diet of Worms.

The Constitutions of Archbishop Arundel in 1408, the statute 2 Henry V., c. 7 (1415), and the Injunctions of

* Foxe, vol. iii., p. 337.

Archbishop Chichely in 1416, all prove the prevalence of gatherings of God's people secretly for worship and conference. The last directs a judicial inquiry to be made in every parish for " secret conventicles," as well as for suspected books in the English language. The first proposition of Lollardism condemned by Archbishop Warham, in 1530, is indicative of the true character of the movement, and denotes the fountain of its energy, for it is, that " Faith ownlee doth justify us."

If the pre-Reformation darkness had been at any time total, it could not have been dispersed as it was by home instrumentality.

In the year 1414, the University of Oxford presented to the King certain articles for the reformation of the Church. The monarch was one whom Shakspeare describes in the eulogistic strains of the priesthood, but whom the poor Lollards prayed for from another standpoint.

> " Hear him but reason in divinity,
> And, all-admiring, with an inward wish,
> You would desire the king were made
> A prelate."

The University articles display the reflex influence of the rising evangelism on the Establishment. The 29th runs as follows :—" Whereas according to the doctrine of our Saviour, all who have the cure of souls ought to feed the flock of Christ with the food of salutary doctrine, and to drive the wolves from the sheep by the barking of holy preaching; yet some are promoted in the kingdom of England who are entirely ignorant of the language of the country, and are therefore dumb, and unable to instruct their parishioners; it seems expedient that no person should hold a benefice in any country unless he understands the vulgar language of that country."

The existence of vital godliness flourishing like the first flowers of spring under inclement skies, is also proved by a work entitled "The Ploughman's Prayer," first printed by Tyndale, but written and circulated long before his time. There is a plaintive tone about this interesting production that rather tells of apprehended than actual violence. No mention is made of Wycliffe or any other person, but the sentiments are given as though they were the thoughts of many hearts. The burthen of the song is the sinfulness of the times, and the perversion of those who should be teachers. The invocation at the commencement, at once shows, that faith in Christ was the ruling principle in the writer's heart. "More need was there never to cry to Christ for help than now." The substitutions of the Church of Rome for the life-giving food of the Gospel were never more powerfully or pithily exposed than in this tract. It is written in earnest, evangelical, forcible language. It concludes by a prayer: "Therefore, we lewd men prayen Thee that Thou wilt send us shepheardes of Thine own that willen feed Thy flocke in Thy lesewe (meadow), and goe before therselfe, and so written Thy lawe in our harts, that from the least to the most all they may knowen Thee." "And, Lord, geue us Thy poore sheepe patience and strength to suffer for Thy law the cruelnes of the mischievous wolues. And, Lord, as Thou hast promised, shorten these dayes.

Lord, we axen this now, for more need was there neuer!"

In the "Creed of Piers Ploughman," written during the Wycliffite agitation, the doctrine is far more antagonistic to Rome than in the "Vision" before referred to. The scope of this poem, like the former, shows the prevalence of very general religious excitement.

The great social problem of those days, the extinction of serfdom, had come to the surface of things. Though it had received some checks from the excesses which led to the death of Wat Tyler, yet it had been well discussed, and had come to be considered as a matter which must be handled at all cost, and would not brook long delay.

There was much individual thought: in the multitude of cogitations the question of questions, "What shall I do to be saved?" was frequently heard. The lethargy was passing away.

A broadside of Caxton's printing was discovered in 1859, between the leaves of a book in Lord Spencer's library. It contains a prayer, comprising an invocation of Christ as a Divine Saviour, God incarnate; a petition for forgiveness through His blood, and for obedience in His love. The intercessory offices of the Virgin are barely acknowledged, whilst sole reliance on the work of our Lord is reiterated with much fervour.*

The complaint of the clergy, presented to Henry the Fifth in 1413, is, "The Heretikes and Lollards of Wicleue's opinion were suffered to preach abrode, so boldly to gather conuenticles unto them, to keep scoles in men's

* See "Athenæum," Dec. 24, 1859.

houses, to make bokes, compyle treatises, and write ballets; to teach privately in angles and corners, as in wodes, fields, medowes, pastours, groves, and in caues of the ground."* A truly graphic account, giving plain testimony concerning the great evangelical ante-Reformation movement then pervading the masses of English society.

About five years after the second Smithfield tragedy, a London tradesman, John Clayden, a currier, suffered death in the same place, for having evangelical books in his house, and evangelical sympathies in his heart. The good man was accused of reading the condemned books, especially one called "The Lantern of Light:" he confessed that he could not read, but "he had heard the fourth part thereof read of one John Tuller," and that "he had great affection for the book from a sermon that was written there." It is a touching picture presented to us by this illiterate man, ignoble on earth, but noble in heaven, groping for divine wisdom as for hidden treasure, finding it in a MS. sermon, and then having the same fairly written on parchment in English, and carefully "bound in red leather," promulgating its truths judiciously, suffering imprisonment, and, ultimately, meekly submitting to martyrdom.

The depositions of the persecutors of Lollardism furnish many glimpses of the dawning light which was beginning to be reflected from the lowliest portion of English society: they also serve to show the connexion between the love of truth and the desire for education.

* "State Trials," folio, vol. i., p. 48.

Thus we read that the wife of an artisan in Martham, in the diocese of Norwich, had, in her anxiety to do good, requested one of her neighbours (from whom the information was extorted) that she "and Jean her maid" would come secretly in the night to her chamber, to hear her husband read the law of Christ unto them, "which law was written in a book that her husband was wont to read to her by night."

From the deposition of a wretched informer named Wright, we gather—"Item, That Anise, wife of Thomas Moore, is of the same sect, and favoured them and receiveth them often ; and also the daughter of Thomas Moore is partly of the same sect, and can read English." "Item, That Nicholas Belward, son of John Belward, dwelling in the parish of Southelmham, is one of the same sect, and hath a New Testament which he bought in London for four marks and forty pence, and taught the said William Wright and Margery his wife ; and wrought with them continually by the space of one year, and studied diligently upon the said New Testament."

The history of the Church largely illustrates the mode of God's moral government of man. We see the highest ends worked out by feeble instrumentality, and often left incomplete, when a slight interference might apparently have been an incomparable improvement or acceleration. But man's freedom is to be preserved at all cost ; miracle is excluded ; the wearisome battle must be fought by the appointed combatants, and by them alone. So, individually, the stores of Divine knowledge cannot be unlocked by any man for his brother. Every one must for himself take the key appointed for him alone, and thereby become divinely wise.

The records of the Privy Council in 1437 disclose a transaction which *may* have been the result of mission work, but may also have been, instead of that, merely an instance of successful mendicancy. We have no criterion whereby to determine the real value of the instance. The entry in question is that of a petition to the council from Guillyaume Pieres, a "Sarasyn," who had been converted to the Christian faith, and had been baptized in the Church of St. Magnus, at the foot of London Bridge, ["*jadys mescreant, ore est convers à loy Dieu, lui Roy omnipotent,*"] setting forth that, from the desire of his heart towards the true God, he had forsaken his country and kindred, and had forfeited all his possessions; whereupon he prays for a contribution towards his support. He is granted by the crown two pence per day.*

We are apt to become restless in the act of contemplating the long periods of time during which the cause of Christ appears to us to have been almost stationary. But, out of our sight, God is ever working, and, as in the case of the earth beneath, preparations are going on with all the unerring precision of physical law.

There was, in truth, much heroism at this time being enacted in obscure places. The meek and lowly followers of our blessed Saviour were now quietly fulfilling His commands, and disappearing one by one. They were hopeful, though they could not unitedly express their

* "Privy Council Proceedings," vol. v.

joyful anticipations; they were content to wait, for so they interpreted their Lord's will concerning themselves. Very few names have escaped the historic oblivion by which they became quickly hidden from view. James Retby, a disciple of Wycliffe, promulgated his master's opinions in Scotland, where they spread in the diocese of Glasgow. The herald of salvation met with the common fate; he was persecuted and burnt for heresy. But he laid the foundation of an extensive and permanent spread of Lollardism throughout the western parts of that kingdom.

As the living experiences of those who are enlightened from above, whereby they perceive the excellency and suitableness of the Gospel as a provision for their souls, display similar principles working in all varieties of cases, so the dying experiences of the sad victims of intolerance also show the identity of the convictions, hopes, and consolations of the sufferers.

The fact of this identity, when there could be no common action, is worthy of note; as is also the tenacious faithfulness of men, many of whom were uneducated and poor.

The humble daisy unfolds its petals at the dawn, and continues open though clouds obscure the sky all day: so these children of God, having once lifted their hearts in faith towards their heavenly Father, continued stedfastly regarding him, though the firmament of his providence was overclouded during all their pilgrimage.

The pen of the English historian now occasionally begins to find materials for notice, besides the territoria wars of princes, and the squabbles of ecclesiastics.

"There was a third party in the country—the only one which, in a true high sense, was of importance at all, and for the sake of which, little as it appeared, the whole work was to be done,—composed at that time nearly of poor men—poor cobblers, weavers, carpenters, trade apprentices, and humble artisans,—men of low birth and low estate, who might have been seen at night stealing along the lanes and alleys of London, carrying with them some precious load of books, which it was death to possess, and giving their lives gladly, if it must be so, for brief tenure of so dear a treasure." *

We obtain indirect proofs of the existence of this third party from the records of subsequent persecutions. Thus it is said of William Cowbridge, who was burnt at Oxford in 1538, that he was the son of the high bailiff of Colchester, a wealthy man of high repute, whose ancestors "even from Wycliffe's time had always been favourers of the Gospel." †

The incurring of penalties by men claiming the right of private judgment in matters of religion, proves that we are not wholly governed by expediency; since the latter would always lead to an accordance with ruling power. There is therefore that within us, which, at the call of God and duty, can rise superior to the claims of self-interest.

The circumstances have changed; truth has been publicly vindicated; the criminals of Lollardism were the ancestors in opinion of the legislators and judges of the present day; the judges of those days would rank with barbarians

* Froude's Hist., vol. i., p. 152.   † Foxe, vol. v., p. 18.

now. The tenets of the Lollards, touching the supremacy of the rights of conscience, are wholly triumphant in the place where once they were trodden under foot. The noble apologies once uttered amidst scoffs have now become axioms of legislative wisdom.

> "The common cry
> Will, as 'tis ever wont, affix the blame
> Unto the party injured : but the truth
> Shall, in the vengeance it dispenseth, find
> A faithful witness." DANTE.

So was it when the great Apostle of the Gentiles stood at the bar of Cæsar; so was it also, when his and our infinitely higher Master stood at the bar of Pilate. On each occasion God's cause in the world seemed to be on the point of becoming extinguished. Yet never was it so grandly triumphant. The times when it has apparently been brought nigh to a perpetual end, have been epochs in which its hidden Divine force has been culminating for future victory.

CHAPTER VII.

The Course of the Movement.

DOUBTLESS, in those confused times, when the religious agitation had fairly begun, there were many persons, both in the ranks of the Romanists and of the Lollards, who were guided to the cross of Christ whilst seeking peace for their souls. Never has the great theatre of human action, since our Lord's advent, been totally free from the presence of His followers. The recognitions of heaven will comprise some strange surprises. The motley liveries of earth often separate brethren. Many who have anathematized each other, have nevertheless been together loving the Lord Jesus Christ, though after a strangely separate and incomplete method.

The literature of evangelic Romanism does not do justice to its votaries; it is greatly defective in Spiritualism, inasmuch as the biographers have been for the most part ritualists, not sympathizing with the deepest feelings and highest aspirations of the soul realised through the influences of the Holy Spirit.

Mysticism, the most attractive form of mediæval piety, never much prevailed in England. On the Continent it has always had a large following. It is still the asylum of personal religion amidst the shows and symbols of Romanism.

> "Oft in stillest shade reclining,
> In desolation unrepining,
> Without a hope on earth to find
> A mirror in an answering mind,
> Meek souls there are, who little dream
> Their daily strife an angel's theme,
> Or that the rod they take so calm
> Shall prove in heaven a martyr's palm."
>
> KEBLE.

It is obvious from the writings of these good men, that they studied one of the highest of human accomplishments,—the successful cultivation of the inner life. The vigour of divine affection thus attained, made all mundane affairs trivial, in comparison with the eternal felicities towards which they were tending, and in the foretaste of which they lived.

But religion in this country has ever been of an active outward turn: it has been regarded, not as an end, but as a means, to regulate the present life, and to attain the future. Even the few of our countrymen who rank within the category of mysticism by their doctrines, were practically active, not dreaming away their lives under the shadow of à Kempis,* but ever before the world of

---

* Hallam says of the work of à Kempis, "It is said to have gone through 1,800 editions, and has probably been read more than any other work after the Scriptures."—"History of Literature," vol. i., p. 140. It is still the permitted channel whereby the faith and fervour of Romanism find their way to heaven.

everyday life. "Life in earnest" is written on every page of English history.

In England there has always been a connexion between vital Christianity and the diffusion of the Scriptures. The men who have been the most distinguished for intense intelligent religious convictions, have been the foremost labourers in the translation or bestowment of the Bible. Such a man was Wycliffe, such also Tyndal. Though the manuscript copies of the former's translation were necessarily costly and cumbrous, yet we find that the fragments still remaining are so numerous as to show that a very considerable diffusion of Divine truth thus took place.

There were two slender sources of public information (independently of preaching) opened before the discovery of printing, but they were far too weak to be of any practical use: one, was the popular dramatic representations of Scriptural subjects common from the thirteenth to the fifteenth centuries, the other, the wall paintings, which during the same period diversified rather than adorned the churches. We can scarcely imagine an instance of the successful influence of these æsthetic methods of instruction. The popular mystery was more usually founded on the apocryphal Gospels than on the true. The mural picture is more frequently a representative of some monstrous monkish legend than of a Scriptural scene. The rood-loft displayed the image of the Virgin more conspicuously than any other symbol.

It is just possible that some stray soul was led into spiritual truth by the representation of the passion of our Lord, which on certain anniversaries in certain towns, as at London, York, and Coventry, was acted during upwards of three hundred years.

The new art of printing now came forward as the great missionary agent. " It is" (says Hallam, Hist. Lit., vol. i., p. 156) "a very striking circumstance, that the high-minded inventors of this great art (printing) tried at the very outset so bold a flight as the printing of an entire Bible, and executed it with astonishing success. It was Minerva leaping on earth in her Divine strength and radiant armour, ready at the moment of her nativity to subdue and destroy her enemies. The Mazarine Bible is printed, some copies on vellum, some on paper of choice quality, with strong black and tolerably handsome characters, but with some want of uniformity, which has led, perhaps unreasonably, to a doubt whether they were cast in a matrix. We may see in imagination this venerable and splendid volume leading up the crowded myriads of its followers, and imploring, as it were, a blessing on the new art, by dedicating its first-fruits to the service of Heaven."

The printers evidently supplied that for which they well knew there was the chief demand. Eager inquiry was everywhere being made of the Divine oracles: no wonder, therefore, that the language and topics of Scripture became household words, and its blessed truths the power of God unto salvation.

D'Aubigné says, " The Reformation in England was essentially the work of Scripture."* If we refer again to

* " History of the Reformation," vol. v., p. 198.

the impartial and richly-furnished historian of the middle age, we obtain valuable testimony of the character of the great religious movement of the fifteenth and sixteenth centuries. He says, "that its vital spirit will be sought for in vain in the theological writings of the age. These were chiefly concerning the two controversies concerning justification by faith alone, and the eucharist." "It was not," he says, "for these trials of metaphysical acuteness that the ancient cathedrals shook in their inmost shrines; and though it would be very erroneous to deny that many, not merely of the learned laity, but of the inferior ranks, were apt to tread in such thorny paths, we must look to what came closer to the apprehension of plain men for their zeal in the cause of reformed religion, and for the success of that zeal. The abolition of saint-worship, the destruction of images—the sweeping away of ceremonies, of absolutions, of fasts and penances—the free circulation of the Scriptures—the communion in prayer by the native tongue—the introduction, if not of a good, yet of a more energetic and attractive style of preaching than had existed before; and besides this, the eradication of monkery which they despised, the humiliation of ecclesiastical power which they hated, the immunity from exactions which they resented;—these are what the North of Europe deemed it gained by the public establishment of the Reformation, and to which the common name of Protestantism was given."*

Other writers, still less observant or cognizant of the

---

* Hallam, History of Literature, vol. i., p. 382.

real character of the movement, attribute it altogether to the political element with which its historical manifestations were so intimately connected. But a deeper insight into the personal history of the actors and sufferers shows beyond all question that its vital energy was personal faith in Christ as the only Saviour, and in God's truth as the only guide. These dogmas, though enfolded in the huge fabric of the Romanist system, had been, practically, wholly withdrawn from common use, or even attainment. The struggle which shook the ancient fabrics to their "inmost shrines," was for the restitution of the lost jewel, the efficacious truth which the Apostle Peter styles "the precious blood of Christ," the "precious" corner-stone, the "precious" object of faith. If the Romanist teachers had only taught the people that which many of them themselves knew,—the true way of salvation,—the revolutions of the Reformation would never have been needed.

Spiritual life at this period of our history appears to have irregularly broken out in various places, and not to have been continuous in its growth. This is a deception arising from the suppression of the connecting links of evidence. The torch-bearers themselves were often unseen; but the flame was borne, the beacons were kindled, the work was done. By the ·bloody footprints of the persecutors we trace their progress through the fair counties of England. Norwich received them in 1422; London, 1450; Westminster, 1511; Colchester in 1511; Coventry in 1519; Lincoln in 1530; York in 1531; Devizes in 1532; Suffolk in 1532; Bedford in 1541;

Bury in 1544; Ipswich in 1544; Tenterden in 1558; Oxford in 1558.

Husbandmen, farmers, carpenters, wheelwrights, millers, turners, shoemakers, glovers, mercers, serving-men, painters, weavers, shearers, cutlers, skinners, glaziers, —all figure in the Gospel muster-roll which is found in the records of the ecclesiastical courts. The word was received everywhere and by all classes with gladness. There was a wide-spread, deep conviction, of the supreme value and importance of saving truth, which led unlettered men to step out of the requirements and habits of ordinary life, to become valiant champions for tenets of belief. The ignorance of many of these spiritual warriors of aught besides the one thing needful, is most affecting. One poor Suffolk peasant (Kerby, at Mendlesham) repeats at the stake all that he knows,—the "Te Deum," the Belief, and some prayers. Another, under similar awful circumstances, from his scanty mental stores sings the " Magnificat." What energy of life is there in evangelic truth, when such power resides even in its fragments!

It has been said that the Reformation in this country was matter of statecraft or priestcraft. Let the assertor, by the aid of old John Foxe, visit the homes of English artisans and peasants, even before the occurrence of the glorious events connected with the Reformation in Germany, and he will find that long ere the Gospel became the subject of contention in courts and camps, it was the dear treasure of the commonalty of the land. The movement was characterized by the fixing of the heart on great ends, with a comparative disregard of all things intermediate. "Every solution of the conduct of the reformers must be nugatory, save one,—that they were men absorbed by the conviction that they were fighting the battle of God."*

In contemplating the sad worldly condition of the majority of the children of God in the past ages of our history, it is consoling to reflect on the abundant compensation which true religion affords for the loss of all outward prosperity. There have been enthusiasts in science, in the pursuit of abstract truth, of learning or poetry, who, for the sake of intellectual pleasures, willingly forfeited all earthly advantages, and could be hardly torn away from their favourite studies; but these are all outdone by the rational enthusiasm of the Christian, whose discovery of the "pearl of great price" is an event far surpassing the surprises of philosophical research. The enchanting sweetness of the interested contemplation of God's work of redeeming love, has been the solace of thousands of persons, whose forlorn condition on earth rendered them the objects only of pity or contempt to the bystanders. Faith in the Divine promises, in the work of our Lord Jesus Christ, is the elixir of spiritual life. Such persons are ever singing to themselves in the strain of one of the Romanist poets of the Elizabethan age—

" Calvarie's Mount is my delight, the place I love soe well;
Calvarie's Mount! O that I might deserve in thee to dwell!
O that I might for pilgrimme goe that sacrede mounte to see!
O that I might some service do where Christ died once for me!

---

* Hallam, History of Lit., vol. i., pp. 292, 308.

> O that I had some hole to hyde my head on thee, to stay
> To view the place where Jesus died, to wash my sinnes away!
> Like words then would I utter there, that Peter sometime did:
> 'Lord! well it is that I am here; let me still heere abide.'
>
> Let me still heere abyde and be, and never to remove—
> Heere is a place to harbour me, to ponder on Thy love;
> To ponder, Lord, upon thy paines, that thou for me hast felt;
> To wonder at Thy fervent love, wherewith Thy heart did melt!
>
> Calvarie Mount, thus would I muse, if I might come to thee;
> All earthlie things I would refuse, might there my dwelling be.
> Might there my dwelling be, no force, no feare should me
>   remove,
> To meditate with great remorse upon my Saviour's love!"

Such persons, not only enjoy here, but actually carry away with them into the unseen world, durable riches and everlasting possessions of the utmost preciousness.

The history of the Church is too often a record of the selfish struggles of ambitious men; but the history of vital religion is remarkably destitute of this element: its promoters have ever acted against their worldly interests, their thoughts have evidently not centred in themselves; the extension of the spiritual kingdom of their unseen Master, and the glory of His great name have been their springs of action.

It needs such examples, to counteract the inference which the world draws from the general correspondence existing between the creed of the governors and that of the people. Too many of the high personages whom the historian delights to honour for deeds of fame, have shown, in this highest matter, subserviency to the powers that be; but when we resort to the cell of the student, or the lonesome dungeon, we find that individual religion is a genuine power, having a real existence, daring to be singular, and willing to do or die.

"Blest prisoners they, whose spirits are at large!"*

Besides the line of strict evangelical witnesses which from the first may be traced running down through society in England, there have never been wanting men of intelligence and force, who have assailed religious error from the stand-point of human reason, though they themselves have fallen short of the acknowledgment of the full truth. The cause of the Gospel has thus had allies in the ranks of the world; men who deemed themselves standard-bearers of reason, have aided the partisans of revelation, fighting earnestly the battle of the church militant. It is not for us now to criticise the various phases of belief which scholars have held, but we may take delight in the retrospect of allthose who, whatever their speculative opinions on other subjects, looked to the atonement made by our Lord Jesus Christ as the only ground of acceptance with God. In 1457, Bishop Pecock, who had been for twenty years, writing and acting against Lollardism, was himself charged with the taint, compelled to recant and burn his books publicly.

The diffusion of short doctrinal tracts on the work of Christ, the way of access to God, and the requirements of true religion, has ever been characteristic of evangelical movement among the people. To the pithy MS. tractates of Wycliffe, succeeded the Confession of Thorpe, the Testament of Tracy, and similar productions, eagerly

* Wordsworth.

copied, and firmly though secretly held. Then followed the prohibited brief printed treatises of the early reformers; afterwards, importations from German theology; next Becon's admirable little books, succeeded by a host of others, issued by the newly-found mighty agency of the printing-press. The narratives of personal history in the pages of Foxe, show how eagerly all these means were used, and how they fed the lamps of individual piety that were burning in a thousand obscure places.

The possession of the Scriptures, during all the future vicissitudes of the kingdom, gave to the followers of Christ the inestimable advantage of a perfect model for their conduct. The path of contumely, trial, and suffering had been well worn by the Saviour; His footsteps were visible in all its windings, and His example is vivified by the constant sense of His ever-living presence. The warriors felt themselves to be not only sustained and blest, but honoured too, by being made spectacles to angels and to men. They acted as though they saw beyond the stars, and lived in the radiant light which flows from the throne of God and of the Lamb. Faith is not, as some pretend, the lowest form of reason, but the highest; the humanity thus manifested is of the noblest style.

> "Into God's word, as in a palace fair,
> Thou leadest on and on, while still beyond
> Each chamber, touched by holy Wisdom's wand,
> Another opens, more beautiful and rare;
> And thou, in each, art kneeling down in prayer;
> From link to link of that mysterious bond,
> Seeking for Christ."

CHAPTER VIII.

Reigns of Henry VII. and Henry VIII.

GEOLOGISTS tell us that convulsions which have riven the rocks, and molten floods which have burst through the earth's crust, have been the means of bringing up to the light of day the mineral treasures hidden beneath: so the heavings of social religious revolution, the fiery outbursts of persecution, have brought to light the golden ore of sanctified character. We know more of the inner religious life of the actors in the Reformation than of any persons before or since. Under the sad compulsion of ecclesiastical inquisition, they were obliged to narrate the rise and progress of religion in their souls. These records we have; to the latest time they will form profitable subjects for study. In the life to come, we shall have myriads of similar biographies; composing the staple of the subjective history of redemption.

The truth which Bradwardine vindicated in his study, which Wycliffe had scattered alongside the highways and byways of the kingdom, now became the dear heritage of many persons who in all parts of England, after an earnest fashion, sought for rest unto their souls. The persecutions under Henry VII., and during the first years of his successor, were nominally founded on the denial of the doctrine of the real presence of Christ in the eucharist; but the opinions thus ascertained to be heretical were invariably accompanied by faith in the atonement as the ground of acceptance with God. The persecutors rejoiced in the supposed extinction of opposition when they triumphed over the extinguished lives of the deniers of transubstantiation, but the main truth lay safe and untouched. It is quite evident that the early sufferers were animated, not by opposition to Romanist teaching, but by the higher power of the Holy Ghost, and the love of our Lord Jesus Christ.

"He being dead yet speaketh," became true in a singular method of one of the landed gentry of England at this time, of whom we should have known nothing but for the preservation of his will. William Tracy was the worthy representative of a worshipful ancient family, seated at Toddington, in Gloucestershire. Though a resident country gentleman, yet he was a scholar, learned in the writings of Augustine, that fountain of mediæval evangelism. During the reign of Henry VII. he had maintained his place in society with a reputation worthy of his lineage. Full of years, he made his will in October, 1530, and died. The document in question is far more than a formal stereotyped statement of the testator's trust in the Supreme: it is a brief, comprehensive avowal of the truth as it is in Jesus:—

"First and before all thing, I commit me unto God,

and to his mercy, trusting without any doubt or mistrust, that by his grace and the merits of Jesus Christ, and by the virtue of his suffering and of his resurrection, I have, and shall have, remission of my sins and resurrection of my body and soul, according as it is written Job xiv., 'I believe that my Redeemer liveth, and that in the last day I shall rise out of the earth, and in my flesh shall see my Saviour.' *This my hope is laid up in my bosom.*" " My ground and belief is that there is but one God and one Mediator between God and man, which is Jesus Christ; so that I do accept none in heaven, nor in earth, to be my Mediator between me and God, but only Jesus Christ."*

Well said, brave old knight! requiring some stoutness of purpose to say it, even in a posthumous manner. He was the type we trust of hundreds more who, in the last day, shall rise from ancestral tombs to join the glorious assemblage around the throne. Little did it boot, that two years after his death, the ignorant priests burnt in the fire the mouldering remains of his body, but much did it signify, in the progress of spiritual life in this land, that the testament of the worthy knight was made a household word by all such as looked for the advent of a purer faith. It spread quickly among the commonalty. They could readily understand both the precept and the example. Tyndale and Frith successively published comments on this unique but characteristic production of the reform before the Reformation.

It is remarkable that Lord Bacon, with his sagacious

* Tyndale's Works. Testament of W. Tracy.

mind, should, in his life of Henry VII., have entirely overlooked the great revolution in opinion then silently but surely taking place. Belief in the church was being superseded by personal faith in our Lord Jesus Christ. The annals of persecution disclose the undoubted fact that the commonalty of England, throughout whole districts, had become extensively evangelized. As old Foxe phrases it, "I find recorded in the register of London between the years of our Lord 1509 and 1527, the names of divers other persons, both men and women, who in the fulness of that dark and misty time of ignorance, had also some portion of God's good Spirit, which induced them to the knowledge of the truth and Gospel."*

At this time there arose a great demand for short practical religious treatises, which by the help of the printing press, could be readily supplied. The accusations of heresy, made against great numbers of citizens, were grounded on their possession of such books as the four Evangelists, the epistles of St. Paul and of St. James, the Revelation of St. John, Wycliffe's Wicket, and the book of the Ten Commandments. The nature of the food thus selected shews the kind of taste which prevailed. No wonder that the anxious inquirers found their way to Divine knowledge. All this was clearly the outworking of the old Lollardism, which had been implanted a whole generation before the great reformation.

We cannot trace the steps by which William Tyndale, during his resort to the newly-opened fountain of Greek literature at Cambridge, or his solitary musings amidst

* Vol. iv., p. 173.

the beautiful vales of his native county, became an earnest devoted Christian; but we find him at the age of thirty-four, at the table of his master, Sir John Walsh, prepared not only for intellectual conflict with the adherents of Romanism, but to do and dare all that was consequential upon deep personal conviction of the power and grandeur of "the truth as it is in Jesus." The light emanating from his example and utterances soon shone around. He had no ambition save to tell others of the Saviour. He replied to his opponent by saying, "That he was contented they should bring him into any county in all England, giving him £10 a year to live with, and binding him to no more but to teach children and to preach."

There are no writings extant which show a more lively image of the writer than those of Tyndale, none more thoroughly imbued with the flow of personal experience.

Take as an instance his definition of the Gospel, how different from that of the mere theologian, how adapted to cheer the heart, as well as enlighten the mind, of the student, as he eagerly glanced at the prohibited pages:—
"Evangelion (that we call the Gospel) is a Greek word; and signifieth good, merry, glad, and joyful tidings, that maketh a man's heart glad, and maketh him sing, dance, and leap for joy : as when David killed Goliath the giant, came glad tidings unto the Jews, that their fearful and cruel enemy was slain, and they delivered out of al danger; for gladness whereof they sung, danced, and were joyful. In like manner in the Evangelion of God (which we call Gospel, and the New Testament), joyful tidings;

and, as some say, a good hearing, published by the apostles throughout all the world, of Christ, the right David; how that he hath fought with sin, with death, and the devil and overcome them; whereby all men that were in bondage to sin, wounded with death, overcome of the devil, are, without their own merits or deservings, loosed, justified, restored to life; and saved, brought to liberty, and reconciled unto the favour of God, and set at one with him again; which tidings as many as believe, laud, praise, and thank God; are glad, sing, and dance for joy."*

Or his description of the same:—

"The law putteth from a man the trust and confidence that he hath in himself, and in his own works, merits, deservings, and ceremonies, and robbeth him of all his righteousness, and maketh him poor. It killeth him, sendeth him down to hell, and bringeth him to utter desperation, and prepareth the way of the Lord, as it is written of John the Baptist. For it is not possible that Christ should come to a man, as long as he trusteth in himself, or in any worldly thing. Then cometh the evangelion, a more gentle pastor, which suppleth and suageth the wounds of the conscience and bringeth health. It bringeth the Spirit of God; which looseth the bonds of Satan, and coupleth us to God and his will, through strong faith, and fervent love, with bonds too strong for the devil, the world, or any creature to loose them. And the poor and wretched sinner feeleth so great mercy, love and kindness in God, that he is sure in

---

* Tyndale's "Doctrinal Treatises," p. 8.

himself how that it is not possible that God should forsake him, or withdraw his mercy and love from him."*

These sentences afford internal evidence of the enjoyment experienced by the writer from his cordial reception of evangelical truth; they serve to suggest to us the existence of inward pleasures which amply compensated for the loss of all that he so bravely forfeited in order to the accomplishment of the great purpose of his life.

> "But Faith
> Her daring dreams will cherish,
> Speeding her gaze o'er time and death
> To realms where nought can perish."

It was not the charm of a rising vernacular literature, nor the pungent sallies of his inextinguishable wit, that induced people throughout the kingdom to peril their lives for the possession of his writings, but it was desire for the word of life. So we learn from a contemporary:—"And then are they also to all Tyndal's bokes, whiche for the manyfolde mortall heresis conteyned within the same openlye condempned and forbydden, they are, 1 saye, yet unto those bokes so sore affectionate, that neyther the condempnation of them by the clergy, nor the forbydding of them by the kings hyghnes, with his open proclamations upon greate paynes, nor the daunger of open shame, *nor parell of painfull deth*, can cast them out of some fond folkes handes, and that folke of every sorte." †

* Tyndale's "Doctrinal Treatises," p. 22.
† Barlowe's Dialogue.

The trying position of intelligent godly persons at this time will be best illustrated by an example. In 1524 a man of good understanding and attainments, married, polite, and pious, named Thomas Benet, having embraced the reformed doctrines, left Cambridge and all hope of preferment, and went to Great Torrington, in Devonshire, where he endeavoured as a schoolmaster to earn a maintenance for his family. This not succeeding, he removed to Exeter, where for six years he successfully followed his calling and at the same time diligently studied the Scripture, and attended all the public services of religion. He first departed from the privacy of his course by seeking out and aiding such as were favourers of the Gospel. Then he became convinced that it was his duty, in spite of the peril, to testify against the prevalent corruption. He acquainted his family and friends with his resolution, disposed of his books, counted the cost, and commenced the warfare by fixing written scrolls upon the doors of the Cathedral, affirming the pope to be Antichrist, and claiming all worship as due to God alone and not to the saints. He was nearly detected by his expressions of ridicule on an occasion when the unknown author of the libels was solemnly excommunicated by bell, book, and candle in his presence; soon after this he was discovered, and then with much calm intrepidity argued for a whole week with his enemies, maintaining not only the anti-papal doctrine, but the still more important truth of the sufficiency of the atonement made by Christ. His poor wife brought food to him in prison, and appears to have sympathised in his views of the terrible necessity of the case. He had no support from without, for in that priest-ridden city the multitude sided with their chiefs, and he experienced the malice and rage of the whole community; but he died a humble, courageous, devoted martyr. Foxe says, " and being brought to his execution, in a place called Livery-dole, without the city of Exeter, he made his most humble confession and prayer unto Almighty God, and requested all the people to do the like for him; whom he exhorted with such gravity, and with such a pithy oration, to seek the true honour of God, and the true knowledge of him; as also to leave the devices, fantasies, and imaginations of man's invention, that all the hearers and beholders of him were astonied and in great admiration; insomuch that the most part of the people, as also the scribe who wrote the sentence of condemnation against him, did pronounce and confess that he was God's servant, and a good man."*

Not until the long rest of the dead is finally disturbed, shall we know what wrongs their graves cover!

When John Tewkesbury, a reputable London tradesman, was examined before the bishops on a charge of heresy in 1529, he avowed that had studied the Scriptures for seventeen years, and by the aid of the New Testament discovered the faults of his soul. He maintained the doctrine of justification by faith, attributed his conversion to Tyndale's Testament and tracts. He was sent from the Lollard tower to the mansion of the able, witty and learned chancellor, Sir Thomas More, who

* Foxe, vol. v., p. 25.

had the baseness to torture in various ways the prisoner whose constancy he could not move by his arguments. Crushed with suffering he recanted, but afterwards withdrew his recantation, boldly but soberly reaffirmed his belief in the sole mediatorship and sufficient atonement of Christ, and was burnt at Smithfield on St. Thomas's eve, whilst his fellow citizens were, in their several wards, electing the members of the corporation for the next year. Truly, the future "weight of glory" must be infinitely great, to bring such sufferings under the category of "light afflictions which are but for a moment!"

The terrific conflicts through which the people of God had now to pass in combating with the enemies of the truth, were greatly augumented by mental struggles. When speedy and cruel death became the inevitable consequence of conscientiousness, it was not unnatural that some persons should attempt to postpone or avoid the result. Bainham, an accomplished London lawyer, with Bayfield, the Bible-hawking priest, followed Tewkesbury's example: first confessed the truth, then recanted to save dear life; then, finding the last state worse than the first, announced their repentance of their recantation, and finally became martyrs. What anguish must the London merchant have felt ere he stood up in his pew in his parish church on a Sunday morning, holding his English New Testament in his hand and Tyndale's "Obedience of a Christian Man" in his bosom, and then, amidst his family and fellow citizens, with a full knowledge that he was dooming himself to an untimely death, declared openly with tears that he had denied God by his former recantation, prayed for forgiveness, and exhorted the people not to do as he had done.

Harding and his wife, of Chesham, were accused of conversing about the Scriptures, and favouring Lollards. For twenty years they had to undergo various penances, fasts, and pilgrimages, which made sad inroad upon their liberty, comfort, and prosperity. Harding was enjoined to wear on both the sleeves of his smock-frock, instead of the quaint embroidery in which rustics still take delight, the image of a faggot. After bearing this for fifteen years, he went into the woods to read in solitude, whilst the villagers went to mass on Easter Sunday. There, whilst he was so occupied with a book of prayers in English, the informers found him. He was denounced and condemned for Lollardism. After sixty years of reputable life spent in his native village, he was burned to death in 1532, at the entrance of the little wooded dell, which contributes to form the exquisite sylvan scenery at the foot of the chalk downs of Buckinghamshire.

A genuine religious revival was taking place in Essex through the faith and firmness of a few intelligent energetic laymen, labouring in the neighbourhood of Colchester, who were joined by one or two converted priests. The leaders of the little band, Tyball, Pykes, Topley, and some godly women of their party, resolved it to be their duty to meet together to hear the word, to pray, and to recognize each other as disciples of the Lord Jesus Christ. Thus, in obscurity and persecution, amidst the fields of East-Anglia, was formed the first true congregation of believers as such, in Britain. Coverdale, Bilney, and

Latimer, willingly acknowledged the right of this gathering to be considered as a true church.* The good women learnt the Gospel by heart, so as to enable them to conduct cottage meetings; the men travelled from one farmstead and town to another, reading the Bible and speaking of Him to whom it testifies. This was about the year 1529.

The cause of personal religion received a large accession from the publication in 1527 of Tyndale's "Parable of the Wicked Mammon," which was introduced into England by stealth. It is a full, hearty vindication of the doctrine of justification by faith in the work of Christ alone. This boon he bestowed on his countrymen immediately after his translation of the Scriptures. Tyndale was far more than a scholar, as this work testifies. "This is therefore plain, and a sure conclusion, not to be doubted of, that there must be first in the heart of a man, before he do any good work, a greater and a preciouser thing than all the good works in the world, to reconcile him to God, to bring the love and favour of God to him, to make him love God again, to make him righteous and good in the sight of God, to do away his sin." . . . "That precious thing which must be in the heart, ere a man can work any good work, is the work of God, which, in the Gospel, preacheth, proffereth, and bringeth, unto all that repent and believe, the favour of God in Christ."

No wonder that the divine, loving truths, and terse language of this little treatise, won many hearts to the

* D'Aubigné, vol. v., p. 519.

Saviour. It was, along with the Bible, the manual of the merchant-martyr Tewkesbury, and of poor Bayfield, the tortured Benedictine of Bury St. Edmunds.

In the short narrations we possess of the personal history of the sufferers during the early reformation-period, we notice an absence of all mere enthusiasm and fanaticism, and the presence of great depth and tenderness of emotion. The occurrences were serious, the men were grave as became the times; but they were men of the market-place, and of the family circle. Never was piety more healthy, because never more active; never was it firmer, for it had been rooted and grounded during continuous storms.

The bishops' registers in the reign of Henry VIII., are full of notices of the succession of spiritual life. A few pages of Foxe in which these are transcribed, will, at a glance, show the prodigious evangelical activity then prevailing. There were devoted laymen who went about every where, instructing the people in the knowledge of Christ crucified, not counting their lives dear to them so that they could accomplish the chosen task. We read for instance, of "a glorious and sweet society" of believers at Newbury, continuing for fifteen years together:— of "a godly and great company" at Amersham, which had continued stedfast for twenty-three years;—of a conventicle at Burford, and conventicles in other places. The Buckinghamshire believers were called "just-fast men," and "known men;" the gathering at Burford was supplied by the "singular good memory" of Alice Colins, wife of Richard Colins, who was a famous woman among them, and could recite much of the Scripture, and other good books, and, when the conventicle met, she was sent for to recite the newly published treatise on the ten commandments, and the older epistles of Peter and James.*

The great revival spread in the land; there was a hunger for the bread of life, prompting persons to gather together in the darkness of night, at all hazards, to listen to some humble Scripture reader. The laity of England were resolved to have the knowledge which they supposed the Bible could impart, cost whatever it might. The poor reader went about at the peril of his life, but still he went. "John Wood, of Henly; William Wood; Lewis, of Henly, a serving-man; Willie and his son," were taken: "This Willie was impeached because he taught the Gospel of Matthew to John Wood and William Wood, after the great abjuration; and father Robert did teach them St. Paul's epistle; which old father was after that burned at Buckingham."†

There is no uncertainty as to the means employed. The instrumentality was humble, but it was "mighty through God." Nothing else will explain its efficacy. There were no political or social or adventitious causes at work. It was wholly a movement for, and of, personal religion. It is high time that the roots of the English reformation should be traced, and its true character vindicated. The messengers who were employed in the work were themselves earnest believers, and this was the secret of their success, and their only title to fame. Again we resort to the registers for proof:—

* Foxe, vol. iv., p. 238. † Ibid., p. 228.

"Thomas Holmes denounced John Phips. He was very ripe in the Scripture; he was a reader or rehearser to the other; also John Butler, carpenter; Richard Butler; William King, of Uxbridge; these three sat up all night in the house of Durdant at Iver Court by Staines, reading all night in a book of the Scripture; also Ioan Cocks, the wife of Robert Laywood, husbandman; for desiring of Durdant, her master, that he being a 'known man' would teach her some knowledge of God's law. Also Nicholas Durdant of Staines; Davy Durdant, of Ankerwyck, the wife of old Durdant; the wife of Nicholas Durdant. These were detected, for that old Durdant of Iver Court sitting at dinner with his children and their wives, bidding a boy, there standing, to depart out of the house, that he should not hear and tell, did recite certain places to them out of the epistles of St. Paul and the Gospels."* "John Butler was also compelled by his oath to detect Henry Vulman and his wife, of Uxbridge; Page, carpenter, of London; a daughter of John Phip; a daughter of William Phip. This Page, carpenter, was detected for having certain books of the Apocalypse in English. Also, for that this carpenter and his wife did bring him, and the wife of Henry Vulman, to a corner house of Friday-street, where the good man of the house, having a stump foot, had divers such books, to the intent they should hear them read." "Thomas Tridway compelled by his oath to detect John Morden, of Ashleygreen, and Richard Ashford his brother. These were accused and detected because John Morden had in his

* Bishop Langland's Registers. Foxe, vol. iv., p. 228.

house a book of the Gospels, and other chapters in English, and read three or four times in the same; in which book his brother Ashford did read once." "John Groser was examined whether he had a book of the Gospels in English; who confessed that he received such a book of Thomas Tykill, morrow-mass priest in Milk-street, and afterwards lent the same book to Thomas Spencer, which Thomas Spencer with his wife used to read upon the same." "Also Richard Colins, of Genge, and his wife. This Colins was among them a great reader, and had a book of Wycliffe's Wicket, and a book of Luke, and one of Paul, and a gloss of the Apocalypse. Also William Colins, brother of Richard. Also Thomas Colins, father of Richard and William. He had a book of Paul and a book of small epistles." "Also John Ledisdall, of Hungerford, for reading the Bible in John Burges's house at Burford, upon Holywood Day, with Colins, Lyvord, Thomas Hall and others." "John Baker, weaver, of Witney; the bailiff of Witney; John Hakker; John Brabant and his wife; John Brabant, his son, with his wife; Reginald Brabant, of Stanlake, for reading in a certain English book of Scripture, they being together in John Brabant's house of Stanlake."

James Brewster, who, together with William Sweeting, was burnt at Smithfield on the 18th of October, 1511, was accused and confessed, "That he had been five times with William Sweeting in the fields keeping beasts, hearing him read many good things out of a certain book, at which reading also were present at one time Woodruff or Woodbine, a net-maker, with his wife;

also a brother-in-law of William Sweeting; and another time Thomas Goodred, who likewise heard the said William Sweeting read. Item, for having a certain little book of Scripture in English, of an old writing almost worn with age."

We read of John Maundrell, of Keevil, in Wiltshire, a husbandman, the son of a farmer, who after the Scripture had been translated by Tyndale, became a diligent hearer and then an embracer of God's truth, so that it was his daily delight. In order that he might constantly hear and speak of the Gospel he kept the New Testament always about him, although he could not read himself. When he came into company where any one could read, his book was always ready and if all were illiterate then he recited the passages fixed in his memory. The pages of old Foxe disclose many similar instances of the pursuit of piety under difficulties. Maundrell was obliged to leave his wife and children, and home and good name and fame, and to wander about as a herdsman. Ultimately he was apprehended, and with two artizans of the same district burnt to death at Salisbury on the 24th of March, 1556; Maundrell at the stake indignantly refusing the offer of pardon if he would recant, with the decided exclamation, "Not for all Salisbury!"

We can, by these aids, reproduce the picture exhibited over a great part of England in and about the year 1520. We see the thoughtful artizan, the scrap of Scripture in his wallet, the tract concealed beneath his doublet, the midnight gathering, the family group, the warm-hearted solemn teaching, the firm resolve with the grateful acceptance. Alas! too often we must add the hypocritical informer, the imprisonment, the trials, mockery of penance, the clamour, and ofttimes the dreadful death. Vital piety shone with singular lustre in these difficult times. Religion, which in the estimation of priest and people theretofore, was a thing to be done by the one for the other, all at once sprang into independent existence.

One well-known character of the kingdom of Christ is illustrated by these details, namely, that it is composed of persons of all worldly sorts and conditions. The stream of life flows with equal purity through the park of the nobleman, and by the hut of the peasant; its waters are equally precious to the prisoner in his cell, and to the monarch on his throne. Of it may be said, as of the sunbeam,

"A joy thou art, and a *life* to all!"

Whilst Christianity was thus springing up amongst the middle and working classes of the country, it also burst out amidst the students at Cambridge, and thence spread to Oxford, in a manner quite independent of the old Lollardism of the provinces. The sound devotion of master Stafford, the sharp convictions and clear insight of Bilney, the loving spirit of Frith, the homely force of Latimer, were all so many powers emerging from the darkness, which were immediately engaged in the active promulgation of the very sum and substance of true religion.. Soon too, the glow from the heat of the Lutheran reformation was felt across the Channel, multitudes of people began to place the teaching of the Church second, and of the Scripture first.

There were some who succumbed in a measure to the force of persecution, by sustaining the modified punishment of degradation and banishment, but who nevertheless continued to promote religion, by going into by-places to teach the knowledge of Christ. Such a man was Becon, who, deprived of all opportunity of rising in his university, went into the uplands of Derbyshire, and there, as an itinerant schoolmaster, preached the Gospel in the districts around. By his godly life, popular addresses, and admirable tracts, he greatly promoted the cause of vital religion. He wrote books for the people, composed in short sentences, full of earnest, persuasive, all-important truth. The titles of some of these proclaim their suitableness to the times. "The Sick Man's Salve," "The Pathway unto Prayer," "The Christmas Banquet," "The New Year's Gift," "The Potation for Lent," "A Pleasant New Nosegay," are all charming little works, in which the doctrines of the New Testament are stated and illustrated, in a sprightly and homely manner.

"In 1526, the promoters of evangelical truth were organized into a society calling themselves the 'Christian Brotherhood,' with a central committee sitting in London, with subscribed funds, regularly audited, for the purchase of Testaments and tracts, and with paid agents, who travelled up and down the country to distribute them."*

The same year witnessed a great development of the lights and shadows of religious life at the English Universities. Wolsey had gathered around his sumptuous new

* Froude, vol. i., p. 153.

foundation of Cardinal College a company of young men who were the ornaments of the age for learning and skill of various kinds—"picked young men of grave judgment and sharp wits." * It so happened, that in the case of the majority of these, the new learning was connected with the re-discovered faith. Among the goodly company, foremost in philology and logic, was Fryth, who had received from Tyndale the love of saving truth. The young men of the University acquired the habit of associating for discussion and enjoyment in the opening field of Biblical learning. Garrett, a zealous pious curate, living in Honey-lane, Cheapside, was in the habit of visiting both Universities with supplies of Tyndale's first translation of the Scriptures, and other volumes of godly learning prohibited by law. This he deemed to be his mission. With zealous heart and winning tongue, he recommended the truths which he bore. Martyrdom speedily became his lot. The young men grew in the knowledge and love of the Gospel. Upwards of twenty of them were seized and imprisoned in the fish-cellar of the New Hall. There they were confined from February until August, save such as death released, and one or two dismissed by less painful agencies. Fryth left this dungeon to cross the sea into Germany, where he visited his spiritual counsellor Tyndale, and aided him in the translation of the Scriptures. Probably, amidst all the discomforts and privations incident to exile, this was a happy period in the lifetime of these rare men. He returned to his own country to carry on the work of

* Foxe.

teaching; was set in the stocks at Reading as a vagrant; released himself by making an appeal in Greek to a passing schoolmaster; was hunted by his brother in learning, Sir Thomas More, the famous chancellor; taken prisoner, confined in the Tower; had to contend before the Chancellor for *dear* life in defence of *dearer* truth; was arraigned and questioned before the Archbishop, again before the Bishop of Winchester, again before the whole episcopal court; would only defend, and would not recant; was condemned and cruelly burnt to death on the 20th of June, 1533. Fryth deserves eminent rank as a vigorous believer, as well as a ripe scholar and bold assertor of the truth. His career was short and bright. He found time to write and publish the most telling books of the day against the sacramentarian errors of the Romanists, which, more than any others, obstructed the career of evangelism. To live "as ever in the great Taskmaster's eye" is a noble attainment; but to do so amidst the undeserved hate and contempt of the world, the penalties of voluntary poverty, the prospect of cruel martyrdom, is heroism of the highest order. We may learn the secret of their strength by stepping into the study of Anthony Delaber, one of the young men at St. Alban's Hall, who favoured the visits of the book-bearer Thomas Garrett from London. After narrating the escape of Garrett, he writes—

"When he was gone down the stairs from my chamber, I straightway did shut my chamber door, and went into my study, and took the New Testament in my hands, kneeled down on my knees, and with many a deep sigh and salt tear did I, with much deliberation, read over the tenth chapter of St. Matthew his Gospel: and when I had so done, with fervent prayer I did commit unto God that our dearly-beloved brother Garrett, earnestly beseeching Him in and for Jesus Christ's sake, His only begotten Son our Lord, that He would vouchsafe not only safely to conduct and keep our said dear brother from the hands of all his enemies, but also that he would endue his tender and lately-born little flock in Oxford with heavenly strength by his Holy Spirit, that they might be able thereby valiantly to withstand to His glory all their fierce enemies, and also might quietly, to their own salvation, with all godly patience, bear Christ's heavy cross; which I now saw was presently to be laid on their young and weak backs, unable to bear so huge a burden without the great help of His Holy Spirit. This done, I laid aside my book safe." *

The opposition made by the ecclesiastics to the spread of Tyndale's Version, appears to have called forth a spirited treatise in favour of the right of the people to God's Word, which is found at length in Foxe.† The sympathy which the writer reckoned upon, is indicated in the closing sentence of this calm and able production: "Who that findeth or readeth this letter, put it forth in examination, and suffer it not to be hid or destroyed, but multiplied; for no man knoweth what profit may come thereof. For he that compiled it purposeth, with God's help, to maintain it unto the death if need be. And therefore, all Christian men and women! pray that the

* Foxe. † Vol. iv., p. 671.

Word of God may be unbound, and delivered from the power of Antichrist, and runne among his people."

It is impossible to attribute the English Reformation either exclusively to the resurrection of the Greek Testament at Cambridge, to the charms of Ann Boleyn at Hever, or to the pen of Luther at Wittenberg. All these things worked together for its good, but its origin was clearly antecedent to any of them; so that when the ripe Christianity of the scholars was promulgated, it was immediately supported by the foregone conclusions of multitudes of thoughtful though unlettered men. The doctrine of justification by the work of Christ alone, was the faith of people in English homes, long ere it was nailed to cathedral doors in Germany or publicly discussed at Cambridge.

We may well conceive the wonder and joy of the poor despised Loilards, when they received the astonishing news that the most learned men in the Universities, and most exalted men at Court, were converts to the faith. On the receipt of these glad tidings, they counted their own individual persecution but a light affliction, and anticipated for the nation a glorious future.

In the year 1531, vital personal religion was burning, with strong but sad-coloured flame, in the breast of "little Bilney," the pensive, strong-minded, faint-hearted Cambridge man. On the Friday before his execution, whilst in prison in the Guildhall at Norwich, talking with his friends about the fiery trial expected on the morrow, and after proving his courage by burning his finger in the candle, he took for his topic the text, "Fear not; for I have redeemed thee, and called thee by thy name: thou art mine. When thou goest through the water, I will be with thee; and the strong floods shall not overflow thee; when thou walkest in the fire, it shall not burn thee, and the flame shall not kindle upon thee: for I am the Lord thy God, the Holy One of Israel, thy Saviour." Which, says old Foxe, "he did most comfortably intreat of, as well in respect of himself, as applying it to the particular use of his friends there present; of whom some took such sweet fruit therein, that they caused the whole said sentence to be fairly written in tables, and some in their books; the comfort whereof in divers of them was never taken from them to their dying day."*

Bilney's Bible, still preserved at Cambridge, has this passage from the 43rd of Isaiah, strongly underscored in the handwriting of the martyr. A few words from Foxe will display the great activity of divine life amongst the scholars at this time, in the very teeth of bitter persecution, and show of what heroic quality was the faith of these good men:—"This godly man (speaking of Bilney), being a bachelor of law, was but of little stature, and very slender of body; and of a strait and temperate diet; and given to good letters; and very fervent and studious in the Scriptures—as appeared by his sermons, his converting of sinners, his preaching at the lazar cots, wrapping them in sheets, helping them of that they wanted, if they would convert to Christ; laborious and painful to the desperates; a preacher to the prisoners and comfortless, a great doer in Cambridge, and a great preacher in

* Foxe, vol. iv., p. 653.

Suffolk and Norfolk; and at the last in London preached many notable sermons: and before his last preaching in London, he, with Master Arthur, Master Stafford, and Master Thistel, of Pembroke Hall, converted Dr. Barnes to the Gospel of Jesus Christ our Saviour, with the assistance of Master Fork, of Bennet College, and Master Send, master of the same college; to whom also were then associate Master Parker and Master Poury. Which Bilney with Master Arthur converted one Master Lambert, being a mass priest in Norfolk, and afterwards a martyr in London." *

The force of personal religion in Bilney is illustrated by his letters to his Romanist priest, and even to his parents: not exhorting them to forsake Romanism as a system, nor opposing their tenets by argument, but persuading them to acknowledge their need of Christ and to embrace him. He tells the Vicar of Dereham, that if he will live according to the Gospel, and speak but one sentence of it every Sunday, yet God would own this one sentence in the conversion of souls: and to his parents he writes, admonishing them to remember the sufferings of Christ, and "howe preciouse thynges He hath bequethed —his remission of our sinnes and everlasting lyffe."

The conversion of Latimer, the fierce young debater for ritualism, by means of the deep gentle voice of Bilney; the story of their subsequent friendship in the dangerous truths, and more dangerous labours, of evangelism; of their walks together to the "Heretics' Hill;" and of their protracted conferences on Holy Scripture,

* Foxe, vol. iv., p. 620.

belongs to this period. The sunlight of the Gospel was gilding the antique towers of college halls, as well as the verdant slopes of Gloucestershire, the broad acres of East Anglia, and the tall gables of the city. The interests of God and eternity seemed to be on the point of becoming universally uppermost. "There is in the realm," quoth Latimer, "(thanks be to God), a great sight of laymen, well learned in the Scriptures, and of virtuous and godly conversation, better learned than a great sight of the clergy." These were the lineal descendants of the Lollards.

The spread of vital religion was at once indicated and promoted by the step taken in 1538, namely, the publication of the Bible in English with free permission to read it, and an injunction that a copy should be placed in every parish church. The proclamation directing this contains a provision singularly adapted to promote the right of private judgment, though expressly denying it:—
"And if at any tyme by reading any doubt shall come to any of you, touching the sense and meaning of any part thereof; that thenne, not geving to moche to your own minds, fantazies, and opinions; nor having thereof any open reasonying in your open taverns or alehouses—ye shall have recourse to such lerned men as be or shall be auctorized to preach and declare the same. So that, avoyding all contencione and disputacions in suche alehouses and other places, unmete for such conferences, and submyttinge your opinions to the judgmente of such lerned men as shall be appointed in this behaalf, his grace may well perceyve, that you use this most heigh

benyte quietly and charitably every of you to the edifying of himself, his wief, and famylye."

The language of this document shows that Scriptural truths had already become leading topics of discussion among the commonalty of England.

The currents were diffusing themselves in all directions throughout English society. The courses of the streams are all unknown to us, but the fertilizing effects remain to this day. Here and there we get a glimpse of the actual process. An incident in the early life of a good man (who was long afterwards living at Stoke Newington) thus admits us into the arcana :—

"When the king had allowed the Bible to be set forth to be read in all churches, immediately several poor men in the town of Chelmsford, in Essex, where his father lived and he was born, bought the New Testament, and on Sundays sat reading of it in the lower end of the church; many would flock about them to hear their reading, and he among the rest, being then but fifteen years old, came every Sunday to hear the glad and sweet tidings of the Gospel. But his father observing it, once angrily fetched him away, and would have him to say the Latin matins with him; which grieved him much. And as he returned at other times to hear the Scripture read, his father still would fetch him away. This put him upon the thoughts of learning to read English, that so he might read the New Testament himself; which when he had by diligence effected, he and his father's apprentice bought the New Testament, joining their stocks together; and, to conceal it, laid it under the bed-straw, and read it at convenient times. One night, his father being asleep, he and his mother chanced to discourse concerning the crucifix, and kneeling down to it, and knocking on the breast then used, and holding up the hands to it when it came by on procession; this he told his mother was plain idolatry, and against the commandment of God, where He saith, "Thou shalt not make any graven image, nor bow down to it, nor worship it." His mother, enraged at him for this, said, "Wilt thou not worship the cross, which was about thee when thou wert christened, and must be laid on thee when thou art dead?' In this heat the mother and son departed, and went to their beds. The sum of this evening's conference she presently repeats to her husband, which he, impatient to hear, and boiling with fury against his son, for denying worship to be due to the cross, arose up forthwith, and goes into his son's chamber, and, like a mad zealot, taking him by the hair of his head with both his hands, pulled him out of the bed and whipped him unmercifully. And when the young man bore this beating, as he related, with a kind of joy, considering it was for Christ's sake, and shed not a tear, his father, seeing that, was more enraged, and ran down and fetched an halter, and put it about his neck, saying he would hang him. At length, with much entreaty of the mother and brother, he left him almost dead." *

Old Strype waxes eloquent in describing the reception of the Bible by the public: "It was wonderful to see with what joy this book of God was received, not only among the learneder sort, and those that were noted for

* Strype, "Memorials," vol. i., p. 92.

lovers of the Reformation, but generally all England over, among all the vulgar and common people; and with what greediness God's Word was read, and what resort to places where the reading of it was. Everybody that could bought the book, or busily read it, or got others to read it to them, if they could not themselves; and divers more elderly people learned to read on purpose. And even little boys flocked among the rest to hear portions of the Holy Scripture read." *

Concurrently with the publication of the translated Bible, was the issue, by John Rogers, of the first Concordance in English. The work, though small, is more than a mere arrangement of the texts, for it contains definitions and short explanations. It must have been very useful to the students who were then beginning to seek the treasure to be found in the long-hidden mine. The preface is worthy of being remembered :—

"As the bees dylygently do gather together swete flowers, to make by naturall craft the swete honny; so have I done the pryncypall sentences conteyned in the Bible. The which are ordened after the maner of a table, for the consolacyon of those whych are not yet exercysed and instructed in the Holy Scripture. In the which are many harde places, as well of the Olde as of the Newe Testament, expounded, gathered together, concorded, and compared one wyth another; to thintent that the prudent reader (by the Sprete of God) may beare away pure and cleare understandynge. Whereby every man (as he is bounde) may be made ready, strong

* Strype, vol. i., p. 92.

and garnyshed to answer to all them that aske hym a reason of their faith."

Far too narrow a view of the great subject of the descent of religion, is frequently taken, by confining the field of observation to the Reformers and their descendants. Not only have there always been people holding with fond attachment the doctrines of grace, but even among the open enemies of the "new way," there were many, who under the armour of opposition, possessed hearts beating in unison with the vital truth. Such a one was Fisher, the anti-Reformation Bishop of Rochester. His lofty intelligence, earnest nature, and popular talents, though devoted to the hopeless advocacy of a failing cause, were accompanied by personal apprehension of evangelical doctrine.

Fisher died for denying the king's supremacy. As he walked from the Tower to the adjoining place of execution, he carried in his hand the New Testament. He was heard to pray that as this book had been his best comfort and companion, so in that hour it might give to him some special strength, and speak to him as from his Lord. "Then opening at a venture, he read: 'This is life eternal, to know Thee the only true God, and Jesus Christ, whom thou hast sent.' He continued to repeat the words as he was led forward: and thus the good old man of eighty, the incipient cardinal, the unflinching adherent of the Papacy, but the equally firm believer in Christ, went with firm heart and tottering step to the block." *

* Froude, vol. ii., from State MSS.

There were many others, too, who retained their ecclesiastical position whilst protesting against the vices of the Church, without a thought of rebelling against her authority, and who nevertheless clearly saw Jesus as the only Saviour. Such was Dean Colet, and such the whole tribe of the followers of Erasmus. They were enlisted soldiers of the Cross, but were not equal to the occasion; they slighted the spirit-stirring call—

> "Awake, my soul, away thy fears,
> And gird the gospel-armour on!"

CHAPTER IX.

Edward VI.

THE accession of the youthful son of Henry and Queen Jane St. Maur, introduced the Evangelical party into absolute power. The people in various places, in their zeal for innovation, outran the Government, and by the demolition of images in the City, at Portsmouth, and elsewhere, showed their reaction against the superstitions which had so long usurped the place of religion. Gardiner, bishop of Winchester, complained to the commander at Portsmouth, calling the people "Lollards" and "worse than hogs." The former epithet was justly applied. It was no new-fangled notion that kindled the zeal of the evangelicals, but the outworking of the old Wycliffite teaching. The Protector writes to the commandant, enjoining him not to meddle with the matter. He wisely says, that "he allowed of his zeal against innovations, but that there were other things that needed to be looked to as much. Great difference there was between the civil respect due to the king's arms, and the worship given to images. There had been a time in which the abuse of the Scriptures was thought a good reason to take them from the people—yea, and to burn them; though he looked on them as more sacred than images; which if they stood merely as remembrancers, he thought the hurt was not great: but it was known that for the most part it was otherwise; and upon abuse the brazen serpent was broken, though made at God's commandment: and it being pretended that they were *the books of the people*, he thought the Bible a much more intelligible and useful book."*

After the people had spoken out by their rejoicings, and the Government had followed suit by the institution of ecclesiastical visitations, the Parliament crowned the whole, by rapidly passing a bill for the repeal of all the penal statutes concerning religion, from the acts against "Lollardies" downwards; followed by an act ordaining the communion in both kinds; and by other legislation, which, after the fashion of that day, sought to settle for all men the modes of Divine worship and homage, which God allows them to settle for themselves, by the aid of His own Word.

As the Reformation advanced in England under the liberal government of the Protector Somerset, the great cry arising from the mass of the people, was for public gospel-preaching. Paul's Cross, usually an engine of state, became a focus of evangelic doctrine. Preachers were clamoured for everywhere; in many places they arose without official authority, and sought to supply the universal demand. Public affairs became strangely

* Burnet's " Hist. Ref.," vol. ii., p. 22.

blended with personal creeds. On April 24th, 1548, a royal proclamation took cognizance and control of itinerant preaching, and forbad it without licence from the king, protector, or primate. Six preachers were specially appointed by the Court to itinerate through the kingdom and spread the new light.

It was a noble thought of those who ruled in the councils of the young king, that the court chaplains should constitute a home mission, as itinerant evangelists; and when we find among the number, such men as Bradford, Grindal, and John Knox, we can easily imagine the effectiveness of such an institution. The journal of the king, written with his own hand, and now in the national library, thus records the appointment: "It was appointed I should have six chaplains ordinary, of which two to be ever present, and four always absent in preaching: one year, two in Wales, two in Lancashire and Darby; next year, two in the marches of Scotland, two in Yorkshire; the third year, two in Devonshire, two in Hampshire; fourth year, two in Norfolk and Essex, and two in Kent and Sussex, &c."*

The face of affairs was changed; piety no longer shrank timorously from the public gaze. The history of religion in England shows that there never has been a time when plain, earnest, intelligent scriptural preaching, failed to prove attractive to the multitude. Such is the evident suitableness of the glorious provision of the Gospel for the need of man's soul. Bishop Hooper, the Gloucester martyr, was one of the popular gospel

* Burnet's "Reformation Records," vol. ii., p. 63.

preachers of his day; and we are told of him, that "the people in great flocks and companies daily came to hear his voice, as the most melodious sound and tune of Orpheus' harp, as the proverb saith; inasmuch that oftentimes, when he was preaching, the church would be so full, that none could enter further than the doors thereof. In his doctrine he was earnest, in tongue eloquent, in the Scriptures perfect, in pains indefatigable." *

Several of the devoted men who soon afterwards suffered martyrdom, preached to overflowing congregations. Eighteen pence was disbursed by the churchwardens of St. Margaret's, Westminster, for mending the benches broken by the crowding of persons to hear Latimer there. The personal knowledge and faith of the converts, so conspicuous shortly afterwards, were now being formed and ripened. The more active partisans on either side, ranged themselves openly in opposition, in almost every parish. The licensed preachers too often found themselves led away from their proper work of ministering the truth, to *controvert* the political and social evils of the day. The famous Thomas Hancock, who had been first licensed and then suspended during the last reign, was now licensed again. Strype gives a curious account of his progresses, in which he made the churches ring with loud controversy between him and the advocates of the former way. The evangelical doctrine was called the "new learning;" and there were, says Strype, great numbers everywhere of the laity, especially in populous towns, who did now more openly show their hearts and their good inclinations

* Foxe, vol. vi., p. 639.

towards it.* At Lyme Regis, the Mayor favoured Hancock; but a rich merchant, with his followers, opposed him openly. Words were leading to blows; "the Mayor had much ado to quiet the hurly-burly; till he got most of them out of the church, and was himself called a knave for his protection of the preacher." †

Licences were granted to pious laymen to preach without any other ordination. We read of Richard Taverner, high sheriff of Oxford, preaching most enthusiastically in the pulpit of St. Mary's there, arrayed in gold chain and sword; and of William Holcot, Esq., of Buckland, ascending the pulpit wearing a velvet bonnet, a damask gown, and gold chain. Taverner, though a learned and earnest man, appears to have successfully cultivated the conceited style then becoming fashionable. Sir John Cheke has preserved a portion of the commencement of one of his sermons, which is as far as possible from simplicity:—"Arriving at the Mount of St. Mary's, in the stony stage where I now stand, I have brought you some fine biscuits, baked in the oven of charity, carefully conserved for the chickens of the Church, the sparrows of the Spirit, and the sweet swallows of salvation."

Various other modes were attempted of ministering to the public religious taste. One, which signally failed, was the revival of dramatic representations, with the facts of gospel history for their basis, instead of the fables of mediæval faith. This soon fell into deserved contempt. It has survived, in very feeble form, down to

* Strype's "Cranmer," A.D. 1547.
† Roberts's "Social History of Southern Counties," p. 222.

our own times, in the occasional introduction of a scriptural scene into the peep-show at the village fair, and, with equal tameness, in the cold "Sacred Dramas" of Hannah More. Art is an illustration, but not a primary teacher of religion.

Such devices were not required in places where the leading reformers were the preachers. At Exeter, for instance, Miles Coverdale, the honoured coadjutor of the martyred Tyndale, and second only to him in his high office as translator of the Bible, preached incessantly the leading truths of the Gospel. So vigorously did he do this, that all other controversy there was thrown into the shade, compared with that controversy which our Lord indicated, when he asked his disciples, "What think ye of Christ?"

Among the men who were at the same time conspicuous examples and considerable promoters of evangelical religion about the Court, was Dr. William Turner, the author of the celebrated "New Herbal," the first original botanical work in our language. He was one of the Cambridge students who, in the first religious revival there, became the subject of decided religious convictions, which through life rendered him the faithful enlightened advocate of the Gospel. Without having been ordained, and renouncing flattering prospects of promotion at the University, moved by missionary zeal, he devoted himself to itinerant preaching, and went out into the cities, towns, and villages of the midland counties, proclaiming Christ as the only Saviour. He settled at Oxford, in order that he might there carry on together his two beloved vocations of preaching and the study of natural history. Under the influence of the shifting policy of the last reign, he was imprisoned and banished; he resorted to Italian, French, and German universities, and, when the times were changed, returned home laden with knowledge and honours. He obtained preferment both as a physician and as a divine, became a standard-bearer for the Gospel whilst practising in high circles as a physician, was banished during the succeeding reign, and afterwards returned and lived a long life of usefulness, glorifying God by the devotion of large endowments, acquirements, and affections, to the great object of advancing the kingdom of Christ.

The eager pursuit and fond appreciation of the doctrines of the Gospel, which now arose, had a far wider range than the geographical limits of the Reformation. The great band of secret brothers in Southern Europe, Juan Valdez, Flaminio, Bernardo Ochino, Peter Martyr Vermiglio, and Aonio Paleario, within and without the Church of Rome, vied with each other in diving for that pearl of great price which lay hid in the depths of divine revelation. Their friends and neighbours who rejoiced with them were amongst the virtuous and the great in many countries. The treatise attributed to Paleario, "The Benefit that Christians receive by Jesus Christ crucified," was first dispersed in MS. in Italy, (having, as is obvious from the contents, been collated with the " Divine Considerations " of Juan Valdez,) printed about 1546, translated into French, and printed at Lyons in 1545; translated from the latter version in 1548, by

Courtenay Earl of Devon, whilst a prisoner in the Tower, and read in MS. by King Edward. The identical copy thus prepared is now in the Cambridge University library, and the young king's handwriting remains in two thoughtful sentences which show us the staple of his reflections. In the page after the dedication he has written, " Faith is dede if it be without workes. Your loving neueu Edward." And in the last page but one, " Liue to die, and die to liue again. Your neucu Edward." *

Thus the glorious riches of God's free grace, the inheritance of every believer in the Lord Jesus Christ, appeared to be on the point of becoming naturalized in the literature of courts and colleges.

The song was again jubilant,—

> "Let all the world in every corner sing,
> My God and King!
> The church with psalms must shout;
> No door can keep them out:
> But, above all, the heart
> Must bear the longest part.
> Let all the world in every corner sing,
> My God and King!"
>
> HERBERT.

The kind and cordial reception given to the eminent foreign Protestant teachers who, at this juncture, came to promulgate the tenets of the German Reformation, and repaid the hospitality, by conduct becoming Christians and learned men, was a token of the earnestness with

* See Mr. Babington's sumptuous edition of this remarkable book, and also Mr. Ayre's admirable edition, published by the Religious Tract Society.

which the truth was then sought. Peter Martyr Vermiglio, Bucer, Fagius, John Alexander, and John A' Lasco, were all treated with honour, and placed in situations where their character and abilities might eminently serve the cause of truth.

The influence of the intercourse between the learned men who had lighted their torches at the same flame of Divine truth in England, and in Germany, produced the happiest results. Every treatise upon evangelical subjects became common property, whether it was published on the Continent or here; letters are still extant showing the mutual delight with which successive works of the reformed press were hailed. Many of these were translated for more extended circulation. The great number of French religious refugees residing in England furthered this operation; and thus we derived from continental sources, much of that well-grounded, though somewhat formal, doctrinal literature, which rendered the Puritan writers so mighty in dogmatic theology. For instance, we find a ponderous folio, printed in 1576, dedicated to Sir Anthony Cook, by Robert Masson, one of the ministers of the French church in London, being the "Common Places" (as such selections were then called) of Peter Martyr Vermiglio. It comprises extracts from such of his works as treat of positive and ethical doctrines; it begins with the psychological consideration of God, then proceeds to consider revelation and nature, then humanity, original sin, salvation, predestination, justification by faith, concluding with the institutions and sacraments of the church.

Every possible topic connected with this large range is discussed. The work forms a body of divinity. It was several times republished; a translation into English was also made in 1583, by Sir Anthony Marten, Lord Chamberlain to Queen Elizabeth. The still more celebrated "Common Places" of Philip Melancthon passed through sixty-seven editions between 1521 and 1595 in the Latin, besides translations. Such were the solid materials from which the learning of the coming age was elaborated. Folios which would appal a modern student, as much as the bow of Ulysses alarmed the effeminate suitors of Penelope.

In this reign commenced that stream of foreign Protestant emigration which, for upwards of a century, served as an outlet for the oppressed ones on the Continent, persecuted by intolerant governments. Commerce and the arts, as well as piety, gained by this accession to our industrial population.

The young king was fond of the French language, partial to A' Lasco, who had forfeited episcopal promotion in Hungary to teach Protestantism in Friesland, and was banished from the latter by the order of the Emperor Charles V. He constituted the Polish refugee superintendent of the foreign Protestants in London, and gave them the old church of the Augustines in Austin Friars, gave them also a charter of incorporation, and otherwise aided them. Edward's translation into French of the texts of Scripture relating to idolatry is still preserved, and brings the royal boy-student before us in an interesting manner. The dedication to the Protector runs as follows:—

"Pourtant, cher oncle, apres avoir noté en ma Bible en Anglois plusieurs sentences qui contradisent à tout idolatrie à cette fin de m'apprendre et exerciser en l'escriture Françoise, je me suis amusé à la translater en la dite langue Françoise : puis les ay fait rescrire en ce petit livret, lesquell de tresbon cueur je vous offre : priant Dieu le Createur de vous donner grace de continuer en vostre labeur spirituel au salut de vostre ame et à l'honneur et gloire d'iceluy."*

Sir John Cheke the king's tutor, a godly and learned man, was, in the language of his biographer Strype, "a fast friend and patron to these outlandish learned confessors." Alas! that Cheke, after services so eminent, —a life so becoming to a pious scholar and Christian gentleman, after banishment for the cause of Christ, suffering and imprisonment,—should have embittered and probably shortened the last few dark days of his life by a recantation of the principles for which he had toiled and suffered! It is an instance of fortitude overcome by wearisome oppression. He afterwards lived only long enough to bewail his weakness; we may still point to him as an earnest, learned man, who successfully carried evangelical Christianity into all the concerns of a busy life in the face of the world.

The new light which was so gladly welcomed in most parts of England, was stoutly barred out and opposed in others. The men of Cornwall and West Devonshire, those of Yorkshire, and some from Buckinghamshire, and even from Norfolk, rose in rebellion in favour of Roman

* Burnet's "Reformation Records," vol. ii., p. 101.

doctrine. Their opposition took a warlike turn, and was opposed successfully by similar weapons. The death of Somerset removed from power the best friend of the "Gospellers." Knots of Bible students had begun to assemble openly in many parts of the kingdom, to consider the Scriptures; but they were broken up by fine and imprisonment, under the councils which succeeded the government of the Protector.

The stimulus afforded by the conjoint effect of the rising reformation and the revival of Greek literature operated powerfully among the educated classes. "It is now no news in England," says Nicolas Udal, "for young damsels in noble houses, and in the courts of princes, instead of cards and other instruments of idle trifling, to have continually in their hands either psalms, homilies, and other devout meditations, or else Paul's Epistles, or some book of Holy Scripture matters."*

The cumbrous romances of mediæval days were fast following into deserved oblivion the warlike rhapsodies of primeval literature. All things were becoming more real, as befitted the serious times which were now close at hand.

This political calm was soon at an end. The death of the young king frustrated the fond hopes of the people. Making ample allowance for the panegyric natural on such occasions, it is impossible to doubt that there remains, in the delineations of King Edward's character given by contemporary observers, the lineaments of a mind of uncommon ability and sagacity, of a

* Strype's Life of Parker.

nature truly gentle and noble; the tokens of extraordinary attainments, great sweetness of disposition, and recognition of a true relationship to God. Death, which was the extinction of one of the brightest prospects ever afforded to humanity, was welcomed by him with a longing desire to be with the chosen ones of his Father in heaven.

In regard to the sorrowing people, the new-born faith of many, yet needed the strength which only trial can impart. The great future of religious life and liberty, was to be heralded by severe and protracted trouble. As a prelude, there was one gentle form of rare mould, which bowed before the first rush of the coming whirlwind.

The humble personal piety of Lady Jane Grey, is as unquestionable, as the facts of her great attainments in learning, and her tragic end. At the place of execution, after acknowledging the justice of her condemnation, for concurring in an act of treason against the queen, and absolving herself from all share in its contrivance, she said, "I pray you all, good Christian people, to bear me witness that I die a true Christian woman, and that I do look to be saved by no other mean but only by the mercy of God in the blood of His only Son, Jesus Christ; and I confess, that when I did know the word of God, I neglected the same, loved myself and the world, and therefore this plague and punishment is happily and worthily happened unto me for my sins; and yet I thank God of his goodness He hath given me a time and respite to repent." Equally is it stereotyped in the well-known letter which she addressed to her sister on the eve of her suffering:—

"I have sent you (good sister Katherine) a book which, although it be not outwardly trimmed with gold, yet inwardly is worth more than precious stones. It is the book, dear sister, of the law of the Lord; it is His testament and last will, which He bequeathed unto us wretched creatures, which shall lead you to the path of eternal joy; and if you with a good mind read it, and with an earnest mind do purpose to follow it, it shall bring you to an immortal and everlasting life; it shall teach you to live, and learn you to die; it shall obtain for you more than you should have gained by possession of your father's lands; for as if God had prospered him you should have inherited his lands, so if you apply yourself diligently to this book, seeking to direct your life after it, you shall be an inheritor of such riches as neither the covetous shall withdraw from you, nor the thief shall steal, nor yet the moths corrupt. Desire, with David, (good sister,) to understand the law of the Lord God. And trust not that the tenderness of your age is an assurance that you will live many years; for (if God call) the young goeth as soon as the old: also endeavour to learn how to die. Defy the world, deny the devil, and despise the flesh, and delight yourself only in the Lord. Be penitent for your sins, and yet despair not; be strong in faith, and yet presume not: and desire, with St. Paul, to be dissolved, and to be with Christ, with whom even in death there is life. Be like the good servant, and even at midnight be waking, lest when death cometh and stealeth upon you, like a thief in the night, you be, like the evil servant, found sleeping; and lest, for want of oil, you be found like the five foolish women, or like him that had not on the wedding garment, and then ye be cast out from the marriage. Rejoice in Christ, as I do. Follow the steps of your master, Christ, and take up your cross; lay your sins on Him, and always embrace Him. And, as concerning my death, rejoice as I do, (good sister,) that I shall be delivered of this corruption, and put on incorruption. For I am assured that I shall, when I lose a mortal life, win an immortal life; which I pray God to grant you, and send you of His grace, to live in His fear, and to die in the true Christian faith, from which (in God's name) I exhort you that you never swerve, neither for the hope of life nor the fear of death; for if you will deny His faith, thinking thereby to lengthen your life, God will deny you and shorten your days. And, if you will cleave unto Him, He will prolong your days to your comfort and His glory, to which glory may God bring me now, and you hereafter when it pleaseth Him to call you. Fare you well, sweet sister, and put your only trust in God, who alone can help you."

CHAPTER X.

The Reign of Queen Mary.

THE materials for our history become more abundant as persecution arose under the change of government. Circumstances develop character in society, just as in the mineral kingdom the intrusion of the molten rock aggregates the shining metal into conspicuous veins. The general views and experience of the Marian martyrs, may be well ascertained from an able manifesto, drawn up with great care by Bradford, Saunders, and their companions in prison, expressly to declare the grounds of their quarrel with the dominant power. They write as men appointed to die for an undying cause. Truth above circumstances is their motto; they appeal heroically to and for the "infallible verity" of God's Word. They write concerning justification a passage which will serve as a specimen of their convictions:—"Fourthly, we believe and confess concerning justification, that, as it cometh only from God's mercy through Christ, so it is perceived and had of none which be of years of discretion otherwise than by faith only, which faith is not an opinion, but a certain persuasion wrought by the Holy Ghost in the mind and heart of man, through whom as the mind is illuminated, so the heart is suppled, to submit itself to the will of God unfeignedly." *

One of the brightest of the shining characters adorning this age is that of John Bradford. He was a native of Manchester, of active habits, and in good business as surveyor of crown lands. In the prime of life, he became a convert to true religion, went to Cambridge, was ordained as a preacher, and was made a prebend of St. Paul's. "In this preaching office," says Foxe, "for the space of three years, how faithfully Bradford walked, how diligently he laboured, many parts of England can testify. Sharply he opened and reproved sin, sweetly he preached Christ crucified, pithily he impugned heresies and errors, earnestly he persuaded to a godly life." He lay in prison for two years before his martyrdom. Nowhere have we on record such a narrative of intense religious action as his experience of these two years supplied. "From the Tower he came to the King's Bench in Southwark; and after his condemnation he was sent to the Compter in the Poultry, in London; in which two places, for the time he did remain a prisoner, he preached twice a day continually, unless sickness hindered him; when also the sacrament was often ministered, and through his means (the keepers so well did bear with him) such resort of good folks was daily to his lecture, and to the ministration of the sacrament, that commonly his chamber was well-nigh filled therewith. Preaching, reading, and

* Foxe, vol. vi., p. 552.

praying was his whole life. He did not eat above one meal a day; which was but very little when he took it; and his continual study was upon his knees. In the midst of his dinner he used often to muse with himself, having his hat over his eyes, from whence came commonly plenty of tears dropping on his trencher. Very gentle he was to man and child; and in so good credit with his keeper, that at his desire in an evening (being prisoner in the King's Bench in Southwark), he had licence, upon his promise to return again that night, to go into London without any keeper to visit one that was sick, lying by the Still-yard. Neither did he fail his promise, but returned to his prison again, rather preventing his hour than breaking his fidelity, so constant was he in word and deed. Of personage he was somewhat tall and slender, spare of body, of a faint sanguine colour, with an auburn beard. He slept not commonly above four hours in the night; and in his bed, till sleep came, his book went not out of his hand. His chief recreation was in no gaming or other pastime, but only in honest company and comely talk, wherein he would spend a little time after dinner at the board, and so to prayer and his book again. He counted that hour not well spent wherein he did not some good, either with his pen, study, or exhorting of others, &c. He was no niggard of his purse, but would liberally participate what he had to his fellow-prisoners. And, commonly, once a week he visited the thieves, pick-purses, and such others that were with him in prison, where he lay on the other side, unto whom he would give godly exhortation, to learn the amendment of their lives by their troubles, and, after so done, distribute among them some portion of money to their comfort. One of his old friends and acquaintances came unto him while he was prisoner, and asked him, if he sued to get him out, what then he would do, or where he would go? Unto whom he made answer as not caring whether he went out or no; but, if he did, he said he would marry, and abide still in England secretly, teaching the people as the time would suffer him, and occupy himself that way. He was had in so great reverence and admiration of all good men, that a multitude which never knew him but by fame greatly lamented his death—yea, and a number also of the Papists themselves wished heartily his life. There were few days in which he was thought not to spend some tears before he went to bed; neither was there ever any prisoner with him, but by his company he greatly profited, as all they will yet witness, and have confessed of him no less, to the glory of God, whose society he frequented."* He was eminently one to whom to live is Christ. All his letters breathe the air of vital personal religion. In the depths of his own inner life he was enjoying the sunshine of God's presence, though outwardly surrounded by the wintry storms of persecution. Open the volume of his letters written whilst waiting for martyrdom, and you are amidst utterances at once manly and heavenly. He writes to his mother, "Perchance you are weakened as to that I have preached, because God does not defend it, as you think, but suffers the Popish doctrine to come again and prevail;

* Foxe, vol. vii., p. 145, 146.

but you must know, good mother, that God by this tries and proves his children and people, whether they will unfeignedly and simply hang on Him and His word. . . . I am at a point, even when my Lord will, to come to Him : death nor life, prison nor pleasure, I trust in God, shall be able to separate me from my Lord God and His Gospel. . . . If it should be known that I have pen and ink in the prison, then will it be worse with me ; therefore keep this letter to yourselves, commending me to God and His mercy in Christ Jesus. Make me worthy, for His name's sake, to give my life for His Gospel and Church. —Out of the Tower of London, the 6th day of October, 1533."

The public materials for the general history of Evangelical doctrine during the reign of Queen Mary are all to be found in the confessions of persecuted and dying men. The proscribed truths were, however, held in secret by many a scholar, and many a peasant, whom the shades of obscurity or the partiality of powerful friendship concealed from the persecutors.

This state of things introduces a new feature into the religious history of our country : it led to the organization of private assemblies ; gatherings of such as found themselves to be under the ban of a common proscription for the sake of their Lord, and who invited each other to share the precarious but precious ordinances of united worship, with the administration of the Lord's Supper, thus forming voluntary churches. Foxe calls them congregations, and says that they first met at the house of one, and then another, in order to elude the vigilance of the authorities. The London congregation first resorted to Sir Thomas Carden's house in Blackfriars; then about Aldgate; then near the great conduit in the City through a narrow alley into a clothworker's loft; then into a shop at Billingsgate; next, into a ship called Jesus ship, moored between Ratcliffe and Rotherhithe, where they had prayer, sermon, and communion; next to a cooper's house in Pudding-lane; then to a house in Thames-street. They were ultimately driven into Islington fields, when several were captured for the last dreadful holocaust at Smithfield. Prompted by the stern necessities of their position on the one hand, and encouraged by the discovery of the suitableness and scriptural propriety of their course on the other, they formally recognized each other in the bonds of the Gospel, and were strengthened. Their contemporaries allege that "they did appoint mere laymen to minister; yea, and lay women sometimes, it is said."* Strype says of them, in his Life of Cranmer, "Sometimes, for want of preachers of the clergy, laymen exercised. Among them I find one old Henry Daunce, a bricklayer of Whitechapel, who used to preach the Gospel in his garden every holiday, where would be present sometimes a thousand people."

On New Year's Eve, 1555, the assembly was in a house in Bow churchyard, "where they were, with their minister, Maister Thomas Rose, devoutly and zealously occupied in prayer and hearing of Goddes word. But whyle they where in the middest of their godly exercise,

* Watson's two notable Sermons, 1554.

they were sodenly betraied (as it is thought, by some false dissembling hypocrite), and about xxx. of them apprehended and sent to the counters: but Maister Rose was had before the Lord Chauncelor, and from thence to the Fleet."*

Joy lies very close to the sorrow which such narratives excite. The rambler through the woodlands in springtime forsakes the beaten path, and, after pushing through tangled underwood, finds an open peaceful glade overhung by the blue canopy, and decorated by the countless beauties of harebell and anemone, which flourish as if the plague of sin were unknown. So, in searching into the past, do we occasionally fall upon the vision of a small community living together in the faith and love of the Lord Jesus Christ, and, like the flowers, giving a character of beauty to the lowly homes where they dwell. But we now look on them only after the ruthless blast of persecution, more bitter than the wind which howls through the woodlands, has crushed them and made the moral greensward a desert. Yet we are thankful that they once lived.

> "As evening's pale and solitary star
> But brightens while the darkness gathers round,
> So faith, unmoved amidst surrounding storms,
> Is fairest seen in darkness most profound."

It is not probable that any true spiritual force ever manifested on earth has been really lost. It may apparently have failed, and vanished from the place of its first occurrence; but the heat which it evolved only

* Foxe, vol. vi., Appendix, p. 775.

entered into some new combination, adding to the amount of moral energy abroad in the world.

Many of the narratives given by Foxe depict the homely strong religious life now growing up in England. The following is an outline of one only amongst many, which may with profit be referred to, in the crowded pages of the old martyrologist. In the early part of the sixteenth century, there dwelt in the parish of Dean, in the county of Lancaster, a young yeoman of simple manners, ingenuous disposition, and kind heart, named George Marsh. He was married, and thought himself, as he says, well settled with his loving and faithful wife and children in a quiet farm. The loss of his wife rendered the pleasant homestead unbearable. He went to Cambridge, and much increased in learning and godly virtue, and became curate to that rare man of God, Laurence Saunders. Here his desires and activities found full scope, and he was once again happy under his most gentle master. He continued for some time labouring, by public readings and preachings throughout Lancaster, to awaken sinners and help God's people. He was reported to hold heretical opinions on transubstantiation. Judicial inquiry was made for him: he was staying with his mother, who advised him to flee, which he had then resolved to do on account of the great sorrow, heaviness, losses, costs and charges, shame and rebuke, it would occasion his friends. His own conscience, whilst allowing the power of this reasoning, yet, on the other hand, suggested the hindrance to the truth that might be occasioned by his supposed defection. He left his mother's house greatly agitated, promising to return in the evening. He went out, met a dear friend on Dean Moor, and at sunset the two knelt down and prayed. He returned home, and found that messengers had been in pursuit of him. He would not harass his mother by staying under her roof, but went away to a friend's house beyond Dean church, where, after broken rest, he was aroused by a message from one of his faithful friends, advising him in nowise to fly, but to abide and confess his faith in Christ. He resolved on this ; whereupon he says that his mind, "afore being much unquieted and troubled, was now merry and in quiet estate." He arose, said the Litany and other prayers, kneeling by his friend's bedside ; went to the houses of various members of his family to ask their prayers, and requesting them to comfort his mother, and to be good to his little children ; and presented himself to the Earl of Derby's messenger, who had been charged to bring him. He was ordered to attend the next day at ten o'clock. He thereupon went to his mother's, took his leave of the household there and at his brother Richard's. "They and I both weeping, went part of the way, slept on the road, arose, prayed, and was at the earl's residence betimes." Then followed his first examination, in which all went well until the point of transubstantiation was touched, when his replies were too much founded on Scripture and common sense to please his judges, and he was remitted to a cold windy prison. On Palm Sunday he was sent for again, and allowed to have a bed, a fire, and liberty to go amongst the servants. He now cried earnestly to God to be strengthened against the allurements and subtlety of his enemies. After a day or two, he was again examined concerning the mass. Another interval and another examination followed, in which he was pressed with the recantation of others. Again on Shrove-Tuesday, again at Easter, did his tormentors ply him with alternate threats and promises; but he answered that he leaned only to the Scriptures, and objected to do as they wished, out of a reverent fear of God. More examined him many times very sharply, plied him with all the resources of learning and logic, lent him books, and ended by rebuking him as intractable and conceited. Poor Marsh answered, that, as for learning, he aimed principally at knowing Jesus Christ, and him crucified; and that his faith was grounded on God's Holy Word. After remaining some time longer in prison at Chester, he was conveyed to Lancaster Castle, and at the sessions held up his hand with the common malefactors at the bar. In Lancaster Castle he was sometimes comforted by the friendly visits of those who sympathized, and at others distressed by the vain attempts of opponents to get him to recant. He and a fellow-prisoner, "every day kneeling on our knees, did read morning and evening prayer, with the English Litany every day twice, both before noon and after, with other prayers more; and also read every day certain chapters of the Bible, commonly towards night: and we read all these things with so high and loud a voice, that the people without in the streets might come and hear us, and would oftentimes—namely, in the evenings—come and sit down in our sight under the windows and hear us read."

Then came the bishop, and complained of the gaoler for being too indulgent, and of the schoolmaster for speaking to such a heretic. After a while, he had to submit to two further examinations, in which every rule of evidence and all courtesy and humanity were violated by the bishop, and at length the fatal sentence was pronounced against him. He was handed over to the city authorities, his former gaoler weeping, and saying, "Farewell, good George!" and consigned to a dark dungeon, communicating with the outer world by a hole in the city wall. At this hole would friends station themselves, as at the windows of the Bishops' prison, and try to exchange sentences of consolation with the forlorn man. "He would answer them most cheerfully, that he did well; and thanked God most highly, that He would vouchsafe of His mercy to appoint him to be a witness of the truth, and to suffer for the same." He was brought out to die; walked through the city with his book in his hand; was offered pardon at the stake if he would recant, but sealed his testimony with his blood. His examinations and prison letters show him to have been a man of singleness of mind, genial loveable disposition and useful abilities, full of all the motive power and philanthropy of the glorious Gospel. Such men did not live or die unto themselves. The people gathering round the prison walls afford the true index to the value of these servants of the Most High. The pulses of spiritual life flowed high and fast in their veins, and, in spite of death, the movement was transmitted onward and outward to an ever-widening circle. Marsh's letter from Lancaster gaol to his brethren advises them—"cleave you fast unto Him which was incarnate, lived, wrought, taught, and died for your sins; yea, rose again from death and ascended into heaven for your justification." Amidst the dismal scenes then being enacted in the professing Church, he might well say that he rejoiced only in Christ, "the glory of whose Church, I see it well, standeth not in the harmonious sound of bells and organs, nor yet in the glistening of mitres and copes, neither in the shining of gilt images and lights, but in continual labours and daily afflictions for His name's sake."

To such men might well be said, as was sung to some of them,—

> "This prison where thou art,
> Thy God will break it soon,
> And flood with light thy heart,
> In His own blessed noon."

After allowing for the state of excited and exalted feeling produced by the apprehension of martyrdom, there still remains a solid substratum of intelligent personal evangelical piety exhibited by these illustrious sufferers. Very superior are they in this respect to the martyrs of the early Church, whose ecstasies led them to court martyrdom as the highest honour. The men and women of England bore it bravely as good witnesses, but did not ignore their own domestic sympathies in the flights of spiritual heroism.

One of the men, educated only in that knowledge which elevates and refines the moral nature by the process of sanctification through the truth, was a Suffolk tailor named George Eagles. During the sunny days of good

King Edward, he, "being eloquent and of good utterance," went about preaching. In the dark days of Queen Mary he forsook not his profession, but went from place to place seeking out the scattered sheep of the flock, in order to instruct and comfort them. We are told that often he spent the night in the woods, or under the open canopy of heaven. The homely name by which he was usually known, "Trudgeover," expresses his habits, and was so well fixed that he was actually indicted as "George Eagles, alias Trudgeover-the-world." He was fervent in faith, strong in prayer;—a representative man, of a long subsequent succession of faithful, useful lay labourers who have ministered the Gospel to their perishing fellow-countrymen. He was cruelly put to death at Colchester in 1557.

During the whole of this fearful period, there were not wanting many who made it their special mission to travel about the country for the purpose of "visiting the professors of the Gospel, and comforting and exhorting them to stedfastness in the faith." Among these were Laurence, of Barne Hall, and his servant; William Pulleyn, otherwise known as Smith; and William "a Scot," who dwelt, Foxe says, at Dedham Heath. These also regularly ministered to a congregation at the King's Head, Colchester, which constantly assembled during the whole period of the persecution, "and, as a candle upon a candlestick, gave light to all those who for the comfort of their consciences came to confer there from divers parts of the realm."*

* David's "Annals and Memorials," 1863, p. 53, from Strype.

In Ridley's most affecting and eloquent "Farewell," written after his sentence, we see the tenderness of his whole nature mingled with unalterable resolution. After sending special loving messages to his kinsfolk by name, he continues—"I warn you all, my well-blessed kinsfolk and countrymen, that ye be not amazed or astonied at the kind of my departure or dissolution; for I ensure you I think it the most honour that ever I was called unto in all my life, and therefore I thank my Lord God heartily for it, that it hath pleased Him to call me of His great mercy, unto this high honour, to suffer death willingly for His sake and in His cause: unto the which honour He called the holy prophets, and His dearly-beloved apostles and His blessed chosen martyrs. For know ye that I doubt no more that the causes wherefore I am put to death are God's causes, and the causes of the truth, than I doubt that the Gospel which John wrote is the Gospel of Christ, or that Paul's Epistles are the very word of God. And to have a heart willing to abide and stand in God's cause and in Christ's quarrel even unto death, I ensure thee, O man, it is an inestimable and an honourable gift of God, given only to the true elects and dearly-beloved children of God, and inheritors of the kingdom of heaven."

It is true that we are no longer attracted by the romance of the early struggles. *Then* so much of marvellous novelty was there in the upburst of the truth, that we feel as though it might at any moment become the dominant profession; but *now* all conclusions are foregone; places are taken, not for deliberation, but for sentence and execution. Argument is a mockery. The truth is persecuted, not as religion, but as treason. Yet, with all these depressing considerations, there is rich instruction for all the Christian ages to come, in the experiences of these Marian martyrs.

If we take Smithfield alone, it will afford a type of what was being done throughout the country at large. Every name is an index to a character rapidly matured for heaven.

The sufferers in this place during the reign were—

1555. John Rogers, the translator.
      Thomas Tomkins, a weaver.
      John Cardmaker, vicar of St. Bride.
      John Warne, or Warren, a citizen and clothworker. His wife soon after burned at Stratford, under circumstances of shocking barbarity.
      John Bradford, " Good Master Bradford, the grete precher."
      John Leaf, an apprentice.
      John Philpot, archdeacon of Winchester.

1556. Thomas Whittle, a priest.
      Bartlett Green, a lawyer of the Inner Temple.
      John Tudson, an artisan.
      John West, an artisan.
      Thomas Brown.
      Isabel Foster.
      Joan Warne, her maid.
      Robert Drakes, minister.
      William Tyms, curate.

Richard Spurge, a shearman.
Thomas Spurge, a fuller.
John Cavel, a weaver.
George Ambrose, a fuller.

1557. Thomas Loseby,
Henry Ramsey,
Thomas Thirtle,
Margaret Hide,
Agnes Stanley,
} For avowing the Protestant doctrine to be the true faith, and denying the mass. Burnt together in one fire.

John Hollingdale.
William Sparrow.
Richard Gibson.
John Rough, a Scottish priest, good preacher, and accomplished, excellent man.
Margaret Mearing, wife of a citizen.

1558. Cuthbert Sympson, deacon of a congregation in the City. Racked twice.
Hugh Foxe.
John Devenish.
Henry Pond,
Reinald Eastland,
Robert Southam,
Mattw. Ricarby,
John Floyd,
John Holiday,
Roger Holland,
} "Godly and innocent persons," who assembled secretly in a back close in the fields by the town of Islington, to pray and meditate on God's word.

The last of this illustrious catalogue was an intelligent, devoted young layman of the City. He uttered at the stake words remarkable for their literal fulfilment: "After this day, in this place shall there not be any put to the trial of fire and faggot." Indeed, such was the augmenting volume of the tide of indignation excited by these spectacles, that even without the change of rulers which shortly ensued, it must have speedily engulfed the authors of the tragedies.

Foxe gives the following account of the closing scene of the Smithfield martyrdoms :—"The day they suffered, a proclamation was made that none should be so bold to speak or talk word to them, or receive anything of them, or to touch them, upon pain of imprisonment, without either bail or mainprize; with divers other cruel threatening words, contained in the same proclamation. Notwithstanding the people cried out, desiring God to strengthen them; and they likewise still prayed for the people, and the restoring of His Word."

Truly,—

"A noble army, men and boys,
The matron and the maid!"

Their godly letters present to us their inner life in a most favourable light. Under the influence of persecution they had been driven and drawn so near to God, that their Christian characters had attained marvellous maturity. The grounds of their individual hope in Christ are shown in all their conversation; and, like the apostles Peter and Paul, they are continually abandoning the high road of their immediate argument to point to the Lamb of God. Take the letters of the Coventry martyr Laurence Saunders as an instance, and study them in the pages of old Foxe, as mirrors of the inner heart and life of men who had been made heroes by the high process of spiritual transformation. He thus concludes an epistle full of high thoughts and noble persuasions :—

"Dear Wife,—Riches I have none to leave behind me, wherewith to endow you after the worldly manner; but that treasure of tasting how sweet Christ is unto hungry consciences (whereof, I thank my Christ, I do feel part, and would feel more), *that* I bequeath unto you, and to the rest of my beloved in Christ, to retain the same in sense of heart always. Pray, pray! I am merry, and I trust I shall be merry, maugre the teeth of all the devils in hell. I utterly refuse myself, and resign myself unto my Christ, in whom I know I shall be strong as He seeth needful. Pray, pray, pray!"

The records of our consistory courts, afford us ample materials for sketching the features of evangelical life at this period. The witnesses depose to the possession of the little Scripture tractate hidden under the doublet, the stealthy gathering for worship by night in woods or fields, as criminating facts for legal action. Then came the sudden alarm, the hurrying cry, the falling away of the feeble, the simple avowal of the faithful, the dark cold dungeon, the tedious examination, the wonderful defence, the unavailing appeal, the useless popular sympathy, the lurid fires of martyrdom. These were the circumstances amidst which there sprung up that tree which, though insignificant in its first appearance, yet grew "like a tree planted by rivers of waters, that bringeth forth his fruit in his season."

The good cause itself survives though its votaries perish. The supposed reflections of the New Zealander on contemplating the ruins of St. Paul's,* can never attach to the spiritual fabric of the true Church. Historical and local ties may be severed, systems fade, institutions be forgotten; but it will still stand, for against it the tooth of time is powerless. Doubtless, the ultimate triumph of the truth was the grand consoling reflection of many a lowly solitary sufferer, as he uttered with the apostle the distinctive cry of faith, "We receiving a kingdom which cannot be moved." Compared with such convictions, how inferior is all ordinary life! The good man endures, "as seeing Him who is invisible," whilst the landscape of the worldly man is bounded by the visible horizon of things present.

The hopes of the Marian martyrs have now become fulfilled history: our sadness, therefore, on account of their personal trials, is tempered by the recollection of the glorious issue of their vital struggle.

"When the shore is won at last,
Who will count the billows past?"

The persecutions naturally alarmed the foreign protestant refugees who had settled in this country. The action of one body of these had an important effect on the subsequent condition of religion in England.

The Walloons, who had fled from Spanish persecution in the Netherlands in 1547, settled in London with Poulain as their minister. They adopted an order of service similar to that which they had used before their expatriation. When driven from England by the government of Queen Mary, they found it difficult to

* Lord Macaulay.

obtain an asylum, because their creed differed from the Lutheran.

At length they found resting places at Wesel, Strasburg, and Frankfort. One party, with Poulain at their head, reached the last-named city in 1554. In June of the same year others followed, including several English. These all adopted the strict reformed church-order which Poulain had established. Though they came from England, and hoped to return thither again, yet they renounced the Liturgy brought over by the English refugees, and thus became the first dissenters within the pale of English protestantism, if such it might then be called. John Knox became one of their ministers. Grindal and the English leaders in vain sought to induce them to conformity. They avowed a preference for their own ritual, as more simple than the Anglican form. They corresponded with Calvin, Vermiglio, Bullenger, Musculus, and Viret, more than with the Englishmen. Their congregations received an increase in 1555, by the arrival of the English and Flemish companions of John A` Lasco, who had left England in 1553, and amounted to 153 persons.*

On their return to England in the subsequent reign, they held fast to their own church-order, and consequently came into speedy collision with the new government and its favoured hierarchy, and were decided Nonconformists.

* Life and selected Writings of the Fathers and Founders of the Reformed Church. Peter Martyr; by Dr. Schmidt, p. 154.

CHAPTER XI.

The Elizabethan Age.

The nation gave an eager welcome to the religious peace which appeared to be inaugurated by the accession of Queen Elizabeth. There had been sufficient personal xperience of oppression in matters of opinion, to render the new freedom, though far from perfect, very acceptable. The contests respecting religion had absorbed more of the public attention than any other subject, and the triumph of Evangelical truth was esteemed as a national victory. Its language became the staple of the utterances both of common life and of literature. If we turn to the pages of Shakspeare, Raleigh, Lilly, or Sidney,—or even of writers who possessed less reverence for the Word of God than these,—we find the constant use of language implying a thorough acquaintance by the reader with the doctrines and facts of Scripture. Religious life, with all its manifestations, had become characteristic of the active portion of the community.

Before this age, the favourite mark of the wits had been the vices of the clergy. These form the fertile subject of mediæval satire. But from the time when true godliness became reputable, the latter has been the chosen object of ridicule. The plays of Ben Jonson seek to bring into contempt the earnestness and Scriptural tastes which evidently then characterized a large portion of the public. The truth overcame the scoffers for the time; but, after the Restoration, the latter had their time of triumph, and the result was most disastrous for the nation. A middle course was taken by such great writers as Raleigh, and after him Lord Bacon, who lauded religion in noble phrases, and copiously referred to Scripture in their writings, without, however, entitling themselves to be regarded as agents in the great work of promoting the spread of spiritual truth for evangelical purposes.

Who cannot but admire the eloquent conclusion of Sir Walter Raleigh's "History of the World?"—

"O eloquent, just, and mighty Death! Whom none could advise, thou hast persuaded; what none hath dared thou hast done; and whom all the world has flattered, thou only hast cast out of the world and despised: thou hast drawn together all the far-stretched greatness—all the pride, cruelty, and ambition of man, and covered it all over with the two narrow words 'Hic jacet.'"

More truly religious, however, is the advice given by him to his wife, in his letter written to her just before his execution:—"Love God, and begin betimes. In Him you shall find true, everlasting, and endless comfort."

Proof complete of the thorough diffusion of the textual knowledge of Scripture in the Elizabethan age, may be found in the plays of Shakspeare. There are above five hundred passages in his works, which may reasonably be referred to direct Scriptural originals, being either verbally, or substantially, founded on quotations from Holy Writ. There are about four hundred sentences, besides these, expressive of sentiments derived from the same source. Nor is this a case of the mere clever adaptation of familiar words. On the contrary, it is evident that the great dramatist thoroughly knew the doctrines of the Evangelical system, though we fail to discover to what extent he rested on them for his own hopes of heaven.

Thus he speaks of the fall of man, and the grace which found its remedy:—

> "All the souls that are, were forfeit once:
> And He, that might the vantage best have took,
> Found out the remedy."—MEASURE FOR MEASURE, Act 2.

And thus of God's righteousness and mercy:—

> "Consider this,—
> That, in the course of justice, none of us
> Should see salvation: we do pray for mercy;
> And that same prayer doth teach us all to render
> The deeds of mercy."—MERCHANT OF VENICE, Act 4.

And thus of the work of faith:—

> "Now God be praised, that to believing souls
> Gives light in darkness, comfort in despair!"
>   2 HENRY VI. Act. 2.

And thus of the atonement:—

> "Then is there mirth in heaven,
> When earthly things made even,
> At one together."—AS YOU LIKE IT, Act 5.

We know not that he himself fled for refuge to—

> "Christ's dear blood, shed for our grievous sins"—
>   RICHARD III.

but the proofs of his own familiarity, and that of his audiences, with the phrases and teachings of the Bible are exceedingly numerous. A modern biographer of Shakspeare says—

"We believe that the home education of William Shakspeare was grounded upon this book (the Bible); and that if this book had been sealed to his childhood, he might have been the poet of nature, of passion,—his humour might have been as rich as we find it, and his wit as pointed; but that he would not have been the most profound as well as the most tolerant philosopher; his insight into the nature of man, his meanness and his grandeur, his weakness and his strength, would not have been what it is." *

If, in the tranquil years of his later life, he joined the gentry of his native town in hearing and supporting the popular Gospel lecturer who officiated there, he must have brought to the exercise a ready fund of ample Biblical knowledge. We would fain hope that he learned to appreciate the deep things of God,—to benefit by his own advice—

"The means that Heaven yields, must be embraced,
And not neglected: else, if Heaven would,
And we will not, Heaven's offer we refuse."
RICHARD II., Act 3.

The extent to which the utterances of the heart were permitted, in the courtesies of high life at this period, is well shown in the language of a remarkable letter written by Bacon to Lord Coke, condoling with him on the occasion of his disgrace at court:—

* W. Shakspere, a Biography, p. 43.

" There is a time when the words of a poor simple man may profit; and that poor man in Ecclesiastes, which delivered the city by his wisdom—found that without this opportunity, both wisdom and eloquence lose their labour, and cannot charm the deaf adder. God therefore before his Son, that bringeth mercy, sent his servant, the trumpeter of repentance, to level every high hill, to prepare the way before him, making it smooth and straight; and, as it is in spiritual things, where Christ never comes before his waymaker hath laid even the heart with sorrow and repentance, so in the rules of earthly wisdom. Afflictions only level the mole-hills of pride, plough the heart, and make it fit for wisdom to sow her seed, and for grace to bring forth her increase. Happy is that man, therefore, both in regard of heavenly and earthly wisdom, that is thus wounded to be cured; thus broken to be made straight; thus made acquainted with his own imperfections that he may be perfected." *

From the same letter, we learn that it had been Lord Coke's practice to take notes of sermons.

The foundation of that grandeur of character which distinguishes the Elizabethan age, and was precursive of the great individuality of the following generation, was the large knowledge of the Holy Scriptures. It induced breadth of mental and moral vision, stimulated the powers of thought, and above all augmented the sense of responsibility in all ranks and conditions of the people. We get a glimpse of its effect from an account of the family of Sir Henry Sidney of Penshurst, father of the

* Original Letters of Bacon, ed. 1736, p. 126.

famous Sir Philip Sidney. In 1536, he was occupying Ludlow Castle, the appropriate official residence of the Lords President of Wales. Little Philip was eleven years old, and was sent to school at Shrewsbury. From school he writes to his father a letter in Latin, and another in French. The father replies in a strain of mingled wisdom and affection. He says—"Let your first action be the lifting up of your heart to Almighty God by hearty prayer, and feelingly digest the words you speak in prayer, with continual meditation, and thinking of Him to whom you pray, and of the matter for which you pray." The mother adds a postscript:— "Your noble and careful father hath taken pains (with his own hand) to give you this his letter, so wise, so learned; and most requisite precepts for you to follow with a diligent, humble, thankful mind, as I will not withdraw your eyes from beholding and reverent honoring the same—no, not so long time as to read any letter from me; and therefore at this time I will write you no other letter than this, whereby first I bless you, with my desire to God to plant in you His grace. Farewell, my little Philip; and once again, the Lord bless you! Your loving mother,—MARIE SIDNEY."

The writer was the sister-in-law of Lady Jane Grey. Sir Henry died in 1585. His widow soon followed him; having spent the last portion of her life on earth in earnest exhortations and persuasions to all around her, to close with the divine offers of mercy through the Redeemer. Their illustrious son, in the following March, lay slowly dying of his wound at Zutphen, agitated by all the ebbs and flows of a true Christian experience, but finally exclaiming, "I would not change my joy for the empire of the world!"

The sacred poetry published during this reign, to which above a hundred writers contributed, affords ample proof of the extent to which evangelical sentiment prevailed. It not only found apt expression in compositions designed for its exhibition, or congruous with its display, but it coloured with its own hue the subject, style, and method of all the writers. The literature of the age is one vast homage paid to the Holy Scripture. Frequently is there a pathetic allusion to the fiery trials which it was hoped had now for ever ceased. At the end of a metrical summary of the martyrdoms, published in 1555, we read—

> "Our wished welth hath brought us peace;
> Our joy is full, our hope obtained;
> The blazing brands of fire do cease,
> The slaying sword also restrained;
>   The simple sheep preserved from death
>   By our good Queen Elizabeth:
> That God's true word shall placed be,
> The hungry souls for to sustain;
> That perfect love and unity
> Shall be set in their seat again;
>   That no more good men shall be put to death,
>   Seing God hath sent Elizabeth." *

The bulk, however, of the poetry of this epoch, is of far higher character than the jingling rhymes in which a grateful people expressed their delight at the auspicious

* Parker Society Select Poetry, vol. i., p. 174.

change of government. The noble strains of Spenser, Sidney, Barnes, and a host of true poets, all conformed to the popular taste; their compositions abound in allusions from which a creed of evangelical doctrine might be readily compiled. A cluster of minor poets, some of the purest water, join in the chorus of compliment to Scriptural truth, and thus the language of theology gained in gracefulness and expression.

Mingled with these, are many productions which breathe the true sentiments of devout hearts and enlightened minds. The following verses, from a piece by an anonymous writer in 1579, afford a fair specimen of this class of productions:—

"The Refuge of a Sinner.

Soyled in sinnes, O Lord! a wretched sinfull ghoste,
To Thee I call, to Thee I sue, that showest of mercie most:
Who can me helpe but Thou, in whom all healp doth rest?
My sinne is more than man can mend, and that Thou knowest best.
On whome then shall I call, to whom shall I make mone?
Sith man is mightlesse sin to cure, I seek to thee alone;
In Thee I knowe all might and power doth remayne,
And at Thy handes I am well sure mercie I shall obtain.
Thy promise cannot fayle, wherein I me repose;
To Thee alone (els to no man) my harte wylle sinne disclose:
The sinner Thou dost save, no Saviour els I finde;
Thou onely satisfied hast for the sinne of all mankynde,
The sacrifice whereof Thou offeredst once for aye,
Whereby His wrath for Adam's gylt Thy Father put awaye." *

The pulpit began to exhibit graces of style, as well as soundness in the faith. It lost in the vehemence of its utterances, but gained in beauty of composition.

* Parker Society, vol. ii., 508.

It argues much for the spirituality of preacher and hearers, when we find Edward Deringe at this period addressing them thus:—"If our hearts cannot comprehend all the wisdom of God in the wind that bloweth, how he raiseth it up or maketh it fall again, how can we understand this wisdom of our uniting with Jesus Christ? Only this can I say: God hath given us faith, in which we may believe it, and out of which such joy shineth in our minds as crucifieth the world, not us. How far our reason is from seeing it, it skilleth not; it is sufficient if we believe it. We believe in the Lord our God; yet we know not what is His countenance. We believe, and apprehend by hope, his glory; yet neither eye can see it, nor ear can hear it. We believe and see immortality; yet our heart cannot comprehend the height, the breadth, the length, the depth. We believe the resurrection of the dead; yet we cannot understand such excellent wisdom, how life is renewed in the dispersed and scattered bones and ashes."

The demand for religious instruction, which sprang up in the train of the English Bible, soon exceeded the means of supply. The beneficed clergy were too few, and many of them too ill-qualified, to satisfy the occasion. In this state of things, a number of educated men, possessing a desire to be useful in this respect, obtained episcopal licence without any cure. They were styled lecturers, and became greatly popular. The benevolent and wealthy landowners and merchants appointed and paid them. They did not exclude or supersede the services of the regular clergy, but came in aid of them.

Four of such lecturers were nominated for Lancashire, and similar proportions in other counties. Henry Smith, one of the most noted preachers of the age, testifies to the fervid religionism which now began to prevail. He says—"The poor receive the gospel; the young men are more forward in the truth and more zealous than the aged,—the son than the father, the servant than his master."

In 1599, Dr. Holland states that there were "in this realm 5,000 preachers, catechists, exhorters; God be praised, who increases the number of them." In the MS. returns of the bishops in 1603, it is stated that, besides the preachers, there are "many honest ministers well able to catechize and privately to exhort, though they have not the gift of utterance, and audacity to preach in the pulpit."*

But, notwithstanding these favourable tokens, it was soon discovered that the golden age of piety had not yet arrived. The fond hopes of the faithful, that the Queen's advent had ushered in the reign of religious peace, were soon destroyed. The squabbles about vestments, the rude interposition of royal authority in ecclesiastical matters, the ordinances against unlicensed preachers, the persecution for attendance at conventicles, the rough usage of the worthy Marian exiles,—all throw their shadows across the path of the historian.

The good citizens of London, about the year 1566, used on Saturdays to send to the house of old Father Coverdale, to know where he would preach on the morrow.

* Haweis' Sketches, p. 306.

For though he was deprived of his living of St. Magnus for nonconformity, yet the authorities did not interfere with him in the prosecution of his lifelong and beloved work. He was now nearly eighty years of age, the last connecting link between the ante-Reformation struggle and the present; an eminent scholar,—one who had been in peril and exile for the Gospel,—a friendly, liberal, loveable old man,—an admirable preacher. His popularity gave offence to the ruling prelates; the good man was obliged at last to tell his friends that he durst not inform them of the place of his preaching, for fear of his superiors; and thus, in the midst of the light which he himself had so much helped to kindle, he died in comparative obscurity, in the year 1568, and was buried, amidst the sorrows of a vast crowd of people, in the chancel of St. Bartholomew's, behind the Exchange,—a place now unmarked save by the traffic of the world, but dear to the memory of all who love to contemplate the heroism of holiness.

In considering the historical development of religion since the dark ages, we must bear in mind that there have been four classes of reformers :—reformers before the Reformation—men who nourished faith and hope when action was impossible; reformers, who from timidity or worldly policy, repudiated public reformation; reformers who added action to conviction, and actually effected the Reformation; and, lastly, reformers of the Reformation itself,—men who would not, under the pretext of peace, accept any finality short of entire conformity to the Scriptures. It is our happiness to know, that there have ever been, holy, eminent, devoted Christians in each of these classes. So infirm are we, even at the best, that the regenerating grace of God, and living faith in the Saviour, by no means produce uniform results, either in clearness of vision, depth of emotion, or courage in action.

The rise of the great religious parties, which still prevail in this country, may be traced back to the commencement of the reign of Queen Elizabeth. First, the Ritualistic, or high-church section; secondly, the Evangelical, or low-church;—the latter again divided into, first, those who accept the order and discipline enjoined by the State; secondly, those who, not denying the right of the State to ordain, yet object to its enactments, agitate for a change, and become Nonconformists. The last again subdivide, into first, such as desire the State to conform to their views; and, secondly, those who deny the right or province of the State to interfere with religion.

The first overt act of Nonconformity, was the hiring of Plumbers' Hall, in the City, for an assembly, and setting up there a separate communion. Those who were resolved on separation from the State Church had met secretly before; but this was a public act, and was followed by the breaking-up of their meeting, and apprehension of the leaders. The latter were brought before the Court of High Commission. The plea of the separatists was, that they entertained conscientious objection to the vestments of the established clergy. The whole question is made quite clear by the record of their proceedings. In the course of the examination, the following took place :—

"*Bishop.*—Have you not the Gospel truly preached, and the sacraments duly administered, and good order preserved, though we differ from other churches on indifferent ceremonies, which the prince has power to command for the sake of order? What say you, Smith, as you seem the ancientest?

"*Smith.*—Indeed, my lord, we thank God for reformation; and that is the thing we desire, according to God's Word. So long, indeed, as we might have the word freely preached, and the sacraments administered without the use of *idolatrous gear*, we never assembled in private houses. But when all our preachers who could not subscribe to your apparel and your laws were displaced, so that we could not hear any of them in the church for the space of seven or eight weeks, excepting Father Coverdale, who at length durst not make known to us where he preached; and then we were troubled in your courts from day to day, for not coming to our parish churches: we considered among ourselves what we should do. We remembered that there was a congregation of us in this city in the days of Queen Mary; and a congregation at Geneva, which used a book and order of preaching, ministering the sacraments and discipline most agreeable to the word of God. This book is allowed by the godly and learned Mr. Calvin, and the other preachers at Geneva, which book and order we now hold. And if you can, by the word of God, reprove this book, or anything that we hold, we will yield to you, and do open penance at Paul's Cross; but if not, we will, by the grace of God, stand to it."

After much argument respecting the vestments, the Lord Mayor interposed, with advice, which, if this were the whole dispute, was certainly worth serious consideration.

"*Mayor.*—Well, good people, I wish you would wisely consider these things, and be obedient to the Queen's good laws, that you may live quietly and have liberty. I am sorry that you are troubled; but I am an officer under my prince, and therefore blame not me. The Queen hath not established these garments and other things for the sake of any holiness in them, only for civil order and comeliness, and because she would have ministers known from other men; as aldermen are known by their tippets, judges by their red gowns, and noblemen's servants by their liveries. Therefore, you will do well to take heed and obey." *

From the days of Wickliffe downwards, we discern occasional traces of gatherings of godly people, who were impressed with the great truths relating to personal Christianity, and under their influence met to strengthen each other, and promote Christ's cause without a wish or a thought beyond. The only organization they knew was fellowship in Christ; their only aim, the enjoyment and propagation of personal faith in Him. They were Nonconformists, but without any party spirit, or political, or even ecclesiastical aim. Though their great principle, if and when carried out, must in due time lead to the

* "Parte of a Register," p. 24.

disowning of regal and hierarchical power, yet this was neither sought nor cared for by them; for their sole concern was the doctrine of Christ crucified, which, whilst it abundantly compensated them for all its inflictions, yet absorbed all their energies. The conventicles of the Lollards, were succeeded by the congregations of the Protestants in the reigns of Henry VIII. and Queen Mary, and these by the assemblies of the Puritans, who dissented from the Queen's ordinances in the reign of Elizabeth. Tyndale's advice to Frith, to conduct their assemblies so as to avoid questions of sacrament and order, and confine the teaching to the great truths of redemption, was much followed, and could not fail to be the means of blessing.

Religion in this country, cannot show exclusive descent through any of the great ecclesiastical parties: truth, like veins of ore split by convulsion, thenceforth lies in varying proportions along all the lines of fracture.

The principle that man is directly accountable to God, and to Him only, for his personal religious belief, lies at the foundation of all the acts of the reformers. They felt, that in spiritual things, Christ is entitled to paramount obedience. They sacrificed reputation, comfort, property, and even life itself, in support of their convictions. They denied the authority of the Government to impose on them a creed at variance with their conscientious interpretation of Scripture. But they never saw the correlative truth, that whatever is not within the jurisdiction of Government, cannot rightly affect the Government with any responsibility. If there is no duty on the one hand, there can be no obligation on the other. From disregard of this principle, arose the multitudinous difficulties which for centuries embarrassed the pure action of religion. The reformers undoubtedly held it to be the duty of the State to select the true faith, and uphold it with the arm of power.

The good men who went into exile in Holland, Germany, and Switzerland, during the Marian persecution, came back with their views unchanged in this respect. On their return, they objected to some of the State ordinances, not on the ground of their origin, but their objects. They would not have had them abrogated, but altered. These were the first Puritans,—men who had never conformed to the regulations of the Government. Their number was speedily augmented, by the addition of those who dissented from the new injunctions of 1559, and of those who preferred the Genevan model of church order to that established by Cranmer.

From these early Puritans the Independents separated. The latter were at first called by their enemies, Brownists, or Barrowists. Browne was a clergyman, a friend of the great statesman Cecil; he was not the originator of the principles associated with his name, but he was the first active able open promoter of them. Browne afterwards conformed; but before this took place, numerous persons, who had recognized in independency, principles already practically known to them, had acted upon the doctrine, and formed isolated self-governing assemblies of professing Christians. Barrow, was a lawyer of Gray's Inn, a self-denying godly man, who was speedily executed for nonconformity. The Independents acknowledged the right of the Government to rule in matters of religion, but claimed for separate congregations the privilege of self-government, subject to the regal control, which, they affirmed, was bound to be exercised in their favour.

From these Separatists, a third offshoot soon sprang,—namely, those who acknowledged the right of the State to control matters of external behaviour, but denied its duty to patronize or interfere with personal religious opinion. The first assertors of this view were Baptists.* So notorious was this, that the term Anabaptist was used reproachfully, to designate the deniers of State authority in matters of religion, irrespective of their sentiments respecting the rite of baptism itself.

The proposition acted upon by the English reformers, is, that Church and State are co-extensive; that adopted by the Genevan reformers, is the papal doctrine of a church-state within and paramount to the civil government: this became the principle of presbyterianism and of high churchism.† The Separatists (in early times comprising the Baptists only) avowed the principle which lay at the root of the action of the martyrs and protesters

* Tracts on Liberty of Conscience and Persecution, 1614-1661. Hanserd Knollys Society, 1846.

† Consult "A Brieff Discours off the Troubles begonne at Franckford, in Germany, Anno Domini 1554, abowte the Booke off Common Prayer and Ceremonies, and continued by the Englishe men theyre, to th' ende of Q. Marie's raigne, in the which discours, the gentle reader shall see the very originall and beginninge off all the contention that hath byn, and what was the cause off the same."

of all ages,—namely, man's individual freedom from all human obligation in the matter of religion, and the consequent impropriety of all human law on the subject. The disputes of subsequent years may be conveniently reduced to these three classes. To examine the ultimate effect of each theory upon the progress of Christ's kingdom is not our task; but the humbler and more grateful office of tracing down in each line, the outflow of vital attachment to the truth as it is in Jesus, which brings its own obligations, and is ever accompanied by its own high hopes.

Though the object of our present inquiry,—vital religion,—is to be traced in all these lines of descent, yet from the nature of things, it is found in most force and frequency among those who attached supreme importance to *doctrine*, rather than to *ritual*.

In the year 1571, the religious desires of the community and the religious convictions of the godly clergy, led to the establishment of meetings called prophesyings; founded upon the practice of the Corinthian church in the days of the Apostles, as indicated in 1 Cor. xiv. 26. The ministers of the district met by appointment; each in his turn gave his views on a chosen portion of Scripture. This institution, begun at Northampton in 1571, soon became popular. It was accompanied by the usual concomitant of free speech,—difference of opinion. The archbishop (Grindal) incurred the decided displeasure of the Queen for patronizing these gatherings. He was required to abridge the number of preachers, and to put down altogether these religious exercises. The good primate remonstrated, but in vain; the imperious Queen issued her mandate forbidding all such associations, and prohibiting all preaching and teaching save by persons lawfully called; which, says the historian, silenced no small number.*

The value set upon these exercises shows the general concern respecting religion. Sir Robert Cotton says,—
"In those days there was an emulation between the clergy and the laity, and a strife whether of them should show themselves most affectionate to the Gospel. Poor country churches were frequented with the best of the shire. The word of God was precious; prayer and preaching went hand-in-hand together; until Archbishop Grindal's disgrace, and Hatton's hard conceit of prophesying, brought the flowing of these good graces to a still water."

The advice of Aylmer, when he became Bishop of London, concerning the Puritans, is a sufficient description of their true character. Strype says—

"In the year 1577, he met with several persons of a contrary way to Papists; of whom he informed the Lord Treasurer, that in respect of their hindering unity and quietness, they were not much less hurtful than they; namely, Chark, Chapman, Field, and Wilcox. These he had before him: the two former he had some hopes of; but the two latter shewed themselves obstinate, and especially Field, who, notwithstanding the Archbishop's inhibition, had entered into great houses, and taught, as he said, God knows what. *His advice concerning these*

* Middleton, Life of Grindal, p. 229.

men was, that they might be profitably employed in Lancashire, Staffordshire, Shropshire, and such other like barbarous countries, to draw the people from Papism and gross ignorance; and that though they went a little too far, yet he supposed it would be less labour to draw them back, than now it was to hale them forward; and that some letters of friendly request might be sent thither for some contribution to be made by the towns and gentlemen for some competent stipend to relieve them. And he thought this might grow greatly to the profit of the Church, and therefore communicated this counsel to the Lord Treasurer, and prayed him at his leisure to think on it. Yet he declared that he said all this, not because he liked them, but because he would have his cure rid of them."*

The first formal outbreak of Nonconformity was occasioned by the articles of Whitgift, on his appointment to the see of Canterbury, in 1583. The Queen charged him to restore the discipline of the Church, and he immediately forbad "all preaching and catechizing in any private family, when any are present except the family. That none do preach or catechize, except also he will read the whole service, and administer the sacrament four times a year. That all preachers, and others in ecclesiastical orders, do at all times wear the habit prescribed. That none be admitted to preach unless he subscribe the three following articles": 1st, to the Queen's supremacy; 2ndly, to the Book of Common Prayer, and to use no other; 3rdly, to the Thirty-nine Articles of the Church of England. This ordinance was enforced by the suspension of several

* Strype's Life of Aylmer, p. 36.

hundred ministers. Supplications for relief were poured in to the Lords of the Council, to the Convocation, and to the Parliament, embodying complaints which show the high value set on the services of an evangelical ministry at that time; but all endeavours to obtain an alteration of the terms were fruitless.

The men who about the year 1590 began to organize their own peaceable Christian assemblies, to choose their own officers to preside, and give to their own poor, were interrupted and branded as traitors. Again and again had they to resort for safety to the shelter of the woods near Islington or Deptford, or the obscurity of the alleys between Shakspeare's theatre and London Bridge. They declared their sole object to be their own instruction and the worship of God; they eagerly disavowed the lower deep of "anabaptistical error;"—meaning thereby the denial of the right of the State in matters of religion;—but, spite of their simple professions and strong disavowals, the thing could not be permitted. It did not comport with the notions of government then current, and hence the opening of another tale of heartburnings, proscriptions, imprisonments, exile, and bloodshed.

It is perplexing and painful to have to recur again to scenes of tyranny and distress. After the full establishment of a reformation grounded only on the sacred right of private judgment, and during the prevalence of great social prosperity and unprecedented intellectual opulence, we are still led to the tribunals, the dungeons, and even the scaffold, in search of the true followers of Christ.

The short life of John Penry, the Welsh apostle, affords much evidence of the state of religious thought and feeling then prevalent in this direction.

Born in the first year of the Queen's reign, he found himself at the University of Oxford at a time when Puritan teaching, though not in the ascendant, was yet the most active thing there. Personally, he had tendencies which led him to Romanism; but soon his quick mind and glowing heart became affected by the simplicity of evangelical truth. He, with a few others likeminded, associated for prayer and Bible-reading. An earnest desire for the spiritual enlightenment of his countrymen now became his ruling passion. He visited the mountains and valleys of the Principality, scattering the good seed of the Gospel with such success, that several places in Breconshire at this day trace their church history to his early activity. He published an eloquent appeal to the Church of England on behalf of Wales, abounding in missionary arguments, though then deemed to be subversive of ecclesiastical order. In this he came under the displeasure of Whitgift, and had to retreat with others into Northamptonshire, where, however, the decrees of the Star Chamber reached the band of church reformers. Penry's sole aim appears to have been the evangelization of his country. This is the burthen of his appeals to Church, State, and people; but the nature of the opposition encountered, led him to attack the hierarchy itself, as an obstacle to the accomplishment of his darling purpose. He had to flee to Scotland. He wished to return, abandon all efforts for higher reformation, and petitioned the Queen for leave to preach in Wales. In 1592 he came back, and found that a lower stratum of Nonconformity than Puritanism had arisen, though in obscurity and amidst difficulties.

Under the opprobrious name of Separatists, united only by a proscription pronounced alike by High and Low Church, Presbyterian, Puritan, and Nonconformist, a number of earnest men had united together in assemblies for worship and edification. In the summer they met in the fields, in the winter in some obscure retreat: even under these difficulties they sought the glory of Christ, by attempting to form and preserve a membership of persons whose lives corresponded to their professions. They were principally tradesmen and artizans of the city of London, with a few professional men and scholars: they met in a house belonging to one of their number in Nicholas-lane,—now No. 80, Cannon-street. The scope of their efforts is thus expressed by themselves:—

"1. We seek, above all things, the peace and protection of the Most High, and the kingdom of Christ Jesus our Lord.

"2. We seek and fully purpose to worship God aright as He hath commanded in His Holy Word.

"3. We seek the fellowship and communion of His faithful and obedient servants, and, together with them, to enter covenant with the Lord; and, by the direction of His Holy Spirit, to proceed to a godly, free, and right choice of ministers and other officers, by Him ordained to the service of His Church.

"4. We seek to establish and obey the ordinances and laws of our Saviour Christ, left by His last will and testament, to the governing and guiding of His Church, without altering, changing, innovating, wresting, or leaving out any of them that the Lord shall give us sight of.

"5. We purpose, by the assistance of the Holy Ghost, in this faith and order to leave our lives, if such be the good will and pleasure of our Heavenly Father, to whom be all glory and praise for ever. Amen." *

The good men had not proceeded far in their career of Christian liberty, ere, as they were about to form a second church, the hand of power ruthlessly broke up their gathering, persecuted the flock, and cruelly put to death their leaders, Barrow, Greenwood, and Penry.

The charge against them was, that they taught opinions subversive of the church as by law established. They had come to the conclusion that the appointment of the higher orders of clergy, and the mode of appointment of ordinary ministers, were contrary to the word of God, and promotive of Popery. They conceived themselves bound to worship God after the manner which is now called Independent; and having strong convictions that the practices they condemned were leading to the re-introduction of Popery, they believed themselves to be contending for important practical ends. Toleration was unknown, and latitudinarianism would have been disavowed by all parties; the terrible consequence was accepted as inevitable: *dissent was treason.* Penry appealed from the actual laws,

* Giffard's Treatise, 1590, quoted in Waddington's Life of Penry, p. 88.

to the principle enunciated in Magna Charta, that the sovereign of these realms should leave inviolable the privileges of the Church of God. The appeal, if conceded, would have issued in the establishment of an inner ecclesiastical state within the outer civil government. This was treated not only with contempt, but as a fresh instance of treasonable audacity. Right principles concerning the office of the magistrate in matters of religion are to be found involved in the manly, pious defence made by the sectaries; but their aims and conclusions are still coloured by the attractive splendours of the Genevan theory, that human governments subsist for the direct outworking of the Divine government in regard to religion. The preachers were, with cruel perversion, charged with assembling in woods and secret places. Penry replied, that this was done, not of their own choice, but from sad necessity; concluding his final examination with words which, though long dormant, are now becoming the creed as well as the experience of nations:—"Imprisonments, indictments—yea, death itself, are no meet weapons to convince men's consciences."*

Although the life of God in the soul of man has become terribly denaturalized, so that it always needs an apology to speak to a stranger concerning God's great mercy, yet, beneath all the conventionalities of mankind, there is a secret longing towards the truth. Society treats religion as if it were the forbidden fruit, but still covets its possession. Thus we find that everywhere, at all times, amongst all people, the earnest, intelligent, pathetic preaching of the Gospel is eminently attractive.

* Life of Penry, p. 166.

It was so in the days when Hooker, the great champion of the Elizabethan Church, preached in the morning at the Temple to a select auditory, "fit though few;" whilst Travers, the representative of the Evangelical school, exercised his persuasive oratory to crowds at the same place in the afternoon. It was likened to ebb and flow. Old Fuller says, " Here might one on Sundays have seen almost as many writers as hearers. Not only young students, but even the greatest benchers (such as Sir Edward Cook [Coke] and Sir James Altham then were) were not more exact in taking instructions from their clients, than in writing notes from the mouths of their ministers."

The public anxiety for the propagation of evangelical religion reached to the municipal and parochial civil institutions of the country. Such orders as the following, made in the borough of Liskeard, in Cornwall, by common consent of the mayor, burgesses, and parishioners, on the 22nd of January, 1586, concerning the poor, were becoming general:—" And for that the said people appear to us to be very ignorant of the knowledge of God and their salvation, we have made petition unto the vicar or his minister to redeem their negligence; or else do order our clerk, in their default, that every particular household, as they are here plotted, shall, by turn in four several Sundays, continually henceforth be taught the articles of their faith, the Lord's prayer and the ten commandments, with the understanding of the sacraments and principles of religion."*

Allen's History of Liskeard, p. 277.

Another proof of the popular attachment to evangelical preaching occurred at the Leicester Assizes in 1596. Mr. Hildersham, a divine of great celebrity, incumbent of Ashby-de-la-Zouch, was appointed to preach the assize sermon before Judge Anderson. The judge considered it to be so puritanical, that he could not conceal his displeasure even in church. No sooner was he seated on the bench, than he required the jury to bring in an indictment against the preacher; but they refused, and it is said that no jury in the country could have been found to do it. When it is borne in mind, how often, in those unhappy days of criminal administration, the juries acted wholly at the bidding of the judge, their conduct shows how extensively and deeply the love of the truth which Hildersham so faithfully preached, pervaded the chief men of the country. Hildersham was afterwards mainly instrumental in promoting stated meetings of ministers for mutual improvement.* There are few epitaphs sufficiently instructive and characteristic to repay transcription. That placed in the chancel of Ashby church over the remains of this good man is a gratifying exception. It is as follows:—

M. S.
Near to this place lieth interred the body
of ARTHUR HILDERSHAM,
honourably descended from Sir Richard Poole,
by his wife Margaret Countess of Salisbury;
but more honoured for his sweet and ingenuous disposition,
his singular wisdom in settling peace,
advising in secular affairs
and satisfying doubts,

* Clarke's "Lives."

his abundant charity,
and especially for his extraordinary knowledge and
judgment in the Holy Scriptures,
his painful and zealous preaching,
together with his firm and lasting constancy
in the truth he professed.
He lived in this place
for the most part of forty-three years and six months,
with great success in his ministry,
love and reverence of all sorts,
and died with much honour and lamentation,
March the 4th, 1631.

In the latter portion of the reign of Queen Elizabeth, and during that of her successor, many godly ministers could neither conscientiously fulfil the commands of the Court on the one hand, or attach themselves to the Puritan party on the other. They lived in continual trouble and distress; but the cause of Christ was actually advancing, in spite of these obstructions, by means of the diffusion of the Scriptures: for it has been well remarked by the historian of our English Bible, that "no section of Christians, of whatever name, can possess any title to rank itself as having been essential either to the progress or to the general prevalence of the English Scriptures."

The mother of the world-renowned Francis Lord Bacon, herself an accomplished scholar, attended one of these assemblies, gathered, in spite of the law and will of the Government, at Rochford Hall, in Essex. The meeting was held daily at eight o'clock in the evening. A church was formed; and though all parties concerned were imprisoned and dispersed, yet many, with her ladyship, testified to the unspeakable advantages derived from these exercises.

In 1592 we find the church at Southwark composed of materials which prove the intelligence and bravery of the lay element in English religious society at that time. Among the members are enumerated, Quintin Smith, aged thirty, of Southwark, felt-maker; Thomas Micklefield, joiner, thirty-two years of age, of St. Mary Overy's; Leonard Pedder, thirty, shoemaker, Blackfriars; Christopher Diggins, twenty-four, weaver; Henry Broadwater, twenty-nine, scrivener, of Nicholas-lane; Edward Grave, fishmonger, of St. Botolph's; William Marshall, thirty-two, of Wapping, shipwright; Arthur Billot, a native of Cornwall, a soldier and scholar, of good family.

Several of the Romish priests who were cruelly executed in the reign of Queen Elizabeth were also evangelicals. What infinite surprises are in store for us in the world to come! Persecutor and victim will, in numberless instances, meet on the same right-hand side of the Judge. The generous, noble-hearted Margaret Clitherow, barbarously pressed to death at York, in 1586, on the charge of harbouring Catholic priests;—the devout and poetical Southwell, so cruelly tortured and executed in 1595, for the crime of being a Jesuit;—will find themselves basking in the same sunshine of Divine favour with their conforming and nonconforming contemporaries of meaner rank but of equal faith. All would have sweetly sung with Southwell—

> "Let us in life—yea, with our life,
> Requite His dying love;
> For best we live when best we love,
> If love our life remove."

In 1573, the before-mentioned treatise of Paleario, the early Italian martyr, was translated from the French edition, and published under the title of "The Benefit that Christians receive by Jesus Christ Crucified." The introduction laments that, "among the greatest evils with which the age is infected, that they which are called Christians are miserably divided about Christ." "In this little book is the benefit which cometh by Christ crucified to the Christian truly and comfortably handled; which benefit if all Christians did truly understand and faithfully embrace, this division would vanish away, and, in Christ, the Christians' household become one."

The leading truths of the evangelical system, having relation to the common spiritual wants of man, and to the all-sufficient provisions of God, have currency everywhere. They have a divine stamp for universal circulation. It was a grand thing when literature, aided by the printing-press, became suffused with the Gospel. As Dean Milman beautifully says—"Eloquence or argument, instead of expiring on the ears of an entranced but limited auditory, addressed mankind at large—flew through kingdoms, crossed seas, perpetuated and promulgated themselves to an incalculable extent."

The foreign Protestant refugees, after a period of reverses during the last reign, again partook of prosperity under regal patronage in the reign of Elizabeth and her successors. Their numbers were so rapidly and considerably augmented in consequence of persecutions in France, that they became quite an influential body of evangelical professors here. Many of them became absorbed into English communities, but at first they formed their own societies. The number of their churches in London rose to thirty-one; others were also established at Wandsworth, Chelsea, Hammersmith, Greenwich, Canterbury Sandwich, Norwich, Thorpe, Southampton, Bristol, Glastonbury, Rye, Winchelsea, Dover, Faversham, Whittlesea, Thorney Abbey, Sandtoft, Ipswich, Plymouth, Dartmouth, and Bideford. This state of things continued until the beginning of the eighteenth century, when the numbers began to decline from the effect of fusion with the English; and, for the last sixty years, the doors have been open for the return to their own country of such of the descendants as retained the desire.* There is now, it is believed, only one left of these original foundations, that in St. Martin's-le-Grand. The abandonment of the old Austin-Friars Dutch church, and the transference of their records, is the work of the year 1863 only.

The fulfilment of history in the gathering of the church of Christ is one long Roman triumph. Group after group pass on in the stately procession, attired in different costumes, with varying physiognomy, each bearing the spoils of its own warfare, but all intent on the one entrance into the city, whence they hear from afar off, the plaudits which arise from around the throne, to which their great Leader has been exalted by the suffrages of an innumerable company.

* Weiss, "Foreign Protestant Refugees."

CHAPTER XII.

James I.—Charles I.

THE harvest quickly followed the seed-time. We begin to read of Gospel influences pervading whole districts; we discern godly *families* where before we saw only *individuals*. Although piety is not hereditary, yet religious biography teaches us that it frequently becomes so. God honours the domestic constitution, by making it the means of accomplishing His own gracious purposes. In the year 1600, a wheelwright, named Sibbes, the father of the great Puritan preacher, was living in Fostock, in Suffolk, with the reputation of being a skilful workman, and sincere Christian, known and esteemed in both characters throughout his native district. Many similar instances are recorded at this time; the growing diffusion of Scripture literature is a marked feature of the age. The published editions of the English Bible, which amounted to fifty-four in the long reign of Henry VIII., rose to forty-nine in the short one of his son; fell to one during the reign of Queen Mary; but again rose to 142 under Elizabeth. In 1644, John Canne, a baptist separatist, compiled the first English Bible with marginal references throughout. It was published at Amsterdam.

The triumphant mental development of the Elizabethan age was grounded on heartfelt reverence for the Scripture, and large use of its divine teachings; and when all else that was peculiar to the times had passed away, the influence of these remained. Their results outlasted the generation, and produced a state of things under which England rose to a pitch of mental, moral, and spiritual greatness before unknown. The controversial literature of the day, though still disfigured by passion and conceit, partook of the improvement. In the ancient times of the Church, the disputes of theologians imperfectly served to eliminate and vindicate the truth; but after the Reformation, improved methods, and fuller subjection to the authority of Scripture, rendered the later productions incomparably superior in utility to those of the Fathers. Hardly an error now springs up in the fertile weed-bearing soil of theology, which has not been already intelligently and exhaustively dealt with, in some portion of the religious literature of the Reformed Church. Good works followed in the train. About the year 1600, some members of the University of Cambridge set on foot a home mission in the villages around that town, which they carried on for many years with much benefit to themselves and the district.*

In the year 1602, Mr. Crook, Fellow of Emanuel College, exchanged the congenial learning of Cambridge for the

* Clarke's Life of Gataker, p. 132.

task of imparting the Gospel to the people living on the Mendip Hills, who had never before, it is said, enjoyed the blessing of a preaching minister. For forty-seven years, he continued to show how a cultivated, active mind, imbued with the love of Christ, may be a means of imparting blessing throughout a large district by efforts and influence exerted in the direct promulgation of Scriptural truth. Other ministers with similar equipments went out to combat the ignorance which still existed in dark spots over the land. The result was a decided and general augmentation of Christian knowledge and piety.

Lord Bacon, in his "Advancement of Learning, Divine and Humane," pays a high compliment to the preaching in his days, when he says, "For I am persuaded that if the choicest and best of these observations upon texts of Scripture, which have been made dispersedly in sermons, within this your Majesty's island of Britain, by the space of these forty years, and more, had been set down in a continuance, it had been the best work on divinity which had been written since the Apostles' times."*

At this time it became the practice of a few serious merchants in the city of London, to select a godly minister, and send him for three years to preach in some town destitute of the Gospel. If his ministry proved acceptable to the people, so as to induce them to desire his continuance, matters were so arranged; but if otherwise, he was removed to be sent elsewhere. This sound Scriptural method of carrying out mission work amidst

* Page 330.

the masses, may well teach a lesson to the promoters of modern missionary enterprise.

Purchas, who published his quaint geographico-theological History of the World in 1613, thus declaims, in his preface, against the appointment of ministers unable to preach : " And let mee have leave to speake it for the glorie of God, and the good of our church, I cannot find any priests in all this my pilgrimage, of whom wee have any exact historie, but take more bodily paines in their devotions, than is performed by not-preaching ministers, especially in countrie villiages, where on the week daies they cannot have occasion for publique prayers ; and therefore if they onely read the service then, and never study for more (which I would it were not the practice of some), even the heathen shall rise up in judgement against them. I subscribe with hand and practise to our *Liturgie*, but not such *Lethargie ;* whose darknesse is so much the more intolerable, in the sunshine of the Gospell, wherein we have a gratious king, so diligent a frequenter of sermons ; and reverend bishops (notwithstanding other their weighty ecclesiasticall employments) yet diligent preachers." *

About the year 1605, the obscure village of Cawk, lying between Ashby-de-la-Zouch and Derby, was the scene of assemblies similar to those which in so many places, and at so many times, have characterized the progress of religion. A good preacher was unknown in those parts, until Mr. Julines Herring came to the parish. His sermons were popular from their faithful exhibition

* Purchas's Pilgrimage. Preface.

of divine truth. The people from the towns and villages within a circle of twenty miles flocked to hear: the building in which he preached could not contain them—they crowded around the windows. After the morning service, an ordinary took place; singing and religious conversation occupied the interval until the afternoon service; after which the multitude dispersed, many having received durable impressions. This continued for many years; and similar results followed Mr. Herring's preaching on his removal to Shrewsbury. A marvellous power has this divine message, vindicating its own character as "worthy of all acceptation" by the fact of its ordinary history!

We read in the records of the Baptist Church at Broadmead, that "there were raised up divers holy and powerful ministers and preachers, in and about this time, in the nation; whereof, in these parts, was one Mr. Wroth, in Monmouthshire, not far from this city of Bristol, who for the powerfulness and efficaciousness of his preaching, with the exemplary holiness of his life, was called the Apostle of Wales; for the Papists, and all sorts almost, honoured him for a holy man."

Mr. Wroth was educated at Oxford. About the year 1620, he became convinced of the vanity of all earthly pleasures by the sudden death of a friend, and thenceforth devoted himself with great success to the ministry of the Word. He was instrumental in the conversion of numbers, during a long series of years, and retained, through trouble and calm alike, the reputation of holiness and wisdom.[*]

[*] Broadmead Records, p. 7.

The same record gives us a pleasing picture of the religious habits of some of the good citizens' wives of Bristol;—how they met to repeat sermon-notes; how they kept days of prayer together; how they grew in humility, spirituality, and faith; how, for twenty years, they went on increasing in numbers and influence, until their gatherings became a mark for persecution.

Dr. Harris, for forty years, from about 1600, was preacher at Hanwell, near Oxford; and he, with Mr. Wheatley, at Banbury, established preaching services on market and on festival days, to which multitudes resorted; upon which the biographer of these worthies observes, in his quaint style,—"In these days godly preachers stuffed not their sermons with airy notions and curious speculations, but sought out profitable matter, which they delivered in sound words, and in plain method of doctrine, reason and use, accommodating themselves to every man's capacity; and God gave them a plentiful harvest in that country." *

The same divine lectured at Stratford-on-Avon every other week, "to which there was a great resort both of the chief gentry, and choicest preachers and professors in those parts; and amongst them, that noble and learned knight, Sir Thomas Lucy, of Charlecote, had always a great respect for him."

As Shakspeare lived in his native town, in the well-earned enjoyment of the competency which had raised him to the position of one of its chief inhabitants, from about 1603 to the time of his death in 1616, it is more

* Clarke's Ten Lives, p. 285.

than probable that he listened with Sir Thomas Lucy to the excellent knowledge of Christ, and Him crucified, which the sermons of Dr. Harris contained. We have not the exact date of the lecture at Stratford; but there were frequent exchanges, and public occasions, on which about this time Dr. Harris preached at Stratford and the neighbouring towns, besides his own constant services at Hanwell, a few miles off.* Dr. Harris was a considerable man in the neighbourhood, well known and much sought after by educated people, as well as others. There were also many in the same locality at that time distinguished as Puritan preachers within the Established Church;—such as Mr. Dods, "the fittest man in England for a pastoral office;" Mr. Cleaver, "a very solid text-man;" Mr. Lancaster, a humble able scholar, by birth a good gentleman, by training Fellow of King's College, and yet a diligent, faithful village preacher, with £40 a year; Mr. Scudder and Mr. Whately. Concerning Mr. Lancaster, Clarke writes,—"When I was young, I knew this Mr. Lancaster: he was a very little man of stature, but eminent, as for other things, so especially for his living by faith. His charge being great and his means so small, his wife would many times come to him, when she was to send her maid to Banbury market to buy provisions, and tell him that she had no money. His usual answer was, 'Yet send your maid, and God will provide.' And though she had no money, yet she never returned empty; for one

---

* Dr. Harris frequently had his will altered, but in the alterations preserved this legacy: "Item—I bequeath to all my children, and to their children's children, to each of them a Bible, with this inscription—*None but Christ*."

or another knew her to be Mr. Lancaster's maid; either by the way or in Banbury town meeting her, would give her money which still supplied their present wants."*

Amidst the graphic portraitures furnished by the biographers of that age, we may find many instances of men and women devoting themselves in their households, to noble purposes, in training their children for God and their country, in spite of the Court influence which had now become hostile to both.

After the year 1600, we read of personal piety within the inclosure of the visible Church, growing to such an extent as to burst the limits prescribed by the ritualism of the former. The Broadmead record states, that at this time "those whose hearts God had touched would get together and pray, repeat their sermon-notes, and upon the Lord's-day would carefully sanctify the Christian Sabbath, and perform other such acts of living piety; as when they could hear of any minister that did savour of God, or of the power of godliness, they would flock to him as doves to the windows; for which they were branded with the name of Puritans." Preachers and teachers sprang up to supply the demand for religious progression. Some of the evangelical clergymen who had been suspended by Laud, other men who had earned amongst their neighbours a reputation for ability with more or less of scholarship, came forward as leaders of the assemblies which in England and Wales now gathered, in spite of the law, and formed centres of spiritual influence throughout the land.

* Clarke's Ten Lives, p. 281.

The patronage of irreligion afforded by the Court of James I. produced division throughout the country, rendering it necessary for persons of the more godly sort to avow their principles, and act openly upon them, whilst those who had no sympathy with personal religion began freely to deride it. Thus in the village of Eaton Constantine, near Shrewsbury, in which Baxter was at this time born (1615), there was scarcely the face of religion left. Not a sermon was to be heard from year to year. The service was run over cursorily; and the congregation adjourned to the village green, and spent the rest of the day in dancing round the May-pole. But the time spent by others in dancing, "his father employed in reading and praying in his family, and recommending holy life. He put him upon a careful reading the historical part of Scripture, which being delightful to him, made him in love with the Bible; and his serious speeches of God and the life to come possessed him with a fear of sinning; so that he became the first instrument of his hearty approbation of a holy life. He found his father reproached for his singularity, and that much affected him. The profane crew derided him as a Puritan."* Young Baxter was no better than others, and particularly partial to robbing orchards. After an expedition of this kind, he found an old torn book which a labourer had lent to his good father. It was a Catholic book of personal repentance, written by Father Parsons, a Jesuit, but altered and edited by a Puritan minister, and called "Bunny's Resolutions." The reading this treatise convinced him of the folly and

* Calamy's Baxter, p. 5.

wickedness of sin. A pedler afterwards brought to his father's door Dr. Sibbes's "Bruised Reed." This completed the process. He found the Great Physician, and thenceforward rejoiced in a lively, grateful apprehension of the love of Christ.

The bent of most of the leading thoughtful minds of the age was towards religion. In 1620, Sibbes, the pungent, earnest preacher, used to ride up weekly from Cambridge, where he lectured, to Gray's Inn, where he was the preacher. Not only did the learned lawyers crowd to listen to him, but many noble personages, many of the gentry and citizens, resorted to the chapel, and lived to confess with gratitude their obligations to the Christian orator. Preston, a divine of similar earnestness and pathos, was at the same time preaching with much acceptance at Lincoln's Inn. Many of the goodly folios of Puritanical literature we owe to the laborious pens of noble ladies, who were accomplished in the art of taking "sermon-notes," then fashionable, and used it on such occasions.

There were many ardent spirits who were dissatisfied with the slow progress made in the diffusion of Scriptural truth after the Reformation, some from political discontent, others from pure zeal for the honour of Christ. Milton expresses their views in his own sonorous, musical fashion : —" The pleasing pursuit of these thoughts hath ofttimes led me into a serious question and debatement with myself, how it should come to pass that England (having had this grace and honour from God, to be the first that should set up a standard for the recovery of lost truth, and blow the first evangelic trumpet to the nations, holding up, as from a hill, the new lamp of saving light to all Christendom,) should now be the last, and most unsettled in the enjoyment of that peace whereof she taught the way to others; although, indeed, our Wycliffe's preaching, at which all the succeeding reformers more effectually lighted their tapers, was to his countrymen but a short blaze, soon damped and stifled by the Pope and prelates for six or seven kings' reigns; yet, methinks, the precedency which God gave this island, to be first restorer of buried truth, should have been followed with more happy success, and sooner attained perfection."*

We have before seen that the historical origin of Nonconformity can be carried back to the commencement of the Reformation. The worthy men who distrusted King Henry, and were not satisfied with his clumsy *via media*, fled beyond seas. They differed among themselves concerning doctrines, but they agreed in holding the rights of conscience to be superior to the demands of the magistrate; whilst Cranmer and his associates weathered out the tempest of the king's tyranny, under the impression that God's glory would be promoted by their accepting such liberty as they could get, and conforming. Looking at the issues of things, we commend the voluntary exiles; but in all history there have been numerous examples of persons who, with the best possible intentions and motives, and with equal personal piety, have judged it to be their duty to accept a settlement which left the attainment of their highest desires still a long way off.

The principle which actuated the exiles of the Refor-

* Treatise of the Reformation.

mation may be traced back into old Lollardism, and thence back into the personal resolve of the solitary protester of earlier days still. A firm grasp of the foundation truth of individual trust in the promise and work of God for the human soul, leads to the assertion of the paramount right that this same conviction should be respected at all cost, and maintained against all comers.

This re-introduces us into the painful portion of our history,—that which deals with the oppressions exercised towards the advanced reformers, by those who accepted as final, the system of doctrine and discipline patronized by the Court and endowed by the State. John Canne, the laborious author of the reference Bible which bears his name, whilst in banishment for Nonconformity in 1634, thus describes the new difficulties which beset the path of conscientious godly men who chose in religious matters to think for themselves:—" Notwithstanding those called Puritans, which will not observe their traditions and beggarly ceremonies, shall be hurried up and down to their spiritual courts upon every occasion, and there be scorned, derided, taunted, and reviled with odious and contumelious speeches, eyed with big and stern looks, have proctors procured to make personal invectives against them: made to dance attendance from court to court, and from term to term, frowning at them in presence, and laughing at them behind their backs, never leaving molesting of them till they have emptied their purses, or caused them to make shipwreck of their consciences, or driven them out of the land; or, lastly, by imprisonment, starved, stifled, and pined them to death." *

The original Nonconformists were clergymen within the Church of England, who simply objected to the prelatical and other ceremonies with which it was re-established by Queen Elizabeth. The term never indicated any dissent from its doctrines or State position. Its historical sense is quite different from the popular modern meaning which it conveniently expresses. This is very apparent in the biographies of good Mr. Clarke. He thus writes of John Carter, vicar of Bramhall, who sustained a holy life and useful evangelical ministry through the troubles of his day, and died before the Act of Uniformity:—"He was sound and orthodox in his judgment; an able and resolute champion against all manner of *Popery* and *Arminianism;* as also against *Anabaptism* and *Brownism*, which did then begin to peep up, and infest the Church, to tear and rent the seamless coat of Christ. He was always a *Nonconformist*—one of the good old *Puritans* of England. He never swallowed any of the prelatical ceremonies against his conscience; so that he was often troubled with the bishops. But God raised him up friends that always brought him off and maintained his liberty." †

But religion is happily ever independent of all names and sects. There were at this time several persons of wealth and station who were occupied in promoting the work of evangelization. Such was Lady Bowes, the

* Canne's Necessity of Separation, p. 160.
† Clarke's Ten Lives, p. 4.

widow of Sir Benjamin Bowes, of Barnard Castle, who spent a thousand pounds annually in maintaining preachers whom she selected and sent into districts devoid of gospel-teaching.

In 1627, a scheme was originated, and a common fund raised by subscription in London, to maintain lecturers in populous places similarly bereft. This was well supported, and extended to the buying-up of advowsons for the same object; but Archbishop Laud considered the scheme as too favourable to the growth of Puritanism, and got an information filed and decree pronounced by the Court of Exchequer, cancelling the association, confiscating by forfeiture to the Crown the impropriations already purchased, and fining the trustees personally.

We get a beautiful sketch of Herbert at Bemerton :— his service twice a day in the chapel of his parsonage ; his congregation made up of gentlemen from the neighbourhood, as well as his own parishioners ; the husbandmen in the fields around letting their ploughs rest when they heard Mr. Herbert's bell ring to prayers, that they might offer their devotions with him, and then return to the plough.

Scarcely less beautiful is the picture of the poet-priest on his deathbed, delivering to his friend the MS. of his volume, now called " The Temple,"—saying,—" Sir, pray deliver this little book to my brother Farrer ; and tell him he shall find in it a picture of the many spiritual conflicts that have passed betwixt God and my soul, before I could subject mine to the will of Jesus, my Master, in whose service I have now found perfect freedom. Desire him to read it; and then if he think it may turn to the advantage of any dejected poor soul, let it be made public: if not, let him burn it, for I and it are less than the least of God's mercies." On the day of his death, he said to another friend,—"My dear friend, I am sorry I have nothing to present to my merciful God but sin and misery: but the first is pardoned, and a few hours will put a period to the latter." His friend took occasion to remind him of his many acts of mercy; to which he made answer,—"They be good works if they be sprinkled with the blood of Christ, and not otherwise." He died realizing his own sweet utterance,—

> "Who goeth in the way which Christ has gone,
>   Is much more sure to meet with Him, than one
>   That travelleth by-ways.
>   Perhaps my God, though He be far before,
>   May turn, and take me by the hand,—and, more,
>   May strengthen my decays." *

The most outlandish parts of England were now being penetrated by evangelical labour. What Bernard Gilpin and Rothwell had done in the North of England, Bagshaw did for the Peak of Derbyshire, Vavasour Powel and Hugh Owen for Wales, Machin in the moorlands of Staffordshire, Tregoss in Cornwall.

In 1625 was the commencement of a revival in the West of Scotland, which illuminated a large district, and originated piety in some who conferred signal benefit on the Church in years long afterwards.†

In the early part of King Charles's reign, there was at Wotton, in Gloucestershire, a gathering of young persons,

* The Temple, lxii.   † See Gillies, vol. i., p. 306.

who used to meet for religious instruction. Joseph Woodward, a graduate of Oxford, master of the free school at Wotton, joined the society, and became eminent at Dursley for his evangelical labours. As he went to church, the people would be waiting at the street-doors of their houses, and fell into procession, so as to accompany the good man, whom they had begun with reviling, and ended with loving. He died before the Act of Uniformity.

To this period, too, belongs the nursing of John Eliot, that great apostolic spirit who was to become the admiration of future ages as the pioneer of mission-work among the heathen. In 1628, Thomas Hooker, a Fellow of Emmanuel College, Cambridge, and lecturer at Chelmsford, had been worried out of the ministry by Laud, and was keeping a school at Little Baddow, in Essex. He was joined by a young Essex man, also a Cambridge scholar, named Eliot, who came to be his assistant, and who writes—"To this place was I called through the infinite riches of God's mercy in Christ Jesus to my poor soul; for here the Lord said unto my dead soul, Live! live! and through the grace of God I do live, and I shall live for ever!" Eliot followed his master to North America, where, moved by the lamentable condition of the Indian tribes, he wrote a tractate entitled "The Daybreaking of the Gospel," and took other effective means of drawing public attention to the subject of their evangelization, acquired their language, and thenceforward devoted all his long life to the work of preaching the Gospel as an itinerant missionary of the Cross. He scorned the notion that either the Red-skin, or the Negro, lay under any inherent disqualification for the Gospel, and he soon produced ample proofs of its triumphs over all the barriers of race and country. The fire which sustained the heroic evangelist amidst the forests of the New World, was first kindled under the Laudean persecutions in Old England.

The home missionary spirit is, at the same time, thus indicated by Sibbes, in 1633 :—" And if it were possible, it were to be wished, that there were set up some lights in all the dark corners of the kingdom, that might shine to those people that sit in darkness and in the shadow of death." *

There were at the time, a great number of godly preachers, both among those who had been deprived by the late Queen's injunction, and those who had escaped these trials. The "Book of Sports," with its surrounding circumstances, was never accepted by the people generally in lieu of religion. Family and personal piety was observed and honoured, laborious evangelical ministers valued and followed. The student of history who will be satisfied with the records of the quiet lives of hard-working ministers, or who will be interested in the kindling of religious feeling in a family or neighbourhood, may still discover much material in the biographies of good men who finished their course in the first half of the seventeenth century, before the political troubles came to a crisis.† Such men were Baines, Stock, Roth-

* The Saint's Safety in Evil Times.
† See Clarke's Lives ; Gillies' Historical Collections.

well, Herbert (famous in another field also), Bolton, Taylor, Sibbes, and others.

Rothwell, in the beginning of his career, was a clergyman without any true sense of religion. What follows will give a picture of the times :—

"I shall set it down as I remember I heard him speak it. He was playing at bowls amongst some Papists and vain gentlemen, upon a Saturday, somewhere about Rochdale in Lancashire. There comes into the green to him one Mr. Midgley, a grave and godly minister of Rochdale, whose praise is great in the Gospel, though far inferior to Rothwel in parts and learning. He took him aside, and fell into a large commendation of him : at length told him what pity it was that such a man as he should be a companion to Papists, and that upon a Saturday, when he should be preparing for the Sabbath. Mr. Rothwel slighted his words, and checked him for his meddling. The good old man left him, went home, and prayed privately for him. Mr. Rothwel, when he was retired from that company, could not rest, Mr. Midgley's words stuck so deep in his thoughts. The next day he went to Rochdale church to hear Mr. Midgley, where it pleased God to bless that ordinance so, as Mr. Rothwel was by that sermon brought home to Christ. He came after sermon to Mr. Midgley, thanked him for his reproof, and besought his direction and prayers ; for he was in a miserable condition, as being in a natural state. He lay for a time under the spirit of bondage, 'till afterwards, and by Mr. Midgley's hands, he received the spirit of adoption ; wherewith he was so sealed, that in the after part of his

P

life he never lost his assurance. Though he was a man subject to many temptations, the devil very often assaulting him, yet God was mightily with him, so that of his own experience, he was able to comfort many. He esteemed Mr. Midgley ever after as his spiritual father.

"He now becomes another man,—forsakes all his wonted courses and companions, preaches in another manner than formerly, opens the depths of Satan and deceitfulness of the heart, so as he was called the 'Rough Hewer.' His ministry was so accompanied with the power of God, that when he preached the law he made men tremble,—yea, sometimes to cry out in the church; and when he preached the Gospel, he was another Barnabas, and had great skill in comforting afflicted consciences. At his first entrance he had great opposition, and sometimes was waylaid to take away his life; but he overcame all that with his patience and courage, and at length his greatest enemies were afraid of him; and he preached few sermons but it was believed he gained some souls. His manner was to spend the forenoon at his studies, and the afternoon in going through his parish and conferring with his people; in which as he excelled, so he gained much upon them, and within four years had so many judicious and experimental Christians, that people came from London, York, Richmond, Newcastle, and many other places to see the order of his congregation." *

It cannot be questioned that, with all this prosperity, the outward form and the inward spirit of religion were again on the point of becoming dissevered. The ten-

* Clarke's Lives.

dency of the Court and Government was decidedly hostile. But it was too late for Christ's cause in England to be blotted out by political movements. The effort to make ritualism under Laud the characteristic of the State church, unhappily was effectual; but it went no further. No effort could be successful to render it, among the masses, a substitute for evangelical religion. The attempt was made, and ended in the ruin of the projectors. Again the people felt that the concerns of eternity were at stake, and they acted accordingly. The sixth article of the London Petition of Grievances made to the Parliament, shows what the commonalty thought of these things:—" VI. The great encrease of idle, lewd, and dissolute, ignorant and erroneous men in the ministry, which swarme like the locusts of Egypt over the whole kingdom; and will they but wear a canonicall coat, a surplisse, a hood, bow at the name of Jesus, and be zealous of superstitious ceremonies, they may live as they list, confront whom they please, preach and vent what errours they will, and neglect preaching at their pleasures, without controul."

The great outworking of the personal religious life of England, continued to spring from the free use of the Scriptures by the people at large. It cannot be too often repeated, that at this period the bulk of the current national literature was composed of sound divinity. The practice of intelligent piety was the most general pursuit. For one instance, amongst hundreds, we turn to the picture given us by Mrs. Hutchinson, of the household of her mother, the wife of Sir Arthur Apsley, governor of the Tower:—"The worship and service of God, both in her soul and in her house, and the education of her children, were her principal care. She was a constant frequenter of week-day lectures, and a great lover and encourager of good ministers, and most diligent in her private reading and devotions." Such was the training of the men of that age. It fostered a faith which was the persuasion of the whole moral nature.

Another sketch, taken from St. Mary's at Oxford, when Usher was preaching there before Charles I. in the beginning of the Civil War, will show how the piety of the family was succeeded by that of the college.

"The persuasion of Armagh's incomparable learning," they say, "the observation of his awful gravity, the evidence of his eminent and exemplary piety, all improved to the height by his indefatigable industry, drew students to flock to him, as doves to the windows. It joys us to recollect how multitudes of scholars, especially the heads of our tribes, thronged to hear the sound of his silver bells; how much they were taken with the voice of this wise charmer—how their ears seemed, as it were, fastened to his lips. Here you might have seen a sturdy Paul, a persecutor transformed into a preacher; there is a tender-hearted Josiah lamenting after the Lord, and with Ephraim smiting on his thigh, saying, 'What have I done?' Others, with the penitent Jews, so stabbed to the heart as they were forced to cry out in the bitterness of their soul, 'Men, brethren, and fathers, what shall we do?' These were some of the blessings from on high which attended his sermons."

The poetry continues to display the deep spiritual tinge of the Elizabethan age. How beautiful is the sentiment of the following lines from Francis Quarles, published in 1642!—

> " Even as the needle, that directs the hour,
> Touch'd with the loadstone, by the secret power
> Of hidden nature, points upon the Pole;
> Even so the wavering powers of my soul,
> Touch'd by the virtue of Thy Spirit, flee
> From what is earth, and point alone to Thee.
> When I have faith to hold Thee by the hand,
> I walk securely, and methinks I stand
> More firm than Atlas."

The early Puritans, doubtless, in domestic life carried too far their profound convictions of the paramount importance of manifested religion at all times and in all places. Yet the result in many instances was the production of characters and actions of the highest value. Oliver Heywood, who was born in 1612, tells us that at a very early age, his mother was accustomed to instruct him "in the deep points of divinity—the fall in Adam, the corruption of our nature, subjection to the curse, redemption by Christ, the necessity of regeneration, the immortality and worth of the soul, the weight and concernment of eternity."* She used the catechism of the famous Puritan schoolmaster, Mr. John Ball; set him to pray in the family, bade him attend the frequent religious conferences held at his father's house, took him to hear the most celebrated preachers in the country round,

* Life of Oliver Heywood, p. 31.

required him to bring home notes of their discourses, and gave him to read Luther and Calvin, with the works of Perkins, Preston, and Sibbes. His mother was noted for ability as well as piety, and was an oracle concerning the time and place of week-day sermons and religious intelligence. At the age of fourteen, young Heywood began to receive the communion in the parish church, and joined a small society of young men who were accustomed to meet together once a fortnight for religious conversation and prayer. It is not to be wondered at that this training, when accompanied by the blessing of God (which it was calculated to bring), resulted in the formation of manly Christian character.

Personal religion had also reached the high places of the land. The piety of Lord Falkland, of Lord Brooke, and several of the conspicuous men of the day, was of the most thorough kind. They lived, acted, and spoke for God. True, the domestic exhibitions of family religion appear to us to have been unduly strict and severe. They, doubtless, were so; but it was an error which shows the high estimation in which piety was then held. In the memoir of Lettice, Lady Falkland, the details of her ordinary routine of daily life are as follows:—"First, she spent some hours every day in her *private devotions* and *meditations;* and these were called, I remember, by her family, her *busy hours*. Then her maids came into her chamber early every morning, and ordinarily she passed about an howr with them, in praying, and catechizing, and instructing them. To these secret and private praiers, the publick morning and evening praiers of the

Church, before dinner and supper, and another form, together with reading Scriptures and singing psalms, before bed-time, were daily and constantly added. Neither were these holy offices appropriate to her menial servants; others came freely to joyn with them, and her oratory was as open to the neighbors as her Hall was."*

The representative men of the best religious life of the age are, however, not only or chiefly to be discovered on the surface of history, but in obscure records, cherished by a few, who hold in reverence memories wholly slighted by the general public. The name of Henry Jessey will serve as an instance. He was a Yorkshireman, born in 1601, educated at St. John's College, Cambridge, where, amidst considerable attainments in human knowledge, he also attained the more excellent divine knowledge of Christ, as his Saviour and friend. After living for nine years with Mr. Gurward, in Suffolk, as domestic chaplain, he obtained a living in the year 1633, but in the following year was ejected for neglecting the rubric and removing a crucifix. He then became chaplain to Sir Matthew Birnton, who brought him to London, where he took charge of a congregation of Protestant dissenters, originally formed in 1616 by Mr. Henry Jacob. Several of the congregation becoming Baptists, Mr. Jessey, after two or three years' attention to the subject, and conference with his ministerial brethren, also espoused and publicly avowed the doctrine of baptism of believers only, and

* "A Letter containing many remarkable Passages in the most holy Life and Death of the late Lady Lettice, Viscountess Falkland." 1648.

that by immersion. "But," says his biographer, "notwithstanding his differing from his brethren in this or any other point, he maintained the same Christian love and charity to all saints as before, not only as to a friendly conversation, but also in respect of church communion. He had always some of the Pædo-baptist persuasion, and blamed those who made their particular opinion about baptism the boundary of church communion. He published the reasons of his opinion in this case; and when he travelled through the north and west parts of England to visit the churches, he made it his principal business to excite them to love and union among themselves, notwithstanding their differing from one another in some opinions; and was also the principal person that set up, and preserved for some time, a meeting at London of some eminent men of each denomination, in order to maintain peace and union among those Christians that differed not fundamentally; and this catholic spirit procured him the love and esteem of the good men of all parties." *

He was famous, too, as a student of the Hebrew (at a time when this study was rare), of the Greek, Syriac, and Chaldaic; for his efforts for the Jews, and for foreigners in general; for his own charities, and his public urgency in favour of benevolence. On the Restoration, he was ejected from a living which he had held under the Commonwealth; was thrown into prison (in spite of his goodness) for his nonconformity, and there died at the age of sixty-three, in the year 1663, beloved and

* Crosby's "History of English Baptists," vol. i., p. 312.

lamented by all, as a man of rare learning, piety, moderation, diligence in doing good, and catholicity of spirit. He was an accomplished, devout Christian gentleman.

An amusing incident in the history of the Pilgrim-Fathers serves to illustrate the general religious habit of the men whom evil legislation was now banishing from our shores. John Fisk, a pious graduate of Cambridge, escaped in disguise with another Puritan preacher, and embarked for New England. When the ship had passed the Land's End, they "made themselves known, and entertained the passengers with two sermons every day, besides other devotional exercises. Indeed, the whole voyage was so much devoted to the 'exercises of religion, that when one of the passengers was accused of diverting himself with the hook and line on the Lord's day, he protested, saying, "I do not know which is the Lord's day. I think every day is a Sabbath day; for you do nothing but preach and pray all the week long."*

In November, 1640, a respectable prebendary of Durham, Mr. Peter Smart, dared to preach against the ritualistic ceremonies then being engrafted on the cathedral service at Durham by Dr. Cosins. He was persecuted, tried, defended himself on the ground of the Prayer-book, Articles, and Homilies,—but all in vain: he was heavily fined and imprisoned, until released by the Long Parliament. We get a glimpse of the family piety from the following letter, written to him by his wife whilst he was in prison:—

* Brook: from Mather's "History of New England."

"Most loving and dearly beloved Husband,

"The grace and blessing of God be with you, even as unto mine owne soule and body, so do I dayly in my harty prayer wish unto you and my children; for I doe dayly twise, at the least, in this sort remember you. And I do not doubte, deere husband, but that both you and I, as we be written in the booke of life, so we shall together enjoy the same everlastingly, throught the saveing grace and mercy of God, our deare Father, in his Soonne our Christ: and for this present life, let us wholly appointe ourselves to the will of our God, to glorifie him, whether by life or by death; and even that mercifull Lord make us worthy to honor him either way, as pleaseth him, Amen. Ye what great cause of rejoysing have we in our most gratious God, we can not but brust fourth into the prasing of such a bountifull God, which maide you worthy to suffer for his name and worde saike: for it is given to you of God, not only that ye should believe in him; but also, that ye should suffer for his saik. 1 Peter, 4, 5. Yf ye suffer rebuke in the name of Christ, that is, in Christ's cause, for his truths sake, then ar ye happy and blessed; for the glory of the Spirit of God resteth upon you, and therefore rejoice in the Lord, end againe I say rejoice; for the distresed church doth yet suffer dayly thinges for her mortification, and for this cause, is contemned and despised. But alas! if thy servant David, if thine onely Soone our Christ livede in shame and contempt, and weere a moking stocke for the people; whie should not we then patiently suffer all things, that we might enter into glory, through many troubles, vexations, shame, and ignominy, &c. ?—The blessing of God be with all, Amen, pray, pray.—Your loving and faithfull wife untill death,

"Susanna Smart." *

Whatever differences of opinion may exist as to the political qualities of Puritanism, there ought to be none as to the reality and depth of the personal religious conviction which lay at its base. Setting aside from the observers all those who are wilfully prejudiced, and from the observed all those who are obviously mere shallow dissemblers, the judgment must be unanimous in favour of the reality, heartiness, truth, and power of the life of God in their souls. The religion which they professed, the interpretation of Scripture which they received, the views of duty which they carried out, were all grounded on the idea of a transaction between God and the individual soul. The work of Christ, the covenant of grace, the promises of Scripture, all had respect to the individual believer. The abuse of this sentiment led to spiritual pride and fanaticism; but its more frequent use led to the manifestation of some of the grandest characters and actions the world ever saw.

* "Illustrations of Neal," p. 61.

CHAPTER XIII.

The Commonwealth.

AFTER the free publication of the Holy Scriptures in the days of Elizabeth, and during the long interval of peace which prevailed in her reign, and in that of her unwarlike successor, we have seen that there was a great spread and growth of individual personal piety. Silently, but surely, the leaven worked; and though many circumstances repressed its outward action, yet the formation of evangelical sentiments and the inculcation of evangelical knowledge became exceedingly prevalent, and with these a large underlying mass of sincere godliness. This is shown by the sudden disclosure made by the troubles of the Commonwealth. No sooner does the strife begin, than there come to the front rank, on both sides, men, whose high principle was sustained by the inner action of a religious life. Nowhere on the page of history do we find so much individuality of character,—nowhere such a solemn realization of the maxim, "No man liveth unto himself." They,

―― "Like a watch-tow'r on the steep of fame,
Shower light upon the sons of distant days." *

* Camoens.

One cause of this lustre of personal religion was the necessity then created for the formation and avowal of individual conviction. In the great political strife now commencing, neutrality was impossible. Religion underlaid all the questions of the day. The mind of every person was compelled, by the surrounding circumstances, to act in an elective manner. Many chose their side, whether for Crown or Commonwealth, under the influence of the highest motives, professedly for the highest ends; and thus were formed the sterling characters which dignify this important period of our history.

So it was with the great theologian Dr. Owen. Whilst quite destitute of evangelical light, as he states, he had at Oxford to choose between the two rising parties. He espoused that cause which he conceived to have the right on its side, though at the cost of the forfeiture of all his worldly prospects. At this juncture, too, he made another choice: he struggled to obtain peace in his soul, which he felt that he needed. Clouds and darkness surrounded his path both socially and spiritually. At this time, says his biographer, "he accompanied a cousin to Aldermanbury Church, to hear Mr. Edmund Calamy, a man of great note for his eloquence as a preacher, and for his boldness as a leader of the Presbyterian party. By some circumstance, unexplained, Mr. Calamy was prevented from preaching that day: in consequence of which, and of not knowing who was to preach, many left the church. Owen's cousin urged him to hear Mr. Jackson, the minister of St. Michael's, Wood-street,—a man of prodigious application as a scholar, and of considerable celebrity as a preacher. Owen, however, being seated, and unwilling to walk further, refused to leave the church until he should see who was to preach. At last, a country minister, unknown to the congregation, stepped into the pulpit, and, after praying very fervently, took for his text Matt. viii. 26, 'Why are ye fearful, O ye of little faith?' The very reading of the text appears to have impressed Owen, and led him to pray most earnestly that the Lord would bless the discourse to him. The prayer was heard; for, in that sermon, the minister was directed to answer the very objections which he commonly brought against himself; and though the same answers had often occurred to him, they had not before afforded him any relief. But now Jehovah's time of mercy had arrived, and the truth was received, not as the word of man, but as the word of the living and true God. The sermon was a very plain one; the preacher never known; but the effect was mighty, through the blessing of God." *

Owen was born in 1616, the year of the death of good Mr. Jacob, who organized the first Congregational church in England.

The extensive development of religion at this time cannot be questioned. Illustrious instances are there, in proof of this, on both sides of the national dispute. Allowing the utmost that can be claimed as a drawback on the score of that hypocrisy which always dogs success, there remains a vast amount of real, enlightened, devout, fervid religious life. Piety was in those days a manly pursuit. Virtuous lives and heroic actions abounded.

* Orme's Life of Owen, p. 27.

The army of the Commonwealth especially bore testimony to the prevalence of real religion, notwithstanding the contemporaneous existence of much dissimulation.

The most famous religious council ever held in England was that which met in Henry VII.'s Chapel on the 1st of July, 1643, in obedience to an ordinance of the Parliament for the settlement of such a government in the Church as should, by common consent, be considered agreeable to God's holy word, and might be enforced throughout the kingdom. If these objects, so long and ardently sought for by statesmen, were in their nature capable of attainment consistently with the sound action of the powers by which they are arrived at, surely they would now have been accomplished. But the protracted labours of the wise, pious, and able men who constituted the great majority of the Westminster Assembly were all in vain. They have left no trace in the religious life of England, and but little record in our literature, save the excellent catechism which bears the name of the Assembly. This great attempt to fix for a nation an inflexible type of faith and worship, was a total failure.

The progress of time rolls away the mists which frequently cloud Divine dispensations during their transit. We can now plainly perceive, that, such was the temper of the dominant sects during the Commonwealth, that all the severe discipline of subsequent reigns was needed to induce clear views of the sacred rights of conscience. The old reformers *acted* rightly; but when they came to *reason the matter*, they admitted false premises, and so their theoretical views lagged behind their practical doings.

It took a century of persecution to institute true toleration, and a century more to inaugurate full freedom. Perpetual strife, on all hands, appears to be the normal condition of Christ's kingdom on the earth,—so inveterate is Satan's opposition. The latter is manifested in all departments of the work, whether in its individual or collective advancement, in its relations to the world or to God. The truces occurring in the course of the conflict are always followed by a resumption of the everlasting hostility. In religion alone, exploded errors of the past are revived by the youth of successive generations.

We gladly escape from these considerations to the more congenial task of delineating the traces of godliness apart from the errors of the times.

The testimony given by Royalist writers to the reality of the piety prevalent in Cromwell's army is remarkable. Chillingworth says—"I observed a great deal of piety in the commanders and soldiers of the Parliament's army; I confess their discourse and behaviour do speak them Christans." This was the army of which Lord Clarendon writes—"An army to which victory is entailed, and, which, humanly speaking, could hardly fail of conquest whithersoever it should be led; an army whose society and manners, whose courage and success, make it famous and terrible over the world." It was in this army that the colonels, including Cromwell, conducted worship and preached.

The growth of this habit greatly shocked the Long Parliament, and served as the topic of many heavy diatribes and light witticisms. It seemed intolerable that whilst all public parties were occupying themselves with the concerns of religion, private individuals should take leave to do the same. But so it was : pious laymen organized a lay mission around London, and began to preach the Gospel to the poor without any other authorization than their own convictions. This was a step as yet too far in advance : five of the offenders were, in 1641, summoned to the bar of the Lower House, and admonished to desist, under the threat of serious penalties for the future.

The preceding age had quickened not only thought, but emotion, on the subject of religion. The solid conviction of the mind was accompanied by the affectionate persuasion of the heart. The familiar correspondence of the day shows with faithfulness sometimes ludicrous, the interest taken in all things pertaining to worship. Preaching and psalm-singing were the favourite occupations of all ranks of the people. By the aid of Mrs. Hutchinson, we may look into the cannoneer's chamber at Nottingham whilst Fairfax lay there. It will illustrate what was going on throughout the host. Presbyterianism was in the ascendant ; but the good cannoneer was not of " that way." He held private meetings in his own chamber, at which Scripture was expounded, and exhortations given by himself and his comrades.

We may obtain an accurate impression of the religious character of this period by examining the numerous details we possess of the inner life of Cromwell himself. His own private letters, written under circumstances which preclude all idea of artifice, may be properly accepted as exponents of his real character, and descriptive of the surrounding circumstances.

It was quite possible for him to have counterfeited in the high places of the world; but in the unobserved current of social every-day life, continued simulation is wholly unimaginable: for private life is a reaction from public life. The hypocrisy of the latter would be flung off in the congenial ungodliness of the former. On the 17th of July, 1650, whilst at Alnwick, marching northwards with the army into Scotland, he writes to Mr. Mayer, the father of Dorothy, his son Richard's wife:—

"I hope you give my son good counsel; I believe he needs it. He is in the dangerous time of his age; and it's a very vain world. O how good it is to close with Christ betimes!—there is nothing else worth the looking after. I beseech you, call upon him. I hope you will discharge my duty and your own love. You see how I am employed. I need pity. I know what I feel. Great place and business in the world is not worth the looking after: I should have no comfort in mine, but that my hope is in the Lord's presence. I have not sought these things; truly I have been called unto them by the Lord; and therefore am not without some assurance that He will enable His poor worm and weak servant to do His will." *

The only letter extant of the Protector's wife to himself, is one written to him at Edinburgh on October 27th, 1650. It cannot be understood without the assumption that both were sincerely religious.

"I should rejoice to hear your desire in seeing me; but I desire to submit to the providence of God, hoping

* Carlyle's Cromwell, vol. iii., p. 13.

the Lord, who hath separated us, and hath often brought us together again, will, in His good time, bring us again, to the praise of His name. Truly my life is but half a life in your absence, did not the Lord make it up in Himself, which I must acknowledge to the praise of His grace." *

Cromwell's letters to Fleetwood are signally decisive not only as to the genuineness of his religious affections, but as to their sound and healthful character. On one occasion of his writing, the Secretary commences the letter; then Oliver takes up the pen himself, writes the page full, then the margin, and then, in the full flow of his emotions, turns the sheet round and fills every part of it.

"Salute your dear wife from me. Bid her beware of a *bondage* spirit. Fear is the natural issue of such a spirit ;—the antidote is Love. The voice of Fear is: If I had done this, if I had avoided that, how well it had been with me!—I know this hath been her vain reasoning.

"Love argueth in this wise: What a Christ have I; what a Father in and through Him! What a name hath my Father: *Merciful, gracious, long-suffering, abundant in goodness and truth; forgiving iniquity, transgression and sin.* What a nature hath my Father: *He is* LOVE ;—free in it, unchangeable, infinite! What a covenant between Him and Christ,—for all the seed, for every one : wherein He undertakes all, and the poor soul nothing. The new covenant is *Grace,* to or upon the soul; to which it, 'the soul,' is passive and receptive.

* Carlyle's Cromwell, vol. iii., p. 136.

I'll do away their sins; I'll write my law, &c.; I'll put it in their hearts: they shall never depart from me, &c.

"This commends the love of God: it's Christ dying for men *without* strength, for men whilst sinners, whilst enemies. And shall we seek for the root of our comforts within us,—What God hath done, what He is to us in Christ, is the root of our comfort: in this is stability; in us is weakness. Acts of obedience are not perfect, and therefore yield not perfect grace. Faith, as an act, yields it not; but 'only' as it carries us into Him, who is our perfect rest and peace; in whom we are accounted of, and received by, the Father,—even as Christ Himself. This is our high calling. Rest we here, and here only."*

The dismissal of the little Parliament by the Protector was mainly owing to his fears lest religion should suffer from their intolerance. This is explained in one of his familiar letters to Fleetwood, proving that his actions, in this respect, were not grounded on reasons of State, but on a desire for the glory of God.

"Cockpit, 22nd August, 1653.

"Dear Charles,

"Although I do not so often as is desired by me acquaint you how it is with me, yet I doubt not of your prayers in my behalf, that, in all things, I may walk as becometh the Gospel.

"Truly I never more needed all helps from my Christian friends than now! Fain would I have my service accepted of the saints, if the Lord will; but it is not

---

* Carlyle's Cromwell, vol. iii., p. 246.

so. Being of different judgments, and 'those' of each sort seeking most to propagate their own, that spirit of kindness that is to them all, is hardly accepted of any. I hope I can say it, my life has been a willing sacrifice, and, I hope, for them *all*. Yet it much falls out as when the two Hebrews were rebuked: you know upon whom they turned their displeasure!

"But the Lord is wise, and will, I trust, make manifest that I am no enemy. Oh, how easy is mercy to be abused! Persuade friends with you to be very sober. If the day of the Lord *be* so near as some say, how should our moderation appear? If every one, instead of contending, would justify his form 'of judgment' by love and meekness, wisdom would be 'justified of her children.' But, alas!—

"I am, in my temptation, ready to say, 'Oh, would I had wings like a dove, then would I,' &c.: but this, I fear, is my 'haste.' I bless the Lord I have somewhat keeps me alive: some sparks of the light of His countenance, and some sincerity above man's judgment. Excuse me thus unbowelling myself to you: pray for me; and desire my friends to do so also. My love to thy dear wife, whom indeed I entirely love, both naturally and upon the best account; and my blessing, if it be worth anything, upon thy little babe."*

And another:—

"Dear Charles, my dear love to thee; 'and' to my dear Biddy, who is a joy to my heart, for what I hear of the Lord in her. Bid her be cheerful, and rejoice in the Lord

* Carlyle's Cromwell, vol. iii., p. 301.

once and again : if she knows the Covenant, she cannot but do 'so.' For that Transaction is without *her ;* sure and stedfast, between the Father and the Mediator in His blood : therefore, leaning upon the Son, or looking to Him, thirsting after Him, and embracing Him, we are His Seed ;—and the Covenant is sure to all the Seed. The Compact is for the Seed : God is bound in faithfulness to Christ, and in Him to us: the Covenant is without *us ;* a Transaction between God and Christ. Look up to *it.* God engageth in it to pardon us ; to write His Law in our heart ; to plant His fear 'so' that we shall never depart from Him. We, under all our sins and infirmities, can daily offer a perfect Christ; and thus we have peace and safety, and apprehension of love, from a Father in Covenant,—who cannot deny Himself. And truly in this is all my salvation; and this helps me to bear my great burdens."*

We may also contemplate the great man in his decline, touched by the death of his dear daughter Elizabeth. The sketch is by one of a class concerning which it is said that no man is a hero before them,—the groom of the bedchamber.

"At Hampton Court, a few days after the death of the Lady Elizabeth, which touched him nearly,—being then himself under bodily distempers, forerunners of that Sickness which was to death, and in his bedchamber,— he called for his Bible, and desired an honourable and godly person there, with others, present, To read unto him that passage in *Philippians,* Fourth : '*Not that I speak*

* Carlyle's Cromwell, vol. iv., p. 23.

in respect of want : for I have learned in whatsoever state I am, therewith to be content. I know both how to be abased, and I know how to abound. Everywhere, and by all things, I am instructed ; both to be full and to be hungry, both to abound and to suffer need. I can do all things, through Christ which strengtheneth me.' Which read,— said he, to use his own words as near as I can remember them : ' This Scripture did once save my life ; when my eldest Son' poor Oliver ' died ; which went as a dagger to my heart, indeed it did.' And then repeating the words of the text himself, and reading the tenth and eleventh verses of Paul's contentation, and submission to the will of God in all conditions,—said he : 'It's true, Paul, *you* have learned this, and attained to this measure of grace : but what shall *I* do ? Ah poor creature, it is a hard lesson for me to take out ! I find it so !' But reading on to the thirteenth verse, where Paul saith, *' I can do all things through Christ that strengtheneth me,'*—then faith began to work, and his heart to find support and comfort, and he said thus to himself, " He that was Paul's Christ is my Christ too !' And so drew waters out of the well of Salvation."*

"All the Promises of God are in *Him :* yes, and in Him Amen ; to the glory of God by us,—by *us* in Jesus Christ."——" The Lord hath filled me with as much assurance of His pardon, and His love, as my soul can hold." —" I think I am the poorest wretch that lives : but I love God ; or rather, am beloved of God."—" I am a con-

* Carlyle's Cromwell, vol. iv., p. 392.

queror, and more than a conqueror, through Christ that strengtheneth me!"*

We feel that we have been in the presence of one who, with all his faults and failings, was a striking exemplification of the life of God in the soul,—a man of prayer and piety.

The explicit testimony of Mr. Richardson, a person of calm judgment, keen mind, and independent habits of thought, a contemporary and a Londoner, probably expresses the exact truth:—"He hath a large heart, spirit, and principle that will hold all that fear the Lord, though of different opinions and practices in religion, and seek their welfare. I am persuaded there is not a better friend to the nations and people of God among men, and that there is not any man so unjustly censured and abused as he is."†

A beautiful picture of the divine power of faith is shown in the closing scene of the life of another great soldier and noble Christian English gentleman, Colonel Hutchinson, who died whilst tyrannically imprisoned at Walmer.

"He was never more pleasant and contented in his whole life. When no other recreations were left him, he diverted himself with sorting and shadowing cockle-shells, which his wife and daughter gathered for him, with as much delight as he used to take in the richest agates and

---

* Carlyle's Cromwell, vol. iv., p. 398.

† Tracts on Liberty of Conscience, p. 241. The scope of Mr. Richardson's mind is characterized by the title of one of his publications: "Newes from Heaven of a Treaty of Peace; or, a Cordiall for a Fainting Heart. Wherein is manifested that Jesus Christ, and all that is His, is freely offered to all who need," &c. 1643.

onyxes he could compass, with the most artificial engravings, which were things, when he recreated himself from more serious studies, he as much delighted in as any piece of art But his fancy showed itself so excellent in sorting and dressing these shells, that none of us could imitate it, and the cockles began to be admired by several persons who saw them. These were but his trifling diversions, his business and continual study was the Scripture, which the more he conversed in, the more it delighted him; insomuch that his wife having brought down some books to entertain him in his solitude, he thanked her, and told her that if he should continue as long as he lived in prison, he would read nothing there but his Bible. His wife bore all her own toils joyfully enough for the love of him, but could not but be very sad at the sight of his undeserved sufferings; and he would very sweetly and kindly chide her for it, and tell her that if she were but cheerful, he should think this suffering the happiest thing that ever befell him; he would also bid her consider what reason she had to rejoice that the Lord supported him, and how much more intolerable it would have been if the Lord had suffered his spirits to have sunk, or his patience to have been lost under this. One day when she was weeping, after he had said many things to comfort her, he gave her reasons why she should hope and be assured that this cause would revive, because the interest of God was so much involved in it that he was entitled to it."*

We trace some of the survivors of the heroic age in the London churches during subsequent reigns. Dr. Owen's

* Life of Col. Hutchinson (Bohn), p. 468.

church numbered Lord Charles Fleetwood, Sir John Hartopp, Colonel Desborough (brother-in-law to the Protector), Lady Abney, Lady Hartopp, Lady Vere Wilkinson, Lady Thompson, Mrs. Bendish (Cromwell's granddaughter), and others, who have all left on the pleasant pages of personal biography some proof that they were examples of the vital godliness prevalent in their younger days.

Presbyterianism was established by an ordinance of the House of Lords on the 6th of June 1646; and in May, 1648, its assembly ordained the punishment of death for certain excesses of blasphemy and heresy. The Presbyterian model was never, however, enforced. It was adopted in Lancashire, Cheshire, and a few other counties; but the spirit of the times favoured liberty. Some church livings were held by Independents, some by Baptists, many by Presbyterians, the majority by the old clergy, who made no difficulty as to the slender amount of conformity to the ruling powers then required. Romanists, Episcopalians, Presbyterians, Independents, all in their turn pleaded divine right, and divine obligation of enforcement and support as its correlation; but religion, as though disdaining such pretensions, did not exclusively dwell with either of the rivals.

Another formal public establishment of religion under the Commonwealth is contained in the ordinance of Government signed and sworn to by Cromwell on the 16th December, 1653, and is as follows:—

"35. That the Christian religion, conteined in the Scriptures, bee held forth and commended as the publick profession of these nations; and that as soon as may bee, a provision less subject to scruple and contention, and more certain than the present, bee made for the encouragement and maintenance of able and painful teachers, for instructing the people, and for discoverie and confutation of error, heresie, and whatever is contrary to sound doctrine: and that, until such provision bee made, the present maintenance shal not be taken away nor impeached.

"36. That to the publick profession held forth, none shall bee compelled by penalties or otherwise, but that endeavors bee used to win them by sound doctrine, and the example of a good conversation.

"37. That such as profess faith in God by Jesus Christ (though differing in judgment from the doctrine, worship, or discipline publickly held forth) shall not bce restrained from, but shall bee protected in the profession of the faith, and exercise of their religion; so as they abuse not this liberty, to the civil injury of others, and to the actual disturbance of the publick peace on their parts: provided this liberty bee not extended to Popery or Prelacy, nor to such as, under the profession of Christ, hold forth and practise licentiousness.

"38. That all laws, statutes, ordinances, and clauses in any law, statute, and ordinance to the contrary of the aforesaid libertie shall bee esteemed as null and void."*

Whenever the force of divine truth presses on the Church with unusual power, the efforts for its diffusion overstep the limits which spiritual ease prescribes in ordinary times.

* Collection of Ordinances, &c., printed 1654, p. 21.

Preaching is then no longer confined, as a practice, to those who are specially and most properly set apart for the work; but others, seeing that the wants of the world can never be overtaken by the efforts of appointed ministers alone, feeling impelled alike by a sense of duty to the cause and regard for their fellow-men, go out, and in the highways and hedges, in market-places and village-greens, in hall and cottage, publish, as best they can, the word of life. This was much practised in the days of the Commonwealth. Sometimes, doubtless, conceit was the moving spring, and shallow teaching the scope of the layman's efforts; but, in the great majority of instances, it was genuine missionary spirit, prompting to the accomplishment of genuine missionary work.

It is easy to detect the incompleteness and inconsistency of the tenets of George Fox, the founder of the Quakers; but it is impossible to regard him otherwise than as a man with many elements of goodness and greatness. The life which he lived was a life of faith. How grand is Penn's testimony concerning him!—"The *inwardness* and *weight* of his spirit, the *reverence* and *solemnity* of his address and behaviour, and the *fewness* and *fulness* of his words, have often struck even strangers with *admiration*, as they used to reach others with *consolation*. The most *awful, living, reverent* frame I ever felt or beheld, I must say, was his in prayer. And truly it was a testimony he knew and lived nearer to the Lord than other men; for they that know him most will see most reason to approach him with reverence and fear."

At this time the practice commenced of requiring from

those who wished to be joined to a church, a statement of their faith. This usually took the form of a biographical sketch of that portion of the life which related to religion. Many of these "experiences," as they were called, were published. By their aid we can demonstrate the actual identity of the Christian life everywhere and at all times, in the divinity of its origin, its vital connexion with revealed truth, its liableness to temptation and fluctuation, its specific individual character, various as the lives and circumstances of its subject. There are passages in the inner life of David, Paul, Augustine, Bernard, à Kempis, Bilney, Rutherford, and Payson, which might be aptly exchanged from one biography to the other with truth and consistency. In like manner they would be expressive of the experience of thousands whose obscurity has never been removed on earth, but will be for ever done away with in heaven.

In the year 1653, John Rogers, the incumbent of St. Thomas the Apostle's, in the City, published, in a curious work entitled "Beth-Shemesh, a Tabernacle for the Sun, or, Irenicum Evangelicum," a statement of the religious experience of several members of his congregation, comprising persons of all ranks in society, including several of Cromwell's soldiers. They are just such as may be found in the volumes of religious biography more ancient or more modern,—the same discoveries, conflicts, lights and shadows. Two short instances, relating to ordinary persons, will serve as types of the whole.

"*Experience of Laurence Swinfield.*

"I have been a travellour for some yeares, and wandred

about in far countries beyond seas till I came back againe into England, and all this while in my natural condition; and so I continued a great while. But I came hither in a sad condition and very comfortlesse, and could not tell what to doe, but to fall to prayer and I did that often, and found (I thank God) much of refreshment from that meanes, but nothing to satisfie my minde, for I have been much troubled in conscience, and could not take comfort, until the Lord was pleased to give me some promises to feed upon, as Matth. xi. 28, 29, 30, where He promised to ease the heavy oppressed, and to make His yoke easy and light: and then I began to long for a reformation, and to desire to be under His yoke, which was before (I thought) a burthen to me; and so Isaiah lv. 1, 'come buy without price and without money:' and soe, I came as freely as I was called, and was presently confirmed by the Spirit of God perswading me to give myself up into God's hands upon these His owne termes; and soe I did to this day. And many other sweet promises I had, whereby I had a great deal of peace and comfort, and can confidently say the Lord is my God; and I have ever since found in me a very great change from what I was before."

"*Experience of Jeremy Heyward.*

"The Lord hath opened my eyes to see sin, and shewne me myself; and I lay under this wrath half a year; and soe long as I sought to make out my own righteousnesse, I lay thus; and yet this while I followed the meanes, heard the word, and I saw at length nothing but Christ would save me, and till then I could have no comfort: wherefore one first day of the week I fell to prayer. I prayed thrice, and at the third time I heard him say, 'Lo! my grace is sufficient for thee;' whereby I was much satisfied ever since, rowling my selfe on Christ, and living in Him alone: and I find soe great a change, that I can say, Whereas I was blind, now I am sure I see."

It will be readily admitted that the two prodigies of human learning in the days of the Commonwealth were John Selden and Archbishop Usher. They took opposite sides in the great political contention of the day, but were one in the ground of their religious hope. Selden, shortly before his death, sought a special interview with the archbishop. They conversed about things transcendently more important in the estimation of both, than were the vast stores of erudition they had each accumulated. Selden bore testimony to the sole sufficiency of Scripture to sustain the soul, and stated that the passage which of all others fixed itself upon his memory, "stuck close to his heart," and imparted comfort to his mind, was that from the Epistle to Titus beginning thus: "*For the grace of God that bringeth salvation.*" (Titus ii. 11—14.*) The ponderous volumes which he had written were all directed to show the origin and constitution of human institutions; but the hope of his soul was in the simple direct gift of God,—*the grace that bringeth salvation.* †

The incomparable Archbishop Usher experienced the

---

* Life of Usher; Society for Promoting Christian Knowledge.

† The reader will be reminded of the exclamation of the dying Grotius: *Heu! vitam perdidi operose nihil agendo.*

trials incident to being deprived of his dignities and possessions by the legislation of the Commonwealth; we find his true character, as one of God's children, shining with an uncommon lustre. His magnanimous mind, though he differed in many conclusions from the great men among the Nonconformists, yet led him to form sanctified friendships with them. Some of his sayings on prayer will serve to show the secret of his strength and peace:—
"No honey is sweeter to the taste than spiritual prayer to God." "God's children, let Him deny them ever so long, yet they will never leave knocking and begging: they will pray, and they will wait still, till they receive an answer. Many will pray to God, as prayer is a duty; but few use it as a means to obtain a blessing. Those who come to God in the use of it, as a means to obtain what they would have, will pray and not give over petitioning till they receive it."*

So do we get an insight into his spiritual condition by the following passage on meditation from one of his sermons:

"If but half the precious time we impertinently trifle or squander away upon employments that will be sure to cost us either tears or blushes were carefully laid out in the cultivating of this kind of thoughts, it might often save our ministers the labour of insisting so long upon the uses of their doctrines, when the whole world would be a pulpit, every creature turn a preacher, and almost every accident suggest all use of instruction, reproof, or exhortation. No burial but would toll a passing-bell to put us

* Life of Usher; Society for Promoting Christian Knowledge.

in mind of our mortality, no feast but would make us aspire to the marriage feast of the Lamb; no cross but would add to our desires to be dissolved and to be with Christ; no mercy but would be a fresh engagement unto obedience to so good a master as the author of it; no happiness of others but would prove an encouragement to serve Him that can give that and much greater; no misery of others but would awaken and heighten our gratitude that we are privileged from it; no sin in our neighbours but would dissuade us from it, though it looks so rich and comely in others, nor any virtue of theirs but would excite our emulation and spur us on to imitate or surpass it."

In the year 1656, at the hospitable priory house at Reigate, the mansion of the Countess of Peterborough, this great man, one of the noblest of the ancient light-bearers, was slowly going down into the dark valley, and closing his life of study and effort by the calm, clear, simple expression of personal faith and hope. The last words of one who was so habitually strong in the assurance of an interest in the Redeemer's work, so anxious throughout life to redeem the time for his Master, were, —" O Lord, forgive me ! especially my sins of omission !"

How he had kept open the affections of his heart amidst the din of great controversies in which his mind had been engaged, may be ascertained from his habit of suspending discussion with his friends on difficult points in theology, history, or chronology, by saying, "Come, let us talk a little now of Jesus Christ."

One of the finest spectacles in the course of the succession of spiritual life, is that which is, from time to time, displayed by men with rare intellects and rich acquirements in philosophy, such as Anselm, Usher, Boyle, and Chalmers, becoming as "little children" before the majesty of the divine oracles, using all their mental endowments as aids to faith, and making all that is written there, conducive to the paramount duty of winning mankind to the loving knowledge of the Saviour, and to the vindication of His cause in the world. Never is man so truly great as when he makes himself of no account in order to magnify his Lord; thus decorating the triumphant car of religious progress with the *spolia opima* of his own moral ability, after he has wandered far and gathered much in the realms of mind and matter.

About the year 1620, Hanserd Knollys was passing through the halls of Cambridge as an under-graduate. He was well born, skilled in polite literature, of engaging manners and address. He began work as master of a grammar-school. Having scruples respecting the Prayer-book, he relinquished his charge; but his diocesan allowed him for two years to preach. Embracing Baptist views, he left the Establishment altogether, and for the remainder of his active life of ninety-three years was eminent as a preacher. Driven once to New England, and at another time to Germany; deprived of his property, harassed and worried by persecution; yet he kept up a constant effort and influence to do good, which was combined with much of the power of religion in his own personal experience. He was a warm-hearted, useful, blameless Christian among his fellows, and before the world. Everywhere, and at all times, he preached the Gospel. Frequently, when preaching in Great St. Helen's, in Bishopsgate-street, he would have a thousand hearers. Persecuted by the Presbyterians, interdicted from his favourite occupation, he managed to disobey without creating any uproar. He was a man of learning, goodness, and force of character, notable in his age.

Such was also Kiffin, the London citizen who began life as a child, left an orphan by the Great Plague. A London apprentice without friends, life dawning upon him without any sunshine, he resolved to run away from turbulent John Lilburne, his master. He fulfilled his design, and used his liberty to wander into a church and hear the preacher discourse on the fifth commandment, which had the effect of sending him back to "honest John" again. He went to the church again, and then heard about peace with God through our Lord Jesus Christ: he saw himself as a sinner in need of this provision, and, as yet, knew not how to attain it. He went again, and heard a sermon from the text, "And the blood of Jesus Christ His Son cleanseth us from all sin." He says that he found this sermon to be a great satisfaction to his soul; his heart closed with the offer of these true riches, his fears vanished, his heart filled with love to Jesus Christ. After some years, he began to visit the sick and to exhort the outcasts in the low parishes of the City to turn to God. He was committed to prison for preaching. He became a successful merchant, trading to Holland; amassed a fortune, but still preached, itinerating through the country for the same purpose. Neither the purity of his motives, nor his known attachment to the Government, nor his loans to Charles II., could save him from frequent annoyance. He always avowed and maintained his principles with courage,—interfered for the oppressed, vindicated the character and claims of evangelical religion through a long and troubled life of eighty-six years.

Baxter, in his "Duty of Pastors and People," published in 1643, argues from Acts viii. 1—4, the obligation of preaching to be incumbent on all faithful brethren. From Boyle's Life, we learn that before the Restoration, Sir Harry Vane used to have preaching in his own house, which was thronged to excess on these occasions. After sermon, discussions were held. Vane was doubtless a fanatic in some of his opinions; but the habit then obtaining amongst the educated class, of meeting together to study the highest of all sciences, was surely not fanatical.

Dr. Gouge's Wednesday morning lecture at Blackfriars, continued from 1608 to 1643, was much frequented by citizens, lawyers, and strangers. It was considered that no well-disposed visitor to the Metropolis had completed his business there until he had been to Blackfriars lecture. The worthy lecturer's "Guide to goe to God" was printed in 1626. Its dedication shows the pains-taking care and diligence with which he inculcated the habit of personal devoutness in the families of his large flock.

Philip Henry, who was trained at Oxford at this time, says that the scholars of Dr. Owen, the then chancellor, used to meet together for prayer and Christian conference, "to the great confirming of one another's hearts in the fear and love of God, and the preparing of them for the service of the church in their generation."

Baxter's preaching at Kidderminster at this period was so well appreciated, that the capacious church required to be enlarged by the addition of five galleries. At Dudley, when he preached, the church would be so crowded that people would hang on the windows.* He had enlisted the able laymen in the place to work with him; they went from house to house, promoting prayer and piety. Meetings for Scripture-reading were common. There were about six hundred communicants, out of a church-going adult population of sixteen hundred. The beneficial effects of this vigorous spiritual cultivation continued visible for a century.

The Lord greatly blesses the efforts of such as simply endeavour to make the most of their opportunities for advancing His cause. Such was the case with Mr. Blackerby, the incumbent of Feltwell, in Norfolk, who after his ejection for Nonconformity settled in the village of Ashen, near Clare, in Suffolk, and there spent his time in educating youth, and in teaching, preaching, and lecturing in the surrounding places. He was a man of eminent piety, spirituality, and steady activity. He acted as "ever in his great Taskmaster's eye," and is said to have been the known instrument in the conversion of two thousand persons in his lifetime. He had so carefully cultivated the Christian virtues, that holiness and self-command became, as it were, habitual to him, though none had a more humbling conviction of personal sinfulness and weakness. His happiness lay in the anticipation of the future peace and glory of the Church.

* Orme's Life, vol. i., p. 150.

Like John Newton, he could, and did declare, that for forty years God had not permitted him to have a doubting thought respecting his salvation. He died in 1651.

The literature of the Puritan age betokens a vast amount of religious attainment and religious attention on the part of those to whom these bulky works were addressed. The sermons on which, for the most part, the great treatises are founded, were evidently adapted to the taste of the times. Doctrinal religion was the staple of thought. It gave substance and colour to the age. The exhaustive discursive expositions, which now serve as mines whence we extract golden ore in fragments, were then welcomed by eager and patient listeners. Taylor, Owen, Howe, Baxter, and their compeers, were not content with doing as Tyndale or Bilney would have done,—stating a proposition from God's word, and leave it with the sanction of its divine authority,—but they set it out in all the glory and variety of language, and showed its congruity with the constitution of things past, present, and to come, and then enforced it with the aid of all the considerations that could be brought to bear on our nature.

In 1658, seven of the London ministers formed themselves into a society for publishing works of practical devotion. The names of these good men who were so far in advance of their age were,—Thomas Goodwin, William Greenhill, Sydrael Sympson, Philip Nye, William Bridge, John Yates, and William Adderley. The incipient book society did not long continue its labours; but it was the model of others which occasionally arose and aided in the diffusion of religious knowledge.

Puritan times were characterized by lengthy and elaborate preaching, ponderous and exhaustive treatises on practical divinity, multifarious and minute personal records. It was at once an age of folios and of diaries. Every one appeared to be acting in the presence of the future. The dignity of life was never exhibited so powerfully as in the sayings and doings of these days. All persons were appealing to each other, to their country, to the world, to God. Many diaries have been preserved and published, fragments of many others are still in MS., showing that the current of inner life ran strong in the souls of men.

We have not yet done with persecution. During the Commonwealth, and subsequently, it pressed hard upon the Quakers.

Many instances of genuine evangelical life are to be found in the annals of their society; for though most of the immediate followers of George Fox were much more mystical than evangelical, yet there have never been wanting, whether in the days of persecution or prosperity, bright instances of Friends who have lived a life of faith on the Son of God, "who loved us and gave himself for us." The mode in which their belief consisted with their peculiar action, and the general state of thought and feeling in religious society during the Commonwealth, will best be illustrated by reproducing from John Tomkins's "Piety Promoted, in a Collection of Dying Sayings of many of the People called Quakers: with a Brief

Account of some of their Labours in the Gospel, and Sufferings for the same;"—one whole narrative.

"John Burnyeat was born in the parish of Lows-water, in the county of Cumberland, about the year 1631. And when it pleased God to send his faithful servant George Fox, with other of the messengers of the Gospel of peace and salvation, to proclaim the day of the Lord in the county of Cumberland and north parts of England, this dear servant of Christ was one that received their testimony, which was in the year 1653, when he was about twenty-two years of age: and through his waiting in the light of Christ Jesus, unto which he was turned, he was brought into deep judgment and great tribulation of soul, such as he had not known in all his profession of religion; and by this light of Christ was manifested all the reproved things, and so he came to see the body of death, and power of sin which had reigned in him, and felt the guilt thereof upon his conscience, so that he did possess the sins of his youth. 'Then,' said he, 'I saw that I had need of a Saviour to save from sin, as well as the blood of a sacrificed Christ to blot out sin, and faith in His name for the remission of sins; and so being given up to bear the indignation of the Lord, because of sin, and wait till the indignation should be over, and the Lord in mercy would blot out the guilt that remained (which was the cause of wrath), and sprinkle my heart from an evil conscience, and wash our bodies with pure water, that we might draw near to Him with a true heart in the full assurance of faith, as the Christians of old did, Heb. x. 22.' Thus did this servant of the Lord, with many more in the beginning, receive the truth (as more at large may be seen in the journal of his life) in much fear and trembling, meeting often together, and seeking the Lord night and day, until the promises of the Lord came to be fulfilled, spoken of by the prophet Isaiah, chap. xlii. 7, and xlix. 9, and lxi. 3, and some taste of the oil of joy came to be witnessed, and a heavenly gladness extended into the hearts of many, who in the joy of their souls broke forth in praises unto the Lord, so that the tongue of the dumb (which Christ the healer of our infirmities did unloose) began to speak and utter the wonderful things of God. And great was the dread and glory of that power, that one meeting after another was graciously and richly manifested amongst them, to the breaking and melting many hearts before the Lord. Thus being taught of the Lord, according to Isaiah liv. 13, John vi. 45, they became able ministers of the Gospel, and instructors of the ignorant in the way of truth, as this our friend was one, who, after four years waiting, mostly in silence, before he did appear in a publick testimony, which was in the year 1657, being at first concerned to go to divers public places of worship, reproving both priests and people for their deadness and formality of worship, for which he endured sore beating with their staves and Bibles, &c., and imprisonment also in Carlisle gaol, where he suffer'd twenty-three weeks' imprisonment for speaking to one priest Denton, at Briggham. After he was at liberty, he went into Scotland, in the year 1658, where he spent three months, travelling both north and west. His work was to call people to repentance from their lifeless hypocritical profession and dead formalities, and to turn to the true light of Christ Jesus in their hearts, that therein they might come to know the power of God, and the remission of sins, &c. And in the year 1659 he travelled to Ireland, and preached the truth and true faith of Jesus in many parts of that nation. About the seventh month, 1659, he met with Robert Lodge, a minister, concerned in the same work, with whom he joined, and they laboured together in that nation twelve months in the work of the Gospel, and return'd to Cumberland the seventh month, 1660. And in the year 1662 he travell'd to London, where he met with G. Fox, R. Hubberthorne, and E. Borroughs; and in his returning home thro' Yorkshire, at Rippon, he was committed to prison, and kept fourteen weeks, for visiting the Friends prisoners there, and exhorting them. After he was discharged of that imprisonment, he returned home, where he abode, except visiting Friends in adjacent counties, till the beginning of summer, 1664. He took shipping for Ireland, and visited most meetings in that nation, and from thence embarqued for Barbadoes, in order to his journey into America, which had lain before him for four years past; and from Gallway he arrived at Barbadoes, after seven weeks sailing, and stayed three or four months there, and had great service, and much exercise also, occasioned by the imaginations of John Parrot, and that fleshly liberty he had led many into, not only there, but in Virginia and other places: from whence he went to Maryland, about the second month, 1665, afterwards to Virginia, labouring in the work of the Gospel; and in the fourth month, 1666, came to New York, so to Rhoad Island, New England, and Long Island, till the second month, 1667. He arrived again in Barbadoes, and spent that summer there; and in the seventh month of the same year, arrived at Milford Haven in England, and labour'd much in the Gospel in this nation, from the time of his arrival from America, till the latter end of the year 1666, that he did spend that winter among Friends in Ireland, and return'd to London in the year 1670, and in the fifth month embarqued for Barbadoes again, in company with William Simpson, who died in peace with the Lord in that island; from thence he went to New York, Long Island, Rhoad Island, and New England, and afterwards to Virginia, and Maryland, where he met George Fox, and several brethren, just come from Jamaica; afterwards having spent much time and labour up and down in America, till the 25th of the second month, 1673, they came from the capes of Virginia, and arrived at Gallaway in Ireland, the 24th of the third month, and to the yearly meeting at London, in 1674; and from that time he continued in this nation, labouring among the churches, until the eighth month, 1683. He went to Ireland again, and tarry'd there till the sixth month, 1684; then he came into Cumberland, and so to Scotland, and into the north parts of England again, visiting the meetings of Friends, and so returned to Ireland, the 25th of the first month, 1685, where he tarry'd till he departed this life."

Dissent now took the specific form in which it has subsequently appeared, so far as separation in worship is concerned. Some of the ministers who held livings during the Commonwealth, formed churches within their parishes, composed of persons whom they accredited as godly. They next proceeded further, and constituted those whom they considered to be worthy communicants, though residing in several parishes, into one church, for the sake of convenience. This practice excited the anger of such as held the communion, and other church rites, to be the common property of the parishioners. The controversy was commenced by the publication of an apology for administering the Lord's Supper in a select company, published by the Puritan party; and was continued by William Morice, of Werrington in Devonshire, in a folio overflowing with misapplied learning, entitled "The Common Right to the Lord's Supper asserted in a Diatribe and Defence thereof." The policy of the Establishment clearly required the adoption of the latter practice; the constitution of Non-conforming associations equally necessitated the former; and thus the breach between the two was widened and rendered impassable by a total difference in discipline. One result was, that those parish ministers who had gathered churches independent of their parishes, during their incumbency, found, on their expulsion from the parishes, such churches ready to receive and support them. This was the case with Caryl of St. Magnus, Bridge of Yarmouth, and a number of others; and in this manner originated several of the Dissenting churches which still exist.

CHAPTER XIV.

The Reigns of Charles II., James II., and William III.

It may be an equally instructive task to follow the downward course of a noble institution as to trace its rise, but it is not so interesting. The study of the causes and courses of degeneracy or misfortune is practically useful to all who are under a common liability to their occurrence; but it has neither the zest of novelty, nor the attractions of hope, to recommend it.

The latter half of the seventeenth century is a period of constant decline: great men lost heart. Persecution from avowed enemies would have been in accordance with precedent, but persecution from avowed friends was hard to bear. Faith and patience were, in many instances, unequal to the trial, and embarrassment led to inaction.

The course of the legislation concerning religion was most mischievous. Piety was mocked, profanity encouraged.

The King soon disappointed the hopes he had excited by his declaration in Holland concerning religious toleration.

The Savoy Conference, in 1661, between the Episcopalians who had now returned to power, and the Presbyterians who had been driven from it, was governed by foregone conclusions. In 1662, the Act of Uniformity, and the resulting Bartholomew evictions, deprived the Established religion of two thousand able, conscientious ministers. In 1665, the Act rendering it penal for any gathering of Nonconformists to be held within five miles of a market town, was a blow at the means for sustaining piety in the provinces. In 1669 and 1670, the legislation against conventicles, pressed sorely against the old Evangelicals. The dispensation with these laws, effected by Royal proclamation in 1672, in order to favour Popery, was not satisfactory to any party. In 1675, the Test Act, making the reception of the sacrament in the Episcopalian Church a necessary qualification for office, degraded religion. In 1685, the accession of James II. and the relaxation of penal statutes, with the view of again establishing Popery, was met by the revolt of the bishops, and led to the abdication and change of government in 1689; after which toleration in matters of religion became a recognized principle of our legislation.

The spiritual declension fostered by the course of these political changes commenced at the Restoration, and first manifested itself in the changed aspect of things at Court and in the upper ranks of society. Godliness was again driven into disfavour and obscurity. Concurrently with this, there also began to prevail amongst the public teachers of religion a lower standard of doctrine respecting the divinity of our Lord, and the value of His atonement. This soon produced visible decay in public piety, for it sapped evangelism in its foundations. In the true church all things languished and became withered. We no longer have to encounter lofty souls prepared for service by a lively sense of the presence and favour of God. The race of Latimers and Bradfords, of Lord Falklands and Colonel Hutchinsons, had passed quite away.

The evil result, however, was not reached all at once. Luminaries of former days continued to shine until they set in the clouds which encumbered the horizon.

> " So, when a ship well-freighted with the stores
> The sun matures on India's spicy shores,
> Has dropp'd her anchor and her canvas furl'd
> In some safe haven of our western world,
> 'Twere vain inquiring to what port she went;
> The gale informs us, laden with the scent."

John Howe, the noble, elegant, large-hearted, accomplished preacher and gentleman, familiar with courts, and now to be contemptuously silenced, lived to adorn his adversity with the same deep individual faith which had kept him sober during the days of his prosperity. Before his death, he insisted that all his private biographical memoranda should be burnt; but the following, written on a leaf of his Latin New Testament, reveals the source and nature of his support :—

" Dec. 26, '89.—After that I had long seriously and repeatedly thought with myself, that besides a full and undoubted assent to the objects of faith, a vivifying savoury taste and relish of them was also necessary, that with stronger force and more powerful energy they might penetrate into the most inward centre of my heart, and there being most deeply fixed and rooted, govern my life ;

and that there could be no other sure ground whereon to conclude and pass a sound judgment on my good estate Godward; and after I had in my course of preaching been largely insisting on 2 Cor. i. 12, 'This is my rejoicing, the testimony of a good consience,' &c.;—this very morning I awoke out of a most ravishing and delightful dream, that a wonderful and copious stream of celestial rays, from the lofty throne of the Divine Majesty, did seem to dart into my open and expanded breast.

"I have often since, with great complacency, reflected on that very signal pledge of special divine favour vouchsafed to me on that noted memorable day, and have with repeated fresh pleasure tasted the delights thereof. But what of the same kind I sensibly felt, through the admirable bounty of my God, and the most pleasant comforting influence of the Holy Spirit, on Oct. 22, 1704, far surpassed the most expressive words my thoughts can suggest. I then experienced an inexpressibly pleasant melting of heart, tears gushing out of my eyes, for joy that God should shed abroad His love abundantly through the hearts of men, and that for this very purpose mine own should be so signally possessed of and by His blessed Spirit. Rom. v. 5."

He began public life amidst the broken sunshine of the Commonwealth, became intimate with the Protector, passed through the evil times of the Restoration, saw the Revolution, outlived William III. and ere he died received the poetical laudations of Dr. Watts. The controversies at the beginning of his career were about forms of church government; to these succeeded disputes respecting conformity, at his death the great Trinitarian debate was beginning. These matters successively occupied the minds of great men, to the exclusion of full primary effort for the spread of the Gospel itself. In all the controversies Howe displayed his profound reverence for God and his great love to humanity. He was an anticipator of the evangelical union of better days to come. The very title which he gave to two of the famous sermons preached by him at the Merchants' Lecture in Broad-street, resounds with the music of peace:—"The Carnality of Religious Contention."

Towards the close of the Protectorate there sprung up a desire for Christian alliance among ministers of different denominations, which evinced itself, in the formation of county associations for mutual counsel and prayer. Such were the Worcestershire Association, that of Cumberland, and afterwards, that of Cheshire.

Philip Henry, who promoted the last-named, observes that there was generally a great change in the temper of God's people, and a mighty tendency towards peace and unity, as if they were, by common consent, weary of their long clashings. They expressly agreed to respect each other's judgment as episcopalian, congregational, or presbyterian, but to lay aside, for the present purpose, the thoughts of matters of variance, and to give each other the right hand of fellowship, that with one consent they might each in his place study to promote the common interests of Christ's kingdom, and the common salvation of precious souls.

The warrantable hopes of these good men expressed

in the year 1658, were no sooner formed, than they were doomed to present disappointment, by the effects of the flood of evil which followed in the train of the Restoration.

Most of the considerable London ministers met after the ejection in 1662, and agreed to hold communion with the Church, not quitting their own ministry, or declining the exercise of it as they could have opportunity. Howe, to whom we are indebted for this fact,* says that as far as he could by inquiry learn, this was also the judgment of their fellow-sufferers throughout the nation. Their spirit had, he says, in it "so much of the spirit of primitive Christianity; such largeness of mind! such reverence of what bears a divine stamp and signature upon it, undefaced! such benignity, even towards them by whom they suffered."

A large proportion of the more celebrated Nonconformist ministers was received into the establishments of the nobility and gentry as chaplains and tutors, where they continued to exercise a good influence, and from which compulsory leisure many of their able doctrinal works proceeded.

About a thousand Nonconforming communities were formed throughout the kingdom, exclusive of Papists and Quakers.†

Others of these good men laid down their special function and adopted secular callings. One of these was Dr. Burgess, who became a physician of some eminence: he did not

---

* Considerations on a Preface, &c., Works, p. 186.
† Life of Oliver Heywood, p. 412.

forget his Master's work, and whilst attending the Duchess of Bedford, so coupled spiritual instruction with medical skill, that the lady became a convert to Puritanism, to the great amazement of her gay connexions. The result was, that the good doctor was forbidden to practise within ten miles of the Court.*

The farewell sermons of eleven of the most eminent Nonconformist ministers, which were published soon after the event, give a favourable view of the scope and method of puritanical preaching. With a large discussion of the text, there is a strict limitation to scriptural argument, and a close personal application of the truth. The references to the all-important event of their compulsory secession are, though slight, in a serious tone, without a trace of bitterness. We can recall the full eloquence of Dr. Bates at St. Dunstan's, preaching his last sermon (with Pepys amongst the crowd in the gallery) descanting on the peace which Christ gives to all who believe in Him; and closing in the morning with the earnest request that every one would pray for the peace of Jerusalem; and, in the afternoon, with the fine sayings—" When Christ died for us, it was not His design only to quiet our consciences, but to quicken our souls;"—" The death of Christ, as there was *value* in it to purchase God's favour, so there was *virtue* in it to restore to God's image." † Well does the preface to this unique historical volume commence,—"The sermons here presented, are the words of dying men who did count their

---

* MS. State Paper Office, quoted by Dr. Vaughan, English Nonconformity, p. 73.

† Farewell Sermons.

dayes by hours, and that time lost that was not spent in labour; their busie thoughts out-vyed the labouring sands, because their lives rid on a dial's point, to end at the arrival of an hour." It speaks of the throngs of people attending to hear the discourses.

Some of the silenced ministers were, like Cincinnatus, sought out and recalled in the time of emergency. Soon after the year 1662, a Wiltshire country gentleman upon the dangerous illness of his wife sent for the clergyman of his parish to pray with her. When the messenger reached the parsonage, the minister was just going out with the hounds, and sent word he would come when the hunt was over. Mr. Grove, the distressed squire, expressed resentment at this; whereupon one of his servants said, "Sir, our shepherd, if you will send for him, can pray very well: we have often heard him at prayer in the field." The shepherd was sent for, and asked whether he could pray: he replied with solemnity, looking at Mr. Grove, "God forbid, sir, that I should live one day without prayer." He then engaged in prayer with fluency and fervour. The master was so much struck, that he urged him to tell who and what he was; and the shepherd then owned himself to be one of the ejected ministers, who, having no means of subsistence in the ministry left to him, was content to earn a livelihood as a shepherd. Mr. Grove, who was an opulent, liberal and learned man, erected a house for worship, and constituted the praying shepherd the minister; for he was a graduate of Brazennose College, a good scholar, a Hebraist, a superior preacher, and of so devout a habit that he was called "Praying Ince," and had been rector of Dunhead.*

* Palmer, Noncon. Mem., vol. ii., p. 503.

The spread of spiritual life has ever been intimately connected with the energetic preaching of the Gospel : the former is promoted by the latter, and, in its turn, each contributes to the other. In times of religious persecution, when faith is brought into lively exercise, and the unseen world is a veritable power, it is impossible to repress the ardent efforts of such as feel themselves under solemn responsibility to deliver to their fellow-men the message which God has committed to them concerning the way of salvation. So was it in 1662 : for whilst many of the two thousand retired into private life, or to become teachers in schools, others possessed of great aptitude for preaching could not be silent, but went everywhere proclaiming the old truth, in spite of pains and penalties. One of these was Mr. Oasland, the ejected minister of Bewdley, who travelled throughout Leicestershire, Northamptonshire, Herefordshire, Warwickshire, Worcestershire, Staffordshire, and Shropshire,—and, as he went, preached in a fervent evangelical strain, to the benefit of very great numbers of people, so that his name became a household word for one or two generations. His style would now be called that of a revivalist; and such was the scope of his ministry.

The occurrence of the Great Plague, in 1665, was the occasion of a general religious concern, which was much augmented by the preaching of the ejected Nonconformist ministers, who, in laudable defiance of the strict letter of the law, under circumstances which virtually worked its abrogation, reoccupied the vacant London pulpits. Their services were attended by crowds of attentive hearers ; so great, that the preacher had frequently, it is said, to be lifted into his place over the heads of the people. The attention was universal, the conversions numerous; many of the hearers were among the subsequent victims of the pestilence, but others outlived the dismal period to date their religious awakening to its terrible and yet gracious accompaniments.

In 1666 the desolation produced in the Metropolis by the Great Fire was the means of calling out much evangelical labour, and of developing some indications of that religious union which had appeared to be a possession lost to the church. About twenty of the silenced ministers hired rooms, or provided tents, and, in defiance of the law, recommenced preaching to crowded auditories; the best and ablest of the conforming clergymen also gave extra services : so that religion, like an angel in the storm, came with messages of love and peace to the affrighted sufferers.

Neither domestic calamity, nor political change, had power to arrest the downward tendency of religious faith and practice throughout the kingdom. Much piety doubtless then existed among the quieter sort of people; but it had apparently lost altogether its progressive action. A plaintive tone is assumed by all who speak of it. The Church had lost hope and heart.

A glimpse of the great argument which should have moved the Church of Christ to attempt the conversion of the world is afforded by the preface to Baxter's "Reasons of the Christian Religion," first published in 1666. He says, "There is no more desirable work in the world than the converting of idolaters and infidels to God and to the

Christian faith. And it is a work which requireth the greatest judgment and zeal in them that must perform it. It is a doleful thought, that five parts of the world are still heathens and Mahometans, and that Christian princes and preachers do no more to their recovery, but are taken up with sad contentions among themselves; and that the few who have attempted it, have hitherto had so small success." The venerable man is still thinking in Genevan channels, concluding that the only hope of the world is from the rulers in Church and State. The duty is recognized; but the obligation, as binding upon all who profess the name of Christ, is considered to be practicable only through the high agency of established leaders.

In 1656 he published his "Exhortation to Unity," which was founded on the rules of a voluntary association which he had actually organized amongst the ministers of Worcestershire. He aimed at effecting a general union of all ministers who sincerely professed the common Christianity. Although the scope of the association was confined to ministers, yet the principles avowed would, had they prevailed, have led to a visible union among all true Christians. In 1680, he published again on the same subject, which was, in fact, connected with his lengthened controversy on "Catholic Communion."

The popularity of Baxter's preaching occasioned crowds to follow him in London, to the frequent endangering of the buildings in which he officiated. This is not to be wondered at; for Dr. Calamy tells us that "he talked in the pulpit with great freedom about another world, like one who had been there and was come as a sort of express from thence to make a report concerning it."

In December, 1657, he gave to the world his "Call to the Unconverted," which he had written at the request of good Archbishop Usher. Twenty thousand copies of this treatise were sold in little more than a year from the date of its publication. The conversions which originated through its persual were unprecedented in number. In the preface to this work he thus laments the irreligious tendencies of his age:—"O Lord! how heavy and sad a case is this, that even in England, where the Gospel doth abound above any other nation in the world; where teaching is so plain and common, and all the helps we can desire are at hand; when the sword has been hewing us, and judgment has run as a fire through the land; when deliverances have relieved us, and so many admirable mercies have engaged us to God, and to the Gospel, and to a holy life;—that after all this, our cities and towns, and countries shall abound with multitudes of unsanctified men, and swarm with so much sensuality as everywhere to our grief we see! One would have thought that after all this light, and all this experience, and all these judgments and mercies of God, the people of this nation should have joined together, as one man, to turn to the Lord."

After unwearied and unexampled labours as a theological writer, (extending to about sixty thick volumes,) ere he laid down his pen at the command of his Master, he thus notes the change which time had made by ripening the spirituality of his thoughts and feelings. He says, "In my youth, I was quickly past my fundamentals, and was running up into a multitude of controversies, and greatly delighted with metaphysical and scholastic writings; but the older I grew, the smaller stress I laid upon these controversies and curiosities, though still my intellect abhorreth confusion, as finding far greater uncertainties in them than I at first discerned, and finding less usefulness, comparatively, even where there is the greatest certainty. And now it is the fundamental doctrines of the Catechism which I most highly value, and daily think of, and find most useful to myself and others. The Creed, the Lord's Prayer, and the Ten Commandments, do find me now the most acceptable and plentiful matter for all my meditations. They are to me as my daily bread and drink; and as I can speak and write of them over and over again, so I had rather read or hear of them than of any of the school niceties which once so much pleased me. And thus I observed it was with Bishop Usher, and with many other men."*

The two great voluminous writers of the Puritan age, Owen and Baxter, terminated their literary labours, the one with his "Meditations and Discourses on the Glory of Christ;" the other, with "Dying Thoughts," of the same noble tenor. Fitting close was this of life-long labours for the advancement of Christ's kingdom on earth. Owen's letter to Fleetwood, written the day before his death, is very characteristic of the man:—"I am leaving the ship of the Church in a storm; but while the Great Pilot is in it, the loss of a poor under-rower will be inconsiderable. Live, and pray, and hope, and wait patiently, and do not

* Orme, vol. ii., p. 457.

despond: the promise stands invincible, that He will never leave us nor forsake us."

It is affecting to find him, amidst the strife of tongues in which he himself was a perpetual actor, sighing for some lone mission station amidst the Indians of the Far West, where he could preach Christ without controversy.

It is clear that the best men in all ages have not regarded their lives as their own, but as belonging to God and mankind. They used their faculties for the accomplishment of an end beyond the interests of themselves or their families; they acted and endured in order to establish and exhibit the reign of God on the earth.

The gloomy days of the Bartholomew Act were relieved in the west end of London by the active piety and winning manners of Mrs. Baxter, who was indefatigable in renting, buying, or building, chapels and schools, distributing books, and collecting the poor together to hear the Gospel. When all her efforts to obtain a peaceful shelter for the preaching of her husband were frustrated, she got others, less obnoxious to the rulers to supply the truth she so much loved. She was one of those ardent, active, devoted, winning, accomplished women, whose admirable example has never been wanting, in any period of our history, to grace the progress of the Gospel on the earth. She possessed in an uncommon degree the faculty of attracting people's affection, and, whilst unwearied in her schemes of evangelical philanthropy, did not neglect the cultivation of her own communion with God. Her lot was cast amidst jars and discords, but personally she everywhere brought music and peace.

A period of decadence is often diversified by the occurrence of some rare temporary instance of prosperity, like a rich autumnal flower blooming beyond its time amidst the decays of the fading year. Thus Flavel, who lived on until after the Revolution of 1688, published, during the godless times of the Restoration, his fine treatise on the Soul;—seeking to win the attention of society, by pathos and persuasion, to the great argument concerning the Unseen. The title-page runs thus:—"The Invaluable Preciousness of Human Souls, and the various Artifices of Satan (their professed enemy) to destroy them, discovered; and the great duty and interest of all men seasonably and heartily to comply with the most great and gracious design of the Father, Son, and Spirit, for the salvation of their souls, argued and pressed." His earnestness and eloquence were not in vain: the nooks and corners of South Devon witnessed many a happy transformation in answer to his appeals: but the fervour did not spread,—the frivolity of the age overcame it. In vain he sought to impress society with respect for the presence of God in their midst. They were unworthy of such exquisite remonstrances as the following:—"No man would light and maintain a lamp fed with golden oil, and keep it burning from age to age, if the work to be done by the light of it were not of a very precious and important nature. What else are the dispensations of the Gospel, but lamps burning with golden oil, to light souls to heaven!"*

Some unknown voice, about 1683, thus pours forth the soul's aspiration for a better—that is, a heavenly country:—

* On the Soul, p. 338.

"THE PILGRIM'S FAREWELL. (HEB. XIII. 14.)

"Farewell, poor world! I must begone;
Thou art no home, no rest for me;
I'll take my staff, and travel on,
Till I a better world may see.

"Why art thou loth, my heart? Oh, why
Dost thus recoil within my breast?
Grieve not, but say farewell, and fly
Unto the ark, my dove! there's rest.

"I come, my Lord, a pilgrim's pace;
Weary and weak, I slowly move;
Longing, but can't yet reach the place,
The gladsome place of rest above.

"I come, my Lord; the floods here rise,
These troubled seas foam nought but mire;
My dove back to my bosom flies:
Farewell, poor world!—heaven's my desire.

"'Stay, stay,' said Earth; 'whither, fond one?
Here's a fair world; what wouldst thou have?'
Fair world! Oh no, thy beauty's gone—
A heavenly Canaan, Lord, I crave.

"Thus the ancient travellers,—thus they,
Weary of earth, sighed after thee:
They're gone before,—I may not stay,
Till I both thee and them may see.

"Put on, my soul, put on with speed;
Though the way be long, the end is sweet:
Once more, poor world, farewell indeed!
In leaving thee, my Lord I meet." *

We have again to note that the history of religion furnishes instances in which piety has become hereditary, through a belief in the promise, coupled with correspond-

* Christian Lyrics, p. 277.

ing life and prayer. This was the case in the family of Philip Henry of Broadoak, where, amidst some strictness, rendered necessary by the shameless dissoluteness then becoming common, the household of the Puritan exhibited a notable example of orderly godliness mingled with intelligence and affection. Among the family muniments still in existence, is a series of formal baptismal covenants, each in the handwriting of the child who subscribed it. Matthew Henry in his Life of his father states that he drew up the following form for the use of his children :—

"'I take God the Father to be my chiefest good and highest end.

"'I take God the Son to be my Prince and Saviour.

"'I take God the Holy Ghost to be my sanctifier, teacher, guide, and comforter.

"'I take the word of God to be my rule in all my actions; and the people of God to be my people in all my conditions.

"'I do likewise devote and dedicate unto the Lord my whole self,—all I am, all I have, and all I can do.

"'And this I do deliberately, sincerely, freely, and for ever.'

"This he taught his children; and they each of them solemnly repeated it every Lord's Day in the evening after they were catechized, he putting his Amen to it and sometimes adding. 'So say, and so do, and you are made for ever.'

"He also took pains with them to lead them to the understanding of it, and to persuade them to a free and cheerful consent to it. And when they grew up, he made them all write it over severally with their own hands, and very solemnly set their names to it, which, he told them, he would keep by him, and it should be produced as a testimony against them in case they should afterwards depart from God, and turn from following after Him."

The custom has hardly yet fallen into desuetude, of inserting in long leases of farms, a covenant by the tenant to keep a hawk or a hound for the landlord. The form of such a covenant is still found in the law books. But, so early as the days of our Puritan forefathers, we find an instance in Shropshire, noted by Philip Henry, of a worthy gentleman who, in renewing his leases, inserted, instead of this condition, a covenant obliging them to keep a Bible in their own houses for themselves, and to bring up their children to learn to read and be catechized.

Vavasour Powell, the apostle of Wales, was an eminent instance at this time of active Christian life. Church or chapel, mountain or moor, fair or market,—wherever and whenever it could be done,—he preached Christ with remarkable success, until his death in 1671.

Hugh Owen was a candidate for the Church when the Act of Uniformity passed. Giving up this, he retired on his own little farm in Merionethshire, and spent his life in preaching the Gospel to the country people in that and the surrounding shires. His regular circuit took him three months to complete, preaching as he went. Thus he lived and laboured until 1699,—a fine instance of a man with one purpose, and that purpose concident and identical with his heavenly Master's will.

From an inspection of the scantily-preserved records of

the first formation of Dissenting churches in England in the early part of the seventeenth century, we gather that the founders were men of strong piety, ardent zeal, and blameless life. Circumstances of persecution had called forth from the bosom of society these "village Hampdens" of the Church. They may have attached overweening importance to their own views of church order and discipline, but amidst obloquy and difficulties, they paved the way for the free action of evangelical principles in English society. Some of such communities had existed from the first dawnings of spiritual life in the Reformation, some took their rise from the Separatists of the Elizabethan era; but the greater number sprang from the effects of the Act of Nonconformity in 1662, and were constituted by a people still attached to their ejected ministers and providing for the continuance of their ministrations as the times and circumstances permitted.

When we pursue religion into the holes and corners whither the Bartholomew Act had driven it in the latter half of the seventeenth century, we find numberless cases of bright personal piety. The records of the ejected ministers display not only their self-denial but their goodness. One instance is an illustration of a multitude of others:—For almost twenty years, Mr. Hughes had faithfully filled the incumbency of St. Andrew's, Plymouth. He found the liturgy laid aside, and did not resume it. He was dismissed by royal commission in 1662 for Nonconformity, and sent to the barren limestone rock in Plymouth Sound called St. Nicholas Island, where imprisonment broke his health. When liberated by the kind influence of his friends, he went to Kingsbridge, where he preached for a short time, and then languished and died. His dying testimony was,—"The dead cause of Reformation for which we now suffer shall rise and revive again: salvation shall come to the Churches." Whilst incumbent he had organized clerical meetings of episcopal, presbyterian, and congregational ministers, for mutual support and prayer. After he was silenced, he happened one day to ride into the neighbouring town of Totnes. It was, though unknown to him, the visitation day of the bishop. The clergy of that large archdeaconry were assembled to meet their diocesan. Upon its being known that the silenced Nonconformist was in the town and about to leave again, all the clergymen, save three only, left the bishop, and accompanied the good old man on horseback for a mile out of the town on his homeward way. Such a procession hastily gathering in the narrow streets of the little town, and then defiling over the crown of the hill along the deep lanes by the ruined castle, was a veritable triumph.

The original Nonconformists now begin to disappear from the scene. Persecution had brought into high relief the features of their personal religion. There is a pensive yet hopeful cast in the meditations of the Christian sufferer. In all ages the glorious future of the Church on earth has been his solace. He has felt, too, that the refining process has been a blessing to his own soul, and is a standing necessity for the Church. There is a noble tone, for instance, in the following words expressed by the spiritually-minded Joseph Alleine, after his own release from prison, to one still unjustly suffering:—

"I can tell you little good of myself; but this I can tell you—that the promises of God were never so sweet in this world to me as in and since my imprisoned state. Oh the bottomless riches of the covenant of grace! It shames me that I have let such a treasure lie by so long, and have made so little use of it. Never did my soul know the heaven of a believer's life, till I learnt to live a life of praise, and by more frequent consideration, to set home the unspeakable riches of the divine promises, to which, I trust, through grace, I am made an heir. I verily perceive that all our work were done at once, if we could but prevail with ourselves and others to live like believers; to tell all the world by our course and carriage, that there is such pleasantness in Christ's ways, such beauty in holiness, such reward to obedience, as we profess to believe. May ours and our people's conversations, but preach this aloud to the world: that there is a reality in what God hath promised; that heaven is worth the venturing for; that the sufferings of the present time are not worthy to be compared with the glory which shall be revealed in us!" *

This good man, in his last publication, thus deplores the decay of godliness:—"Friends, it is matter of astonishment to consider how very few lively Christians there are to be found amongst us. Thus we every one talk." †

* Stanford's Alleine, p. 304.
† "Instructions about Heart-work," p. 114.

T

During the indulgence granted in 1672, there was, once more, open and frequent and fervent preaching, in houses and conventicles. Lectureships were established, and for about three years the word of the Lord was again freely disseminated. But a suspicion of the object of government, and a sense of the precarious tenure of the new liberty, clouded the minds of God's people. Nevertheless, there was a commendable amount of activity in the supply of religious teaching,—very much confined, however, to the gathered flocks, and not outward in its scope.

A bright beam of light falls upon the religious condition of the working classes in England from the record of Bunyan's early life. His wife's father was counted for a godly man: though he had no other worldly goods to leave to his daughter, he gave her "The Plain Man's Pathway to Heaven," and "The Practice of Piety." The daughter fondly recounted to her husband, how her father would reprove and correct vice, both in his house and among his neighbours; and what a strict and holy life he lived in his days, both in words and deeds. Although Bunyan himself at this time had no relish for the beauty of holiness, yet the possibility and pattern of it in his own sphere had an attraction for his spirit, which greatly helped him to leave off sinning and turn to the Lord. Another illustration of the same kind is afforded by the well-known incident in his youth, of the godly women at Bedford sitting in the sunshine, discussing the things which concern the kingdom of heaven.

"Upon a day, the good providence of God called me to Bedford, to work at my calling; and in one of the streets of that town, I came where there were three or four poor women sitting at a door, in the sun, talking about the things of God; and being now willing to hear their discourse, I drew near to hear what they said, for I was now a brisk talker of myself, in the matters of religion; but I may say, I heard but understood not; for they were far above, out of my reach. Their talk was about a new-birth, the work of God in their hearts, as also how they were convinced of their miserable state by nature; they talked how God had visited their souls with his love in the Lord Jesus, and with what words and promises they had been refreshed, comforted and supported against the temptations of the devil: moreover, they reasoned of the suggestions and temptations of Satan in particular; and told to each other, by what means they had been afflicted and how they were borne up under his assaults. They also discoursed of their own wretchedness of heart, and of their unbelief; and did contemn, slight, and abhor their own righteousness, as filthy, and insufficient to do them any good.

"And, methought, they spake as if joy did make them speak; they spake with such pleasantness of scripture language, and with such appearance of grace in all they said, that they were to me as if they had found a new world; as if they were 'people that dwelt alone, and were not to be reckoned among their neighbours.'

"At this I felt my own heart began to shake, and mistrust my condition to be naught; for I saw that in all my thoughts about religion and salvation, the new-birth did never enter into my mind; neither knew I the comfort of the word and promise, nor the deceitfulness and treachery of my own wicked heart. As for secret thoughts, I took no notice of them; neither did I understand what Satan's temptations were, nor how they were to be withstood and resisted, &c.

"Thus, therefore, when I had heard and considered what they said, I left them, and went about my employment again, but their talk and discourse went with me; also my heart would tarry with them, for I was greatly affected with their words, both because by them I w s convinced that I wanted the true tokens of a truly godly man, and also because by them I was convinced of the happy and blessed condition of him that was such a one.

"Therefore I would often make it my business to be going again and again into the company of these poor people : for I could not stay away; and the more I went among them, the more I did question my condition; and as I still do remember, presently I found two things within me, at which I did sometimes marvel, especially considering what a blind, ignorant, sordid and ungodly wretch but just before I was. The one was a very great softness and tenderness of heart, which caused me to fall under the conviction of what by scripture they asserted, and the other was a great bending in my mind to a continual meditating on it, and on all other good things which at any time I heard or read of."*

John Bunyan is one of the most vigorous Christian characters enrolled in history. He lived in and for both worlds; the things of time and sense, and the things of eternity and faith, obtained proportionate measures of his

* "Grace Abounding," ch. ii.

sympathy, thought, and care. As a neighbour, friend, counsellor, preacher, teacher, administrator, and author, he shone, without any other effort than the unwearying desire to serve Christ and glorify God.

Very rarely, in the nature of things, can we obtain a glimpse of that fellowship of the Spirit which yet to a large extent, pervades the Church in all ages;—the sympathy which is enkindled by common resources in heaven above, and kept up by common liabilities in the world below. In the MS. records of a small church gathered at Cockermouth in 1676, we read, that on April 14th the congregation met, and spent some hours in prayer for the Church of Christ in New England, on account of troubles by the Indians. So again on the 9th of June: and on the 22nd of September they kept a day of thanksgiving for "God's appearing for his people in New England: 'Blessed be God, who is a God hearing prayer.'"

A pleasant instance do we get of religious friendship from an entry in the diary of Ralph Thoresby, the historian of Leeds, in the year 1692:—

"September 10th, afternoon. Had a letter recommendatory from Lord Wharton, for the eminent Mr. Howe of London; whose excellent company, with the Rev. Mr. Todd's, I enjoyed rest of day; and evening, his assistance in family duty.

"12th, morning.—Enjoyed Mr. Howe's assistance in family prayer; then accompanied him to Pontefract. Lord, preserve him from the danger of his journey, and convey him safe to his own habitation, that he may be continued as a blessing to his nation!"

A more touching one occurred six years afterwards, when Howe thus writes to his venerable friend Spilsbury, the aged Baptist minister, then drawing near his end:—" If I tell thee I love thee, thou knowest it before as to the *quod sit;* but for the *quid sit,* no words can express it; therefore the offer at it is vain. When—when shall we meet above? That will make us pure good company when dulness and sluggishness are shaken off and gone, and we shall be all spirit and life. Cordial salutations from me and mine, to thee and thine. Farewell in our dear Lord: and still remember thy entirely affectionate J. HOWE."

Piety was, however, by no means confined to the illustrious sufferers for conscience' sake who differed from the dominant party. Let it not be supposed that there were not bright lights and loving hearts amongst those who saw not and felt not the necessity for separation.

Let us contemplate the work of Mr. Thomas Gouge, the old vicar of St. Sepulchre's in London. For twenty-four years he preached the Gospel there faithfully, catechized in the church every morning,—instituted industrial reformatory operations, by purchasing a stock of flax and hemp, setting the poor to work, and reclaiming them from poverty and vice. He diligently taught all the children, gave a Bible to every person of age to read it, and required from them an account of their progress. In order to promote education and Bible-reading in Wales, he made an annual journey thither. He established between three and four hundred schools in the Principality, published a large translation into Welsh of the Bible and Liturgy, and distributed them either gratuitously or at a low rate. The house of the Bible Society in Earl-street, and the Ragged School and Reformatory in Field-lane, have appropriately sprung up within sound of the bells of St. Sepulchre.

In fact, the essential identity of Christian doctrine in all ages is paralleled by the close correspondence of Christian action in all time.

In the middle of this seventeenth century, there was a young man of burning zeal and fair abilities passing through the halls of Cambridge,—Thomas Wadsworth. He there formed religious classes among the under-graduates. He became rector of Newington in Southwark by election, and distinguished himself there by carrying out alone many enterprises of mercy in the then scattered suburb, similar to those which have made it renowned in modern times. He preached faithfully and constantly, taught the people from house to house, gave Bibles to the poor, expended his estate and time in works of charity among his parishioners. He was a man of singular ability in work, of good judgment and healthy piety; mighty in prayer, diligent in doing good. After he was ejected by the Bartholomew Act, he still went among the people preaching. Similar testimony might be given concerning hundreds of other good men who pursued the practice of piety and evangelical virtue under difficulties and worldly disfavour.

This similarity of religious action in all times may be discerned in the first formation of Young Men's Christian Associations. In 1632, a number of London apprentices, having no other opportunity for religious conversation save the Lord's Day, united together to meet at five o'clock on Sunday mornings for an hour's prayer and religious conversation, and at six o'clock attended the morning lecture at Cornhill or Christ Church.* In the Life of Dr. William Harris, we find mention of a similar association, meeting once a week for "prayer, reading, and religious conversation ; for the mutual communication of knowledge ; and with a view of strengthening each other against the solicitations of evil company."† This was about 1695.

The course of life in the gay world is sometimes interrupted by the conversion to religion of some eminent votary of fashion. This was the case in the year 1680, when the society of infidel libertines, among whom John Earl of Rochester was ranked as a leader in ability, attainments, and impiety, was startled by the report that he had become a saint. He lay at Woodstock for five weeks, languishing of an illness from which he did not recover. In poignant distress, he repented ; and, as the result of the intelligent direction of his mind to the whole subject, he sought and accepted the mercy of Him whom he had so long ridiculed. The letters and advice of Bishop Burnet, and, above all, the counsels of Mr. Parsons, the evangelical chaplain of his mother, were instrumental to this end. The former gives the following account :—" He said he was now persuaded both of the truth of Christianity and

---

* Wilson's "History of London Dissenting Churches," vol. i., p. 407.

† Ibid., p. 66.

of the power of inward grace, of which he gave me this strange account:—He said, Mr. Parsons, in order to his conviction, read to him the fifty-third chapter of the Prophecy of Isaiah, and compared that with the history of our Saviour's passion, that he might there see a prophecy concerning it, written many ages before it was done; which the Jews, that blasphemed Jesus Christ, still kept in their hands, as a book divinely inspired. He said to me that, as he heard it read, he felt an inward force upon him, which did so enlighten his mind and convince him, that he could resist it no longer; for the words had an authority which did shoot like rays or beams in his mind, so that he was not only convinced by the reasonings he had about it, which satisfied his understanding, but by a power which did so effectually constrain him, that he did after as firmly believe in his Saviour as if he had seen him in the clouds. He had made it to be read so often to him, that he had got it by heart, and went through a great part of it in discoursing with me, with a sort of heavenly pleasure giving me his reflections on it."*

In the year 1671 was published a treatise entitled "The Causes of the Decay of Christian Piety; or, an Impartial Survey of the Ruins of Christian Religion undermined by Christian Practice. Written by the Author of the Whole Duty of Man." It displays on the frontispiece an engraving of a ship at anchor being consumed by fire, and sets forth in lachrymose vein, but in the strongest terms, the degeneracy of the times in relation to religion.

* Burnet's "Life and Death of John Earl of Rochester," p. 82.

sister, describing his first visit to the Metropolis, he writes, in 1680, that the crowd flocking to hear good Mr. Shower preach was so great, that "you could scarce get any room, it was so crowded." Wherever and whenever the clear ring of Gospel truth is heard in the air, it acts as an effectual call-note to the souls of men.

In the year 1682, Traill notices the commencement of the great defection :—" In the beginning of the reformation from Popery, the worthies whom God raised up in several countries did excellently in retrieving the simplicity of the Gospel from the popish mixtures. But that good work took a stand quickly, and is on the declining greatly. How little of Jesus Christ is there in some pulpits! It is seen as to success, that whatever the law doth in alarming sinners, it is still the Gospel voice that is the key that opens the heart to Jesus Christ."*

In 1685, the current of vital godliness is still frequently running in prisons. The father of Dr. Watts, who was persecuted and imprisoned for Nonconformity, writes to his children,—" I charge you frequently to read the Holy Scriptures ; and that not as a task, or as a burden laid on you, but get your hearts to delight in them : there are the only pleasant histories which are certainly true, and greatly profitable ; there are abundance of precious promises made to sinners, such as you are by nature ; there are sweet invitations and counsels of God and Christ to come in and lay hold of them ; there are the choice heavenly sayings and sermons of the Son of God, the blessed prophets and apostles. Above all books and

* Traill's Works, vol. i., p. 247.

writings, account the Bible the best : read it most, and lay up the truths of it in your hearts : therein is revealed the whole will of God, for the rule of man's faith and obedience, which he must believe and do, to be holy here and happy hereafter." *

Dr. Horneck, who died in 1697, was for many years a popular evangelical preacher at the Savoy Chapel. In an age of frivolity and form, he was earnest in his life, pure in his aim, pathetic in his pulpit, loving in his deportment to others, and ingenious in efforts to promote the knowledge of Christ. His church was so crowded, that it was difficult to obtain admission. He was eminently a man of spiritual mind; for, unmoved by the rationalistic tendencies of the current literature, he published in his book entitled "Delight and Judgment," the following noble description of the true pleasures of a Christian, declaring them to flow from "a spiritual delight in God, in a crucified Saviour, and in the blessed effects and influences of the Holy Spirit,—in feeling the operations of the Divine power and glory upon our souls, in the precious promises of the Gospel, in the revelations God hath vouchsafed to mankind, in the good we see wrought in ourselves and others, in the providences of God, and in contemplation of His various dealings with the several states, orders, and degrees of men,—in psalms and hymns and praises of the Divine Majesty—in the thoughts and expectations of a better life—in the treasures which God hath laid up for them that fear Him, in another world, and in the various privileges, prerogatives, and advantages of holy men."

* Montgomery's "Christian Correspondent," vol. iii., p. 178.

The close of the seventeenth century witnessed good Matthew Henry at Chester working to the full extent of man's life-power, in the promulgation of his favourite doctrine. "I am most in my element," he says, "when I am preaching Christ and Him crucified." All that could be done to methodize time, to economize and apply ministerial opportunity, was done by this diligent, able, affectionate man. He catechized, expounded, visited, fasted, prayed, counselled, wrote, preached, with unflagging diligence, and yet maintained a full flow of personal piety and communion with God. He was greatly successful. A credit he would have been to any age, but a particular contrast in his own.

Soon after the Restoration, the Institutions of Episcopius were substituted as a text-book in our Universities for the Institutes of Calvin. Apart from all controversy, this fact is the indication of great deterioration in the standard of religious thought. From the first, there have been evangelical champions on both sides of the everlasting controversy respecting grace and free will. On both sides multitudes of combatants, equally loving and trusting Christ, have ranged themselves. But it is nevertheless a historical fact that vital Christianity has flourished mostly in the times of Augustinism, Jansenism, and Calvinism. When the first declined in the Romish Church, the second in the Gallican, the third in the Anglican, the whole religious power of each body became less effective and its action less scriptural. Religion has been frequently injured by the tactics of the combatants, and by the partial successes on either side. The fashionable

extreme Arminianism which prevailed in high places
after the Restoration, led to a reaction in low places of a
dogmatic, unlovely Calvinism: both have left their blight-
ing influences on succeeding church-growth in our land.
In the present day, the deliverances of Scripture as it
is, are wisely accepted on all hands as the true limits of
religious thought, to the infinite advantage of the common
cause. In the unity of a common work, the labourers find
their individual differences are practically overcome, without being either despised or solved.

> "O could we bear *that* sacrifice,
> What lights would all around us rise!"

The religious publications of the period partook, with
rare exceptions, of the somnolency creeping over the
visible kingdom of Christ. The first age of the Reformation produced controversial writers whose chief employment was the manifestation and defence of the new doctrines
on the basis of holy Scripture. The second age was distinguished by men who strove to vindicate the reform, on
the footing of its accordance with the tenets of the Primitive Church. The third age found the controversy shifted,
for strife had arisen in the reformed camp as to the finality
of the measure. In the first stage, learning was subordi-
nated to personal assurance of salvation; in the second,
both were used together; in the third, personal assurance
no longer appears as the energizing motive. Every page,
for instance, of Tyndale, brings us into acquaintanceship
with the man and his hopes of heaven. Taylor's affluent
sentences show us far less of himself, but introduce a
cloud of witnesses; whilst Tillotson and his contemporaries

leave us altogether strangers to the writers, in regard to their personal, cordial, pervading reception of Christ crucified.

The closing years of the seventeenth century were, however, characterized by some few premonitions of future revival. The Honourable Robert Boyle bears a name which cannot well be left out in any history of the progress of experimental philosophy, and is worthy of still higher commendation in the history of personal religion, for he is the first notable instance of the acknowledgment of those personal obligations for its diffusion which lie at the basis of modern religious manifestations. He not only sustained by his "nursing" letters, and ample contributions, good John Eliot, the missionary to the Red Indians, but attempted, as a director of the East India Company, to connect missionary efforts with mercantile undertakings in the East. He printed 500 copies of the Four Gospels and Acts in Malayalim at his own expense, contributed largely to the Turkish New Testament, printed and distributed tracts in Arabic, had types cast and Bibles printed in Gaelic, and published and distributed the Bible in Welsh. This great man had been converted by the impression made on him whilst a student by a storm at Geneva, and attained to a peace and rest in believing, which, though often tried by intellectual doubts, yet became more and more fixed and operative as life advanced. His works abound in passages which show the workings of the inner life. The following passage, on meditation, will serve as a specimen :— " There is a thing," he says, in one of his pieces, " wondrously wanting amongst us; and that is meditation. If we would give ourselves to it, and go up with Moses into the Mount to confer with God, and seriously think of the price of Christ's death, and of the joys of heaven, and the privileges of a Christian; if we would frequently meditate on these, we should have these sealing days every day—at least, oftener. This hath much need to be pressed upon us; the neglect of this makes lean souls. He who is frequently in that, hath these sealing days often. Couldst thou have a parley with God in private, and have thy heart rejoice with the comforts of another day, even whilst thou art thinking of these things Christ would be in the midst of thee. Many of the saints of God have but little of this, because they spend but few hours in meditation."

There are very few poetical productions between the age of the Commonwealth and that of Watts, which denote the existence of religious experience in the writer. Exception must be made in favour of a popular volume entitled "Spiritual Songs," issued anonymously towards the close of the seventeenth century. The following is a fair specimen of poetry which must have quickened the pulsations of spiritual life in this dull time:—

"JOY IN THE HOLY GHOST.

"There is a stream that issues forth
　From God's eternal throne,
And from the Lamb a living stream,
　Clear as the crystal stone!
This stream doth water Paradise,
　It makes the angels sing:
One cordial drop revives my heart,—
　Hence all my joys do spring.

U

"Such joys as are unspeakable,
   And full of glory too;
Such hidden manna, hidden pearls,
   As worldlings do not know.
Eye hath not seen, nor ear hath heard,
   From fancy 'tis concealed,
What thou, Lord, hast laid up for thine,
   And hast to me revealed.

"I see thy face, I hear thy voice,
   I taste thy sweetest love :
My soul doth leap : but, oh for wings,
   The wings of Noah's dove!
Then should I flee far hence away,
   Leaving this world of sin;
Then should my Lord put forth his hand,
   And kindly take me in."

CHAPTER XV.

The Eighteenth Century. First Part.

PREVALENT contempt for evangelical religion produced its inevitable consequence,—universal degeneracy in morals. Lady Mary Wortley Montague's comic proposal implies the whole truth. Her ladyship suggested that in the next session, Parliament should pass a law to have the word "not" taken out of the Commandments, and "clapped into the Creed;" "the world being entirely *revenue de bagatelle*, and honour, virtue, reputation, &c., which we used to hear of in our nursery, being as much laid aside and forgotten as crumpled ribands."

Prudent men took the alarm: the opening of the eighteenth century witnessed several attempts to ameliorate the corrupt state of things.

The first movement was made by voluntary societies, under high patronage, for the direct suppression of vice. Queen Anne inaugurated one of them; another was formed by and of London citizens; a third, of the City constables, for the due execution of the laws against

Sabbath-breaking and immorality; a fourth, for the impartial discovery and prosecution of evil-doers; and so on, to the number of eight distinct incorporations for similar purposes in the Metropolis alone.

These, not being founded on the sound principle of dealing with the root of the matter, soon fell into formality, and died out.

Another series of societies arose in a different manner, and were somewhat more effective. It appears that, in the year 1667, two pious clergymen in London—the Rev. Dr. Horneck and Mr. Smithies,—preached so pungently as to produce considerable effect, in exciting anxiety respecting religion, in the minds of great numbers of people. Under the influence of this feeling, various small, isolated religious societies were formed in the Metropolis and other places.

In 1699, Dr. Woodward published an account in which he enumerates forty of these associations in and around London. The public progress of spiritual things first showed itself by faithful, simple gospel-preaching; next came the manifestation of personal concern and inquiry respecting the way of salvation; then mutual communication, and meetings for religious conversation and prayer. Thus the first symptoms of the returning current of spiritual life became visible.

These voluntary gatherings were the fosterers and forerunners of the subsequent outflow of religious energy. They were mainly promoted by young persons in whose hearts religion had newly become a power. When Wesley began his work, he everywhere went to these societies, and used them as the first stations in his great movement.

The societies were governed by rules which might be conformed to by any serious, sober-minded person. The non-evangelical character of these regulations proved the causes of the comparative failure, and early extinction of the associations. That burning zeal for the proclamation and prevalence of Christ's Gospel which overleaps the barriers of ecclesiastical topography, was lacking; and hence, though they were the precursors, yet they had not the honour of restoring the fainting religious life of the nation.

The Society for the Propagation of the Gospel was formed in 1701; but the defective theology at this time patronized by the Church of England, effectually neutralized all official efforts at evangelization. The degenerate views of Bishop Bull's "Apostolic Harmony," published in 1669, gained extensive acceptance: the doctrine of justification by faith was displaced; faith and works were to be united as joint conditions; salvation was considered to be a pursuit only, and not as an attainment in any sense, on this side of the day of judgment. King William, in 1695, and King George, in 1721, prohibited anti-Trinitarian teaching; but the prohibitions were ineffectual, and now only serve to indicate the extent of the evil.

Nor was the prospect more attractive in other parts of the field. The original Nonconformist ministers had no successors in the proper sense of the term. The learning and orders which they brought to their work, came to be considered as necessary qualifications. When these could no longer be had, they were substituted by such approximations towards learning and orders, as could be provided by dissenting academies and ministerial ordination. The original positions of the separated congregations, would have led to the selection of ministers, in whom fervid piety and ability to preach, should be the first,—perhaps the only qualifications; but under the influence of a supposed propriety, derived through the good men who had been thrust out of the Establishment, they established a clerical institute of their own, sustained it by the best educational apparatus they could command, produced a few able men, and gave authority to a host of mediocre youths, to monopolize ministerial work, on the ground of their formal training for the purpose. The burning zeal of the Lollard missionary, the lofty self-sacrifice of the Tudor reformer, the great power of the Commonwealth puritan, were lost. All things ran in prescribed channels. Forms, such as they were, usurped the chief place. The doctrine of our Lord's divinity, guarded only by creeds, fell into less prominence, and extensively dropped altogether from the system of many preachers; and with it vital Christianity died out. Aggression was no longer the law of the kingdom. A kind of ecclesiastical stagnation prevailed. General society became eminently anti-religious. Godliness, banished from polite circles, was regarded as an eccentric weakness. Men everywhere became ashamed of Christ; the waters from the wells of salvation, flowed only in secluded dells, hidden from the public gaze. In the midst of the thirty years political peace, there was an absolute decay of all that exalts a nation, or ennobles and blesses individuals.

The voice of Christian song, which has so often heralded the better time coming, did so now. About 1706, Dr. Watts's hymns furnished aliment for the hopeful. In 1709, his "Horæ Lyricæ," prefaced by laboured apologies, proved that evangelical piety might be allied to taste, and that poetry might be found in the neighbourhood of religion. In 1719, he published his versification of the Psalms, which was adapted to the most advanced and joyous state of the Church. Rising above the surrounding mist, like the lark, he greeted the heavens, and sang—

> "Jesus shall reign where'er the sun
> Doth his successive journeys run;
> His kingdom stretch from shore to shore,
> Till moons shall wax and wane no more."

These utterances continued, for nearly half a century, to be in advance of the average amount of religious feeling amongst evangelical Christians. They were certainly far in advance of the style of sermonizing then current.

It was not from want of learning that the preachers of this period failed to lay hold of the public mind, nor was it from want of opportunity, but from the entire absence of *individuality* both in the subject and mode of their addresses. They presented learned disquisitions and able vindications, to minds needing to be interested in elementary principles, to souls needing a personal supply of the knowledge of salvation, to hearts requiring a personal awakening. The feelings were not aroused, affections not engaged; people were tired of being convinced without being persuaded. Fervour and zeal were condemned qualities; spiritual life sank into inanition. In a few places the Gospel was still preached with genial hearty plainness of speech: in these cases it proved to be, as it ever has been and must be, "the power of God unto salvation," and thus life was continued in the land. Watts blamed Doddridge for patronizing the Methodists and Lady Huntingdon; but the affectionate pastor of Northampton saw further than his brethren,—he felt that themes classically correct and chastely polished, were not adapted to accomplish the work of converting the world. Never before had Nonconformity attained so genteel a position as in the times of the first monarchs of the Hanoverian succession, never were its spirituality and usefulness at so low an ebb.

We miss from the picture altogether the public interest in the Gospel. There was nothing like the exhibitions which might have been witnessed at Paul's Cross when Hooper was the preacher; or at St. Margaret's, when Latimer preached; or at St. Mary's at Oxford, when Cartwright had the pulpit, and the sexton was obliged to take out the windows to make more room; or at a meeting-house on the Surrey side of London, in a dark winter morning, when Bunyan preached to thousands; or at the Barbican Chapel, when worthy John Gosnold, an ejected minister, had three thousand stated hearers; or at Bristol, where there were fifteen hundred regular listeners at one chapel, in the later days of Puritanism.

The press was almost equally cheerless in regard to productions of an evangelical spirit, with the exception of the works of Dr. Watts and Doddridge.

The religious literature of the Reformation period, save so far as it dealt with Romanist controversy, was essentially expository. The Bible was used with unquestioning faith. It was felt to be God's truth. Afterwards, when Christian scholars were allowed some breathing-time from persecution, they began to indulge freely in controversy respecting doctrines: as this abated, there arose argumentative discussions touching the evidences. It was fondly hoped by Baxter and others, who opened the defensive batteries of the citadel, that a solid demonstration of the transcendental claims of the Bible and of the world to come, would bear down the stream of frivolity, and create a generation of dignified, thoughtful men. The event did not answer the expectation. The life of God in the soul, is not often kindled by mere study, and real students are always few in this busy world. The noblest considerations concerning God's ways are devoid of interest, until the soul is touched with power from on high. The latter sometimes surprises with its genial glow the earnest scholar, for it is ever the reward of devout research into the oracles of God, but the multitude are wrought upon by fervid, repeated exhortations, and not by the slower process of study.

If standards of orthodoxy could have availed to prevent declension, then the perspicuous, decided Articles of the English church on the one hand, and the full definitions of the Assembly's Larger Catechism on the other, would have prevented the subscribers to the first from becoming Arminian, and the southern partisans of the second from becoming Arian, both which perversions became almost universal in spite of unexceptionable dogmatic forms.

The general decline was quite obvious to the good men who had been trained up in the preceding age. It is difficult to assign a reason for the mournful acquiescence with which many of them regarded it. Some were still found faithful, but no hero arose. We may read in the life of Samuel Harvey, a devoted young London minister in 1722, that, "he took great pains to press upon his hearers the vast importance of the mediation of Christ, and the standing influences of the Holy Spirit, as the great peculiarities of the Christian dispensation, and feared that the want of due regard to them was one great reason of the languishing state of religion, and of the frequent revolts from the Christian interest." *

To the same effect writes Mr. Hayward in 1751, in his correspondence with Dr. Conder :—" I am sorry to find you complain of the state of religion amongst you. Infidelity abounds, and churches grow cold and lukewarm; ministers labour, and in a great measure in vain. It requires courage and resolution now to confess Christ before men : things cannot continue long in the present posture; either there must be a reformation, or some sore judgment." †

Dr. Watts, in the preface to his "Humble Attempt to Revive Religion," published in 1731, laments "the decay

* Wilson's "History of Dissenting Churches," vol. i. p. 87.
† Ibid, vol. iii. p. 109.

of vital religion in the hearts and lives of men, and the little success which the ministrations of the Gospel have had of late for the conversion of sinners." He calls upon "every one to use all just and proper efforts for the recovery of dying religion in the world." Archbishop Secker, in 1738, says, "In this we cannot be mistaken, that an open and professed disregard to religion is become, through a variety of unhappy causes, the distinguishing character of the present age, that the evil is grown to a great height in the metropolis of the nation, and is daily spreading through every part of it."

All contemporary literature bears testimony to the same dismal conclusion. Doubtless the lines of Wesley express the suitable conviction and prayer,—

> "I pass the churches through,
> The scattered bones I see,
> And Christendom appears in view,
> A hideous Calvary.
>
> "Can these dry bones perceive
> The quickening power of grace,
> Or Christian infidels retrieve
> The life of righteousness?
>
> "All-good, Almighty Lord,
> Thou knowest thine own design,
> The virtue of thine own great word,
> The energy divine.
>
> "Now for thy mercy's sake,
> Let this great work proceed,
> Dispensed by whom thou wilt, to wake
> The spiritually dead."

There can be no doubt about this decline of piety in the

dissenting churches in the middle of the eighteenth century, for we have the statement from the ministers themselves. Mr. Barker, morning preacher at Salters' Hall, in a letter to Lady Huntingdon, says:—" Alas! the distinguished doctrines of the Gospel—Christ crucified, the only ground of hope for fallen man,—salvation through his atoning blood—the sanctification by his eternal Spirit, are old-fashioned things, now seldom heard in our churches. A cold, comfortless kind of preaching prevails almost everywhere; and reason, the great law of reason, and the eternal law of reason, is idolized and deified." The Countess replies that " were the Gospel of our adorable Saviour preached in purity and with zeal, the place would be filled with hearers, and God would bless his own word to the conversion of souls. Witness the effects produced by those whom He hath sent forth of late to proclaim His salvation. What numbers have been converted to God, and what multitudes attend to hear the word wherever it is proclaimed in the light and love of it."* Dr. Doddridge testifies to the same effect concerning both the disease and the remedy.

Defoe, in 1712, published his tract entitled, " Present State of Parties in Great Britain, Particularly an Enquiry into the State of the Dissenters," in which he contrasts the degenerate piety and puny religious attainments of the age then coming, with those of the former days. His essay affords a fine description of English Puritanism. He says:—

" Their ministers were men known over the whole

* "Life of Countess of Huntingdon," vol. i. p. 144.

world; their general character was owned even by their enemies; generally speaking, they were men of liberal education, had a vast stock of learning, were exemplary in piety, studious, laborious, and unexceptionably capable of carrying on the work they had embarked in.

"As were the ministers, so, in proportion, were the people; they were conscientious, diligent hearers of the word preached, studied the best gifts, encouraged, but not worshipped their ministers; they followed the substance, not the sound of preaching; they understood what they heard, and knew how to choose their ministers; what they heard preached, they improved in practice; their families were little churches, where the worship of God was constantly kept up; their children and families were duly instructed, and themselves, when they came to trial, cheerfully suffered persecution for the integrity of their hearts, abhorring to contradict, by their practice, what they professed in principle, or, by any hypocritical compliance, to give the world reason to believe they had not dissented but upon a sincerely-examined and mere conscientious scruple.

"Among these, both ministers and people, there was a joint concurrence in carrying on the work of religion: the first preached sound doctrine, without jingle or trifling; they studied what they delivered; they preached their sermons, rather than read them in the pulpit; they spoke from the heart to the heart, nothing like our cold declaiming way, entertained now as a mode, and read with a flourish, under the ridiculous notion of being methodical; but what they conceived by the assistance of the great

Inspirer of his servants, the Holy Spirit, they delivered with a becoming gravity, a decent fervor, an affectionate zeal, and a ministerial authority, suited to the dignity of the office, and the majesty of the work; and as a testimony of this, their practical works left behind them are a living specimen of what they performed among us: such are the large volumes of divinity remaining of Dr. Goodwin, Dr. Manton, Dr. Owen, Dr. Bates, Mr. Charnock, Mr. Pool, Mr. Clarkson, Mr. Baxter, Mr. Flavell, Mr. Howe, and others, too many to mention.

"It will be a sad testimony of the declining state of the Dissenters in England, to examine the race of ministers that filled up the places of those gone before, but more especially the stock springing up to succeed those now employed, and to compare them with those gone off the stage."

The prevalent irreligion attracted the attention of all classes. The House of Commons presented an address to the King on April 6th, 1711, declaring their opinion that the want of churches had contributed to this sad result, and asked for fifty new churches in the metropolis. Public morality was at its lowest ebb. The Duke and Duchess of Marlborough and the famous Robert Walpole were censured and deprived of place for separate systematic plundering and misappropriation of public money. A proclamation was issued, offering a reward of £100 to any one who should discover a "Mohock"—the name given to a set of fashionable brawlers who infested the streets at night, and diverted themselves with maiming and wounding whomsoever they met and could overcome. The political preface to Bishop Fleetwood's sermons was ordered to be burnt in Palace Yard by the common hangman. Duels were frequent and sanguinary. Clubs for the express purpose of promoting blasphemy and irreligion (Hell-fire Clubs) were in vogue. So rapid had been the progress of degeneracy, that all this occurred ere Richard Cromwell, the last of the actors in the previous period, had died. He ended a religious, though inglorious life in July, 1712, in the 90th year of his age.

Lewis, the historian of the English Bible, writing in 1738, says: "Whatever reputation the Holy Bible *has* been had in, it is *now* treated with the utmost slight and neglect, and is scarce anywhere read but in our Churches! So far, too, are many of our modern Christians here in England, from reading this book, meditating on it, and letting the sense of it dwell richly or abundantly in them; that everybody knows, the writings of the most silly and trifling authors are often preferred and read with greater pleasure and delight. What surer sign can be given that we have a name that we live, and are dead?" Yet the weapons were already forged which, in Butler's hands, should vindicate the ways of God to men, and in Wesley's should persuade men everywhere to be reconciled to God through the living, loving Saviour.

Good men had given up all hope of general success for the Gospel; they had consigned to spiritual cloud-land the fulfilment of God's promises to his Church. This was the case even with Doddridge, who lived in advance of his age. His religious affections were warm and demonstrative, his catholicity as wide as possible, his temperament sanguine; and yet, in his personal religious exercises, publications, sermons, and letters, we discover the faintest symptoms only of pity for the wants of an unconverted world. His highest ambition was to be able to furnish a due supply of orthodox preaching to the then existing dissenting congregations. The heroic aspirations and noble presages of former days had departed, and the rushing tide of modern missionary zeal, resounding on every shore,

" Wide as the world is thy command!"

had not yet come.

In Dr. Doddridge's six rules for the government of his ministerial conduct at Kibworth, the 1st, 3rd, 4th, and 6th refer to the maintenance of his own piety; the 2nd to the choice of topics suitable to his congregation: the 5th is, "I will more particularly devote some time every Friday to seek God, on account of those who recommend themselves to my prayers, and to pray for the public welfare—a subject which I will never totally exclude."* The good man speaks of the "*curious* life of Count Zinzendorf," and says of the greatest revivalist of the coming age, "I take Mr. Whitfield to be a very honest, though a very weak man." Dr. Watts writes to Doddridge, "I am sorry that since your departure I have had many questions asked me about your preaching or praying at the Tabernacle, and of sinking the character of a minister, and especially of a tutor, among the dissenters so low thereby." The leading laymen of his

* "Doddridge Correspondence," vol. ii. p. 3.

party also remonstrated with Doddridge on the impropriety of his showing sympathy to any extent with the rising leaders of Methodism.

All this is calculated to give grave warnings concerning ecclesiastical associations of every kind, endowed or unendowed, in respect of the inherent tendency of such bodies to change the promotion of truth into its guardianship, and then to allow the latter to pass into conservancy of form only, and so to become, first coldly affected, and afterwards even hostile, to the fundamental object. The glad welcome given to the free, open proclamation of the Gospel came again once more, not from the great, or even from the good, but arose in shouts from the multitude who had suddenly become awakened into newness of life. Christ was preached throughout the land; and, as in the days of the first Reformation, the ploughman, the smith, the artisan, the shopkeeper, the farmer, the collier, the miner, with here and there a yeoman, a gentleman, and a priest, heard the word with gladness.

Doddridge was on the brink, at times, of departure from the settled modes of action; but during his short life his zealous, diligent soul found enough to do in the particular path before him. In 1742, when he preached in London, it was to "vastly crowded auditories." In 1744 he published his incomparably moving treatise on the "Rise and Progress of Religion in the Soul," a book which has been of signal service to the cause of personal religion. The good men of this period appear to have been unable to benefit the cause of Christ, save by way of legacy.

A bright instance of personal piety was during a quarter of this dull century, from 1720 to 1745, afforded by the brave Colonel Gardiner. The sense of religion which had been kindled in his mind, in a manner truly remarkable, appears to have kept his soul in a continual glow of love and praise to the Saviour, rendering his society elevating and delightful. He first met Dr. Doddridge on the occasion of a sermon preached by the latter at Leicester, on June 13, 1739, from the 158th verse of Psalm cxix., when, after the sermon, one of Doddridge's beautiful hymns (then only existing in MS.), was sung— "Arise, my tend'rest thoughts, arise." This was the commencement of an interesting friendship, to which we owe a memoir which has greatly enriched the Church of Christ. The two good men hailed the news of the revival at Kilsyth with true appreciation of its character; but it did not apparently occur to them that a like blessing might be sought and found elsewhere. The soldier rode on his journeys, loving the communion with God which such solitude permitted; singing as he went the new compositions of his friend,—his two favourite hymns, "Hark the glad sound! the Saviour comes," and "Jesus, I love thy charming name,"—strains well fitted for the raptures of his soul. Doddridge's estimate of his character is worth transcribing, as a good type of a noble, manly, earnest Christian:—"On the whole, if habitual love to God, firm faith in the Lord Jesus Christ, a steady dependence on the Divine promises, a full persuasion of the wisdom and goodness of all the dispensations of Providence, a high esteem for the blessings of the heavenly world, and a sincere contempt for the vanities of this, can properly be called enthusiasm, then was Colonel Gardiner, indeed, one of the greatest enthusiasts our age has produced; and in proportion to the degree in which he was so, I must esteem him one of the wisest and happiest of mankind."*

In the year 1734 William Grimshaw, a Lancashire clergyman of the ordinary type in those degenerate days, a worldly sportsman, without the least sympathy with his work, was attacked by earnest anxiety respecting his own salvation. After a year or two of conflict he became a hearty, ardent, devoted promoter of evangelical doctrine. In 1742 he began to preach on the excellency of faith in Christ, and on salvation by Him alone. It was with great surprisethat he discovered that the way of life he had now entered upon was the good old way of God's people at all times. He went literally from house to house exhorting and warning all concerning the truths of the Gospel; he preached with readiness, liveliness, and fervour. Crowds flocked over the rugged hills to Haworth, which was his parish. He extended his ministrations, and proclaimed the glad tidings constantly, not only in the hamlets of his own parish, but throughout the West Riding of Yorkshire, and even in the houses of the unwilling, if he could overcome their reluctance. Thus he went on for twenty years, preaching fifteen, twenty, or sometimes thirty sermons a week, until the whole country side was thoroughly awakened to the necessity and nature of true religion. He died in 1763, but his influence and his name still survive.†

* Doddridge's "Life of Colonel Gardiner," p. 84.
† Middleton, "Biographia Evangelica," vol. iv. p. 324.

In November, 1729, Charles and John, the sons of Mr. Wesley, the rector of Epworth, went to Oxford to follow their father's footsteps into the ministry. With two others, they agreed to meet three or four evenings in the week to read classics, and on Sunday evening, divinity. In the following summer, one of their friends several times mentioned to them, that he had called at the gaol, to see a man condemned for killing his wife, and that, whilst there, one of the debtors suggested that it would be a good thing for some one, now and then, to come to speak to the prisoners. After some delay the Wesleys went, and were so well satisfied that they appointed to go twice a week. Next, they were asked to visit a sick woman in the town. The success of this step led them to resolve to devote a few hours a week to the occupation, if the consent of the clergyman of the parish could be obtained. Diffident of their own judgments, they wrote to the old rector, their father, for advice; and he warmly and thankfully bade them go on; telling them that in his day he preached to the prisoners at the Castle at Oxford; urging them to be superior to fear, promising to pray for them at the set periods of their duty, and concluded, "accordingly, to Him who is everywhere, I now heartily commit you, as being your most affectionate and joyful father." Opposition, which was soon manifested, led to a formal temperate defence; the controversy became public. The young men were styled the Godly Club, Supererogation-men,—*Methodists*. At this time they were merely conscientious from a sense of duty. The Wesleys went to Georgia. John Wesley, after his return, visited the

Moravians at Herrnhut in search of earnest piety. A sermon preached by Christian David there, first conveyed to his mind correct views concerning the ground of a sinner's acceptance with God, the nature and force of the Atonement. He became a new man. Immediately on his return to England, he began to proclaim freely and fully the abounding grace of God. His journal well shows the upspringing of forces which had recently become dormant in the Church, though vital to the Gospel from age to age. The movement thus commenced has in effect reanimated the whole Christian world, and, we trust, is never again to subside. He writes, in the year 1738,—

"Sunday.—I began again to declare in my own country the glad tidings of salvation, preaching three times, and afterwards expounding the Holy Scriptures to a large company in the Minories. On Monday I rejoiced to meet with our little society, which consisted of thirty-two persons. The next day I went to the condemned felons in Newgate, and offered them free salvation. In the evening I went to a society in Bear-yard, and preached repentance and remission of sins The next evening, at a society in Aldersgate-street. Some contradicted at first, but not long: so that nothing but love appeared at our parting.

"On Monday I set out for Oxford. In walking, I read the truly surprising narrative of the conversions lately wrought in and about the town of Northampton, in New England. Surely this is the Lord's doing, and it is marvellous in our eyes.

"On Thursday, March, 1739, I left London, and in the evening expounded to a small company at Basingstoke.

"Saturday, 31.—In the evening I reached Bristol, and met Mr. Whitefield there. I could scarce reconcile myself at first to this strange way of preaching in the fields, of which he set me an example on Sunday, having been all my life (till very lately) so tenacious of every point relating to decency and order, that I should have thought the saving of souls almost a sin if it had not been in a church."

John Wesley's own testimony to the nature of the Christian life and its counterfeits, is invaluable. He gives it in a letter to one of his correspondents:—

"From the year 1725 to 1729 I preached much, but saw no fruit of my labour. Indeed, it could not be that I should, for I neither laid the foundation of repentance, nor of believing the Gospel, taking it for granted that all to whom I preached were believers, and that many of them needed no repentance.—2. From the year 1729 to 1734, laying a deeper foundation of. repentance, I saw a little fruit. But it was only a little; and no wonder.—3. From 1734 to 1738, speaking more of faith in Christ, I saw more fruit of my preaching and visiting from house to house than ever I had done before; though I know not if any of those who were outwardly reformed were inwardly and thoroughly converted to God.—4. From 1738 to this time, speaking continually of Jesus Christ, laying Him only for the foundation of the whole building; making Him all in all, the first and the last, preaching wholly on this plan—'The kingdom of God is at hand;

repent ye, and believe the Gospel;'—the word of God ran as fire among the stubble; it was glorified more and more: multitudes cried, 'What must we do to be saved?'"

In the year 1739, the first society was formed by John Wesley in London: it consisted, in the beginning, of eight or ten persons, who desired him to spend some time with them in prayer, and to advise them how to flee from the wrath to come. In the same year, a deserted building called the Foundry, in Moorfields, was opened by them for worship; a chapel was built at Bristol, classes formed in that city; and the brothers published their "Hymns and Sacred Poems" for the use of their followers, and the Church Universal.

There was never any obscurity respecting the nature and object of the reform promoted by the Wesleys and Whitefield. It struck at the innermost stronghold of moral evil, and aimed to bring the individual man into a state of peace with God, through faith in the work of our Lord Jesus Christ. It dragged him first to the tribunal of his own conscience for condemnation, next to the bar of God for a confirmation of the verdict, and then opened up to him the infinite love of God in the gift of a Saviour, urging immediate acceptance on the ground of imminent danger. It produced a reform truly radical. Of course there were some persons who counterfeited penitence and peace; but, in the main, genuine spiritual religion has been from the first the product of the movement. John Wesley, in his own succinct and lucid manner, published his opinions at the commencement of his career, and, as is well known, his sentiments have ever been characteristic of his followers. He says, in answer to the inquiry, Who is a Methodist?—

"I answer—A Methodist is one who has the love of God shed abroad in his heart by the Holy Ghost given unto him; one who loves the Lord his God with all his heart, and with all his soul, and with all his mind, and with all his strength. God is the joy of his heart, and the desire of his soul; which is constantly crying out, 'Whom have I in heaven but Thee? and there is none upon earth that I desire beside Thee! My God and my all! Thou art the strength of my heart, and my portion for ever!'" After a statement of Christian disposition and duties, he continues:—"If any man say, 'Why, these are only the common fundamental principles of Christianity!'—thou hast said, so I mean; this is the very truth. I know there are no other, and I would to God both thou and all men knew that I, and all who follow my judgment, do vehemently refuse to be distinguished from other men by any but the common principles of Christianity;—the plain old Christianity that I teach, renouncing and detesting all other marks of distinction; and whosoever is what I preach (let him be called what he will, for names change not the nature of things), he is a Christian, not in name only, but in heart and life. He is inwardly and outwardly confirmed to the will of God, as revealed in the written word."

In the mean time, Whitefield, an equally powerful instrument for resuscitating the decayed spiritual intelligence of the country, had arisen, and was progressing in the same track. He began, at Christmas 1738, by preaching nine times, and expounding eighteen times in one week, in London, being at the same time employed from morning till midnight in conversing with those who called on him for religious advice. On the 17th of February, 1739, he yielded to what appeared to be a necessity, and preached his first open-air sermon to the Kingswood colliers, at Rose Green. A few only attended; but on each repetition of the service the numbers increased, until thousands formed his audience. His own feelings he thus describes:—" As the scene was quite new, and I had just begun to be an extemporary preacher, it often occasioned many inward conflicts. Sometimes, when twenty thousand people were before me, I had not, in my own apprehension, a word to say. But I was never totally deserted. The open firmament above me, the prospect of the adjacent fields, with the sight of thousands and thousands, some in coaches, some on horseback, and some in trees, at times all affected and drenched in tears together, to which was added the solemnity of the approaching evening, was almost too much for me, and quite overcame me."* His journal shows the man and his work:—

" Chepstow, April 7.—Oh, how swiftly has this week passed off! to me it has been but as one day. How do I pity those polite ones who complain that time hangs heavy on their hands! Let them but love Christ, and spend their whole time in His service, and they will find no dull, melancholy hours. Want of the love of God I take to be the chief cause of indolence and vapours. Oh

* " Life of Countess of Huntingdon," vol. ii., p. 359.

that they would be up and be doing for Jesus Christ! they would not complain then for want of spirits.

"May 6.—Preached this morning in Moorfields to about 20,000 people, who were very quiet and attentive, and most affected. Went to public worship morning and evening, and at six preached at Kennington. But such a sight did I never see before. I believe there were no less than 50,000 people; and what was most remarkable, there was an awful silence among them, and the word of God came with power. God gave me great enlargement of heart. I continued my discourse for an hour and a half.

"May 7.—Received several letters of the fruits of my ministry in several places, and had divers come to me awakened, under God, by my preachings in the fields.

"Friday, June 1.—Preached in the evening at a place called Mayfair, near Hyde-park Corner. The congregation, I believe, consisted of near 80,000 people. It was by far the largest I ever preached to yet. In the time of my prayer there was a little noise, but they kept a dead silence during my whole discourse. A high and very commodious scaffold was erected for me to stand upon; and though I was weak in myself, yet God strengthened me to speak so loud that most could hear, and in such a manner, I hope, that most could feel. All love, all glory, be to God through Christ."

When we analyze the effects thus produced, we find the same product, and trace the same power, as have been effected and manifested in all ages of the Church. One case will not only serve as representative of the whole contemporary movement, but will also serve to link this with all other phenomena of conversion. In 1747, a few obscure persons in Barnard Castle, who had heard of the fame of Mr. Wesley, and began to think about the salvation of their souls as their chief personal interest, met together to read the Scriptures, the books which John Wesley had published, to sing hymns, and to pray. This they did nightly, though frequently mocked and disturbed. Among the mockers was a young man named Thomas Hanby. In the midst of his mirth, he felt a secret persuasion that the poor people whom he had been despising were right. He begged to join them, and endured the fate of those who turn from the ranks of the persecutors to those of the persecuted. Finding direct opposition to be unavailing, the clergyman of the parish proposed to him to be at the head of a class for moral reformation. This position he took, and his class soon outnumbered the Methodists. This negative association did not last, and Hanby rejoined the society in the upper room for reading and prayer. He says, " God continued to draw me with strong desires : I spent much time praying in the fields, woods, and barns. Any place, and every place, was now a closet to my mourning soul, and I longed for the Day-star to arise in my poor benighted heart. And it pleased Infinite Mercy, while I was praying, that the Lord set my weary soul at liberty. The next day the Lord was pleased to withdraw the ecstasy of joy, and I had well-nigh given up my confidence ; but the Lord met me again, while I was in the fields, and from that time I was enabled to keep a weak hold of the precious Lord Jesus." *

* "Arminian Magazine," vol. iii.

We have heard similar utterances so often, that they would be properly considered to be conventional, were it not that they have come from solitary hearts utterly unacquainted with each other, and ignorant of any other expressions than those which their own experience dictated. It is not merely the similarity which arises from common agreement or sympathy, but the operation of the same Divine Spirit which worketh all in all.

The reappearance of vital religion at this time did not result from any restitution of forgotten doctrines, but from the newly-awakened concern respecting eternal things produced by fervent Gospel-preaching. The masses of the people were so far gone in insensibility, that the very sense of spiritual things appears to have been practically lost. The world that now is, had succeeded in ignoring the world that is to come. Correct standards of belief were still displayed in some places; but they kindled no attachment or enthusiasm, and were really deserted. There was no extraordinary obloquy, no virulent persecution, but all parties accepted as sound reason, the maxim that worldly-mindedness was the whole duty of man.

Meanwhile, the kingdom of God was coming, not with observation, not in one mode only, not by formal announcement or contrivance, but in its own spontaneous way.

In 1735, Mr. Howell Harris, a Christian gentleman, of Trevecca in Brecknockshire, of good attainments, ardent piety, and ready utterance, began to go from house to house in his own parish, exhorting sinners to "flee from the wrath to come." He next traversed the whole district, read, expounded, and finally preached God's word.

Multitudes flocked to listen; many were converted and saved. In four years he established four hundred gatherings of believers in South Wales. Many ministers joined the ranks: a general itineracy for preaching was established. Again the necessities of the soul broke through human systems. A great revival of religion took place. For twelve years the work progressed. The preaching was in the open air, or in any public building that could be secured. The people then began to build chapels. The first was opened at Builth in 1747.

About the year 1743, a few poor persons in Scotland associated themselves together for a service of prayer for the revival of religion. Mr. Robe, minister of Kilsyth, speaks in this year of thirty societies of young people then existing in Edinburgh for united prayer. The example spread: there were forty-five in Glasgow, others in Aberdeen and Dundee. In October of the next year, 1744, a number of Scottish ministers resolved to promote this method. They fixed a time when, on every Saturday evening, every Sunday morning, and every first Tuesday in the quarter, special prayer should be made for the extension of Christ's kingdom on the earth. They began the holy practice. Before the first season had closed, they felt their hearts so warmed, that they agreed on a memorial on the subject, to be addressed and sent to the Churches of Christ in England and America. This precious document is dated August 26th, 1746. The request was well received, and acted upon. England, Wales, Ireland, and North America responded to the appeal. The reign of apathy had ceased. We are standing over the upburst of the great stream of divine life, which has ever since flowed in augmenting volume.

Another instance, lying quite apart from the currents of public life, is afforded by the case of the Rev. Thomas Adam, the worthy rector of Winteringham, in Lincolnshire. About the year 1740, he was fulfilling his routine of duties with exactness, living so as to satisfy himself and stand well with the world. He became acquainted with the writings of Mr. Law and the mystics. These induced within him the desire for peace with God, but showed him not the way of its attainment. After stumbling for a year or two amidst theological difficulties, consulting commentators in vain, striving for inward satisfaction so strenuously that his friends deemed him to be insane, he emerged into the glorious liberty and divine peace of the Gospel. The process is narrated by his biographer, Stillingfleet, as follows :—" One morning, in his study, being much distressed on the subject, he fell down upon his knees before God in prayer—spread his case before the Divine Majesty and Goodness, imploring Him to pity his distress, and to guide him by his Holy Spirit into the right understanding of his own truth. When he arose from his supplication, he took the Greek Testament, and set himself down to read the first six chapters of the Epistle to the Romans, sincerely desirous to be taught of God, and to receive, in the simplicity of a child, the word of His revelation ; when, to his unspeakable comfort and astonishment, his difficulties vanished—a most clear and satisfactory light was given him into this great subject. He saw the doctrine of justification by Jesus

Christ alone, through faith, to be the great subject of the Gospel, the highest display of the Divine perfections, the happiest relief for his burdened conscience, and the most powerful principle of all constant and unfeigned holiness of heart and life. He was rejoiced exceedingly : he found peace and comfort spring up in his mind ; his conscience was purged from guilt through the atoning blood of Christ, and his heart set at liberty to run the way of God's commands without fear, in a spirit of filial love and holy delight ; and from that hour he began to preach salvation, through faith in Jesus Christ alone, to man, by nature and practice lost and condemned under the law, and, as his own expression is, always a sinner."*

In the year 1739, Mr. Ingham, one of the small clerical Wesleyan band at Oxford, on his return to his native Yorkshire, began to hold religious meetings in his mother's house, at which the neighbours attended, and from which a considerable religious awakening originated. He went to Georgia, afterwards to Germany ; but in 1738 preached with great fervency and power in the populous towns of the West Riding ; and when the churches were denied to him, he went out into the fields, or into barns, and there proclaimed his message, until the whole country rang with the fame of the Gospel, and forty religious societies were formed. A number of lay preachers likewise went out to meet the urgency of the times.

Among those who went to hear the first preaching of the Methodists, was a noble lady, the sister of Lord Huntingdon,—the Lady Margaret Hastings. The truth

* Life of Adam, by Dr. Stillingfleet, 1785.

was blessed to her conversion: she immediately urged her own beloved relatives to seek for themselves the peace which she herself had gained. She found a willing auditor in the young Countess of Huntingdon, her sister-in-law, who was much struck with Lady Margaret's assertion, that "*since she had known and believed in the Lord Jesus Christ for life and salvation, she had been as happy as an angel.*" This gave direction to her thought; sickness gave the opportunity for reflection; God gave the blessing; and thus commenced the foundation of a movement the good effects of which will endure longer than time itself. With characteristic vigour, she first vanquished the moderation of the bishop who was sent to remonstrate and reconvert her, then sent a message of encouragement to the Wesleys, and went herself and took her husband to hear Whitefield.

Some of those who were thus brought to the knowledge of the truth had to endure great domestic persecution: they were compelled to forsake home, with all its attractions; and in many cases, as in that of Lady Anne Frankland, of London, and Mrs. Scudamore, of Bristol, sank under the sorrows of social desertion, broken-hearted, but happy in the assurance of their Saviour's love.* Lady Huntingdon was a member of the first Methodist society formed in Fetter-lane: here she induced Mr. Maxfield (who had been left by John Wesley in charge of the society, and to lead their devotions) to expound the Scriptures, and afterwards to preach; and thus was begun at that time the systematic movement of

* "Arminian Magazine," 1793.

the great engine of lay preaching, which has subsequently acted so considerable a part in the history of the kingdom of God amongst us, in connexion with Wesleyan and Nonconforming organizations. With marvellous inconsistency, her ladyship resolutely opposed the extension of the principle she had thus aided to inaugurate, and brought under the discipline of the Church those who speculated on the possibility of dispensing with orders in the administration of the sacraments.* But though the infant body of revivalists was thus disturbed in relation to ecclesiastical questions, the grand glorious work of preaching and conversion, went on upon a scale and with a success hitherto unknown.

About 1748, Lady Huntingdon began the practice of making progresses through selected parts of England and Wales, accompanied by a considerable staff of able preachers. She travelled slowly, in order that two of the ministers might daily preach in some town or village on the route. Her following absorbed into its ample ranks godly clergymen, and all persons of local eminence who were willing to join in the crusade. Thus armed, she literally attacked the country; and taking possession of market-place, village-green, field, or public place, Whitefield, or Wesley, or Berridge, or one of the fiery Welshmen, or other of her chosen heralds, would declaim with such fervour and force as to give rise to scenes of Pentecostal character. Hymns were sung as they had never been sung before,—sometimes both hymns and music made for the occasion. Never did merry England resound

* See "Life of Countess of Huntingdon," vol. i., p. 35.

to more joyful melodies. Opposition sometimes showed itself; but on the whole the message was well received, and its welcome acceptance laid the foundation of extensive, powerful, religious life.

In the year 1748, the Countess inaugurated a series of remarkable services, which were held in her drawing-room for many years afterwards, and could only have been brought about by such a rare union of talents and opportunities as she possessed. Whitefield was the preacher; Lord Chesterfield, Lord Bolingbroke, and others well known to fame, attended as hearers. It became an established mode of procedure. Her ladyship's ministers were required to obey the welcome call, and urge in the gilded saloons of May Fair, the same great truths which they declared to the thousands in Moorfields, or at the Tabernacle. Many persons were thus converted and instructed in the ways of righteousness; adding thereby to the privileges of an earthly aristocracy, the nobler rank of heirship to God.

The general spread of religion at this time, was much promoted by the step taken by the Countess of Huntingdon, in organizing a system of direct evangelization, by commissioning well-known ministers to go out once a year on a preaching tour. Their services were principally conducted in the open air: the audiences were numbered by thousands. The results were the formation, in many places, of distinct religious communities, and in all places the advancement of Christ's kingdom in the hearts of individual believers. Her ladyship's circular letter on the subject shows the holy simplicity of her aim :—" It appears an important consideration to us, and alike to all, that every means in our power should be engaged for those many thousands lying in darkness and in the shadow of death, that the voice of the Gospel by our faithful ministers should, by every means in our power, reach them also. For this best end it was concluded, at a late meeting, that the only means effectually to reach the multitudes was, that the four principal ministers—Mr. Glascott, Mr. Wills, Mr. Taylor, and Mr. Piercy—should for three months visit universally in four different departments, and, thus severally taken, preach through the towns, counties, and villages of the kingdom, by a general voice or proclamation of the glorious gospel of peace to lost sinners."*

Thus the patriotic idea of a home mission, which Wycliffe had attempted, which King Edward's advisers had commenced, which many a lover of his country had hoped for against hope, was now actually set on foot. Christianity again, as at the first, became aggressive on its own account. Those who thus proclaimed it were free from all bye-ends, and aimed simply and only to bring into play "the power of God unto salvation."

Lady Huntingdon, from her position, combined with the fervour and force of her mind, possessed the power of fusing together the active Christian zeal of the revival period. What joyful meetings there must have been, when Whitefield and Hervey, Wesley and Romaine, Cennick and Lady Frances Shirley, and even the rigid Nonconformist doctors, Dr. Gill and Dr. Gifford, were

* Life, vol. ii., p. 432.

assembled at her ladyship's invitation, and alternately prayed, sang, preached, and conversed together, like persons on the verge of a new golden age of the Gospel! In after days, when many of these good men had become leaders of different regiments in the Lord's army, there were meetings at which, though each rejoiced in the other's welfare, yet they were no longer one; but at the first, the gatherings were like those of the young Church, when "all that believed were together, and had all things common." Such were the days when Whitefield, writing to the Countess Delitz, says of a visit at Lady Huntingdon's,—"We have the sacrament every morning, heavenly conversation all day, and preach at night."

The members of the new society formed in Fetter-lane Chapel (now the Moravian Chapel, Neville's-court, Fetter-lane) comprised the Wesleys, Whitefield, Ingham, Howell Harris, and many others who afterwards became famous as preachers. They sometimes spent whole nights in prayer. Their earnestness, the singleness of their purpose, and the adaptedness of the Gospel message to the souls of men, soon drew a numerous assembly to the constant services.

Many clergymen now caught the holy enthusiasm. Fletcher in Shropshire, Perronet in Sussex, Griffith Jones in South Wales, Berridge in Cambridgeshire, Venn and Grimshawe in Yorkshire, Thompson in Cornwall, and several others, began to work in harmony with the movement.

One of the most effective labourers in the great revival was Mr. Berridge, the vicar of Everton. His decided individuality renders him conspicuous wherever present in the picture. A burning zeal for his Master, resolute determination to preach the Gospel everywhere and at all times, moulded a character in which wit, learning, ready power, and unbounded benevolence were all trained to contribute to the good work. No ecclesiastical bonds or topographical limits were allowed by him to interfere with the great purpose of his life,—the preaching of Christ crucified. "Such was the powerful import and piercing sharpness of this great preacher's sentences, so suited to England's rustic auditories, and so divinely directed in their flight, that eloquence has seldom won such triumphs as the Gospel won with the bow of old eccentric Berridge. Strong men, in the surprise of sudden self-discovery, or in joy of marvellous deliverance, would sink to the earth powerless or convulsed ; and in one year of 'campaigning' it is calculated that four thousand have been awakened to the worth of their souls and a sense of sin." *

The early records of Wesleyanism now begin to furnish augmenting materials for the pleasing picture of spiritual revival. They reveal the sighs and struggles of many a lonely soul panting for peace with God through a reconciling Saviour. As the originators of the great movement passed through the country, they drew out the latent evangelism of society. From persons of gentle birth, down to the factory girl, there were instances in which the advent of Methodism caused the pre-existing embers of spiritualism to kindle into a flame. The hope and faith cherished in the obscure recesses of social life

* "North British Review," vol. vii., p. 324.

came out in open profession and glad acknowledgment. Then, the kindling ardour of sympathy, the contagion of holy fellowship, acted and reacted ; the circle widened every day, until the whole kingdom was aroused as if by an invader.

One of the first helpers in this work was John Nelson, a British stonemason. After his conversion, he felt that as he had the power, so he owed the duty, of making known to others the sufficiency of Christ's salvation. At Christmas, 1740, he returned to his native place. Mr. Wesley narrates the rest :—

"His relations and acquaintances soon began to inquire what he thought of his new faith, and whether he believed there was any such thing as a man knowing his sins were forgiven. John told them, emphatically, that this new faith, as they called it, was the old faith of the Gospel, and that he himself was as sure his sins were forgiven as he could be of the shining of the sun. This was soon noised about, and more and more came to inquire concerning these strange things. Some put him upon the proof of the great truths which such inquiries naturally led him to mention, and thus he was brought unawares to quote parts of the Scripture. This he did, at first, sitting in his house, till the company increased, so that the house could not contain them ; then he stood at the door, which he was commonly obliged to do in the evening as soon as he came from work. God immediately set his seal to what was spoken, and several believed, and, therefore, declared that God was merciful also to their unrighteousness, and had forgiven all their sins. In this manner John Nelson was employed as a teacher of Christianity at this early period. He afterwards extended his labours by preaching during his dinner-hour, and in the week-day evenings as well as on the Sabbath, and in the surrounding towns and villages. By his early preaching many of the greatest profligates in all the country around were changed, and their blasphemies turned to praise. Many of the most abandoned were made sober, many Sabbath-breakers remembered the Sabbath-day to keep it holy. The whole of Birstal wore a new aspect. Such a change did God work by the artless testimony of one plain man; and from thence his word sounded forth to Leeds, Wakefield, Halifax, and all the West Riding of Yorkshire. For preaching, the magistrates interfered, and sent him into the army, where he maintained his integrity, and nobly confessed his Lord." *

The workers multiplied; divisions of creed broke out, but did not quench their ardour or divert their aim from preaching repentance towards God, and faith in our Lord Jesus Christ.

In 1741, Mr. Deacon, a farmer, of Ratby in Leicestershire, working in his field, was told that a man had been preaching in the streets in a village hard by, and was going to preach again. This man was David Taylor, one of Lord Huntingdon's servants, who, being a person of some education and considerable ability and piety, was sent out by the Countess as a village missionary. Deacon laid down his scythe and went to hear Taylor, was struck with the vein of new thought opened up to him, read,

* "Local Ministry," p. 128.

studied and prayed, found peace and joy in believing, became himself a preacher, gathered a flock at Barton-Fabis, which became the mother church of 113 societie in the Midland Counties, now forming the new connexion of General Baptists.

Many from the ranks of life both below and above that of the Leicestershire farmer, and in different parts of England, took a similar course. Some afterwards consorted with the Wesleys, some with Whitefield, others remained unincluded in any organization; but all cared little for party, and much for Christ and the souls of men.

Meanwhile the New World echoed back its welcome. The lofty soul of Jonathan Edwards kindled into enthusiasm under the force of long-pent feelings. With all the perspicuity of his capacious intellect, with all the mighty instinct of intense personal religion, he responded to the address from British Christians by a still more emphatic memorial. The title-page is as the sound of a trumpet addressed to the sleeping host :—"*A* HUMBLE ATTEMPT *to promote an explicit Agreement and visible Union of God's People through the world, in extraordinary* PRAYER *for the* REVIVAL *of Religion, and the Advancement of Christ's Kingdom on Earth, pursuant to Scripture promises and prophecies concerning the last time.*"

CHAPTER XVI.

The Eighteenth Century. Second Part.

SPIRITUAL religion must always, in the nature of things fail to be thoroughly understood by such as are strangers to its power in themselves. "The natural man receiveth not the things of the Spirit of God, for they are foolishness unto him; neither can he know them, because they are spiritually discerned." * But, however this may be, men should at least give each other credit for sincerity. This, however, had ceased to be the case in the early part of the eighteenth century. The progress of degeneracy had been so rapid, that the profession of piety, which before this time had always commanded a kind of respect from the world, now came to be considered as consigning a man to contempt. It was not until after the lapse of nearly a century, marked by the labours of two generations of good men, that evangelical religion was restored to any recognized standing among the forces actuating society. Even at the present time, the irreverent tone in which sacred things are usually dealt with in our periodical literature, is altogether

* 1 Cor. ii. 14.

at variance with the awe and tenderness displayed by the Elizabethan writers on the same topics. It was not until many years after Sir Richard Hill and Wilberforce had avowed it in Parliament, Lady Huntingdon and Lady Glenorchy in the saloons of the nobility, Romaine and Newton in the London pulpits,—Berridge, Whitefield, and the Wesleys to the multitudes,—Hervey and Cowper to the tasteful, Hannah More to the sensible,—that it ceased to be a proscribed topic amongst genteel people. It was usually treated with contemptuous superciliousness by the votaries of fashion, and it is quite ignored in the dismal, soulless literature of those dull, frivolous days.

Nor is the religious landscape brighter in any other direction; for with few exceptions, the darkness had overspread the land, in high and low places alike. The utmost efforts of the leaders of small Nonconformist societies, scattered in provincial towns and villages, could scarcely keep out the chilling frosts of unbelief. There were, among these lowly pastors, some persons of great piety and good parts, who, though lost to the world and uninfluential in the Church, will yet have a niche in the true Temple of Fame. Such a man was old Robert Hall of Arnsby, himself a strong minded Northumbrian, having an afflicted wife and numerous young family, and struggling to uphold God's cause, as his minister, in a village of graziers, in the fat pastures of Leicestershire, with a salary of fifteen pounds a year. Thus he narrates the workings of his soul :—

"I have had in the course of the last year many afflictions, and many mercies, under which I desire to be humble and thankful. O Lord! hear my prayer, and make me holy, and in the enjoyment of Thyself happy. I never before saw such need of the Lord to satisfy my soul. Nothing but God can support me; and were everything in the world quite as I could wish, I find something in me that would be dissatisfied without God as my portion. Lord, keep fast hold of my heart; let it never desert from Thee, or sin against Thee." This was written about the year 1760.

In seeking to trace out the windings of the river of life, we are constantly meeting with proofs of its continuity and freshness. No sooner are its sparkling streams discovered by the needy, than there is a rush towards them. One company after another drinks, and then gratefully proclaims the glad tidings, until the welkin rings with the report. Such an instance do we find in the dark days of 1757, when Mr. Abraham Maddock, a lawyer of mature age, who had become a clergyman, aroused the dormant population in Northamptonshire. For nearly thirty years he preached with fidelity, with what results his own letter to Erasmus Middleton shows:—

"When I came the first Sunday to this place in October, 1773, I had not above twenty, which was the usual congregation. Even the sound of the Gospel was unknown in these parts. The very next Sunday, which was the next time I preached, I could scarcely get into church. In less than two years, viz., June 1775, I built the gallery, for the church would not contain the people. I preached one year at Naseby. God was pleased to work so mightily there, that in that time (for the rector would not let me preach any longer, because the church was crowded) many were converted—how many God knows, but there were so many that they built a meeting-house at Clipson, the next parish to Naseby, because Creaton was too far for them to attend constantly with their families. About eight years ago I was ill six weeks with the gout. My people feared I should die: upon this they built a meeting-house at Guilsborough, and both these places are crowded. As soon as I lost these two congregations, my church was immediately filled with new faces, who before could not get in; so I never missed them; and I am so full, that every Sabbath very many stand in the churchyard under the windows, because they cannot get in even into the porches. But why should you urge me to say more? It was the same at Kettering. It was the same twenty-four years ago, when I left Weston-Favell. Mr. Ryland had above a hundred of my people, and owns at this day that his meeting is greatly indebted to my leaving his neighbourhood. There are four, if not more, who are now Dissenting ministers, who were converted under me, and who, because they could not get ordination in our Church, preach among that people. Three have stated meeting-houses: one in Huntingdonshire, one near Aylesbury in Buckinghamshire, and one in Shropshire. Thus hath God wrought! But if it is boasting, remember you have compelled me to do it, and therefore I hope you will pardon me. But, blessed be God, the best of it is, the work is not yet at an end."*

* Middleton, "Biographia Evangelica," vol. iv.

An "Earnest and Affectionate Address to the people called Methodists" was published by "The Society for Promoting Christian Knowledge, at the Bible and Key in Ave-Mary Lane," and went through several editions. The object of this publication was to recall the Methodists to the sole teaching of the Church, on the ground of its sufficiency and authority. It purported to come "from a person who has been long grieved to see so much honesty and well meaning, as I yet believe and hope to be among you, so greatly imposed upon; to find you ignorantly going on in serving the designs of Enthusiasm, and in giving credit to the most extravagant and groundless Pretences." * But the call "to leave those teachers, who have hitherto deluded you with vain pretences," † fell unheeded; nor did the contemporaneous publication, by the same Society, of various short essays on the practice of devotion, stay the progress of the life-giving Gospel. As old Berridge writes,—"The people who are chiefly loaded with morality are booksellers; and they have got their shops full, but are sick of the commodity, and long to part with it." ‡

In 1754, Henry Venn, who had been passing through the phases of religious thoughtfulness, self-reliance, and penitence, to faith in the work of Christ, became curate of Clapham. He preached fervently and intelligently the doctrines which had given peace and joy to his own soul.

* "Earnest and Affectionate Address," &c., 5th edition, 1751, p. 3.
† Ibid, p. 47.
‡ "Christian World Unmasked."

The enmity which he had to encounter from one party, and the warm attachment of another, soon made it manifest that the truth he proclaimed was calculated to revolutionize society as then constituted. He went to Huddersfield, and impressed the great West Riding with excitement for the Gospel. He then retired to a secluded incumbency near Cambridge, where he was the foster-father of the young men who became famous as the preachers of the next age,—Thomas Robinson, Simeon, and others,—the fathers and founders of the modern Evangelical school of the Church of England. Personally, Mr. Venn fully illustrated the value of the doctrines which he prominently preached.

The self-taught architect of the "Rainbow Bridge," Pont-y-Prydd, over the Taff in South Wales, William Edwards, in addition to his business as farmer and engineer, preached for forty years, from 1750, conveying the truth to successive generations in his native country, earning a reputation for godliness and charity which wore brighter to the last. The example of such a man, undaunted by successive failures at the commencement of his career, triumphing over obstacles and ridicule, rising from obscurity into fame by the exercise of genius and patience, and all the while preserving his modesty, religious fervour, and steady zeal for the diffusion of saving truth, in an age of dull indifference, is truly refreshing.

The contemporaries of such men pitied them as fanatics, and socially persecuted them. They little anticipated that, within a century, legislators and philosophers would come to regard them as the benefactors of their country by their earnest goodness and practical virtues.

The scheme of a formal alliance between all those who love the Lord Jesus Christ, (that ever-recurring ideal in the minds of his followers,) was attempted by John Wesley at this time. He addressed a circular letter to every evangelical clergyman then known, proposing that they should be allied for the purpose of their great work, leaving each free in regard to doctrine and discipline. Finding this fail, he again attempted it, in 1766, among the leaders only: but the times were not propitious; or else there is inherent, and perhaps insuperable, difficulty, in forming into an organization, that which can only exist in the independent action of personal religious conviction.

In 1767, a second outburst of zealous piety occurred in the English Universities. Dr. Stillingfleet, and about a dozen students, formed the band at Oxford, of whom six were expelled from St. Edmund's Hall for the offence of meeting together to read and expound the Scriptures, sing hymns, and pray. At Cambridge, Rowland Hill headed an equal number of similar offenders. Personal devoutness, belief in the necessity and spiritual nature of regeneration, in the duty of preaching the Gospel to the poor, and nonconformity to the worldly habits of the gay crowd around them, constituted the peculiarities which were ridiculed and complained of.

But, notwithstanding the discouragements, the avowed helpers of evangelical religion amongst the ministry of the Church of England began to increase, though still comparatively few. To the isolated instances of the previous fifty years, now succeed the honoured names of the Venns, Grimshawe, Fletcher, Hervey, Romaine, Toplady, and Milner, who all died before the close of the century; after having lived to witness the successful establishment of the great work which had been commenced in the midst of social difficulties and popular opposition.

About this time a retired soldier, of simple, unostentatious piety, settled in a village in the Weald of Sussex. He first admitted his neighbours to attend his family worship, then began to expound the Scripture read by him at these little gatherings; next visited the adjacent hamlets and villages, to speak to the people concerning their souls; then began to preach; and during the remainder of a long and blameless life, statedly announced the glad tidings of the Gospel throughout the scattered villages of the Kent and Sussex Weald. This was George Gilbert, whose name is still honoured by many a ploughman and many a yeoman as the "Apostle of Sussex." He continued his trade as a carpenter and preserved his bearing as a soldier, but ever sought the glory of God in the simple diffusion of the Gospel.

Ere long the battle was rife all over the United Kingdom. Spiritual life was once more openly struggling for the mastery. The resistless artillery of Whitefield, the incessant swift attacks of the Wesleys, occasional sallies of earnest laymen, the continuous fire from the regulars enlisted in the service, the long-withheld sympathy of the Nonconformists, the newly-found boldness of many hidden ones who now came out and gathered around their proper banners, made the whole country, from Caithness to Cornwall, resound with the proclamation of free mercy. Some of the nobility, ladies who had place in Court, men who sat in the Council, promoted the movement. Lady Huntingdon, with a choice band of earnest, fervent preachers, went from place to place, disarming all opposition; so that, by all means and everywhere, salvation through a crucified Redeemer might be practically and plainly offered to the people.

In one of the letters of the pious Lord Dartmouth, written to Mr. Hill probably about the year 1760, he narrates an instance of the pleasure received and given by the discovery of sympathizing fellow-labourers in the Christian cause. "My dear Mr. Hill,—As often as you have any such accounts to give of the experience of a soul made subject to the power of Divine grace, and such indisputable instances to produce of the Holy Spirit's agency upon the soul during its abode in the flesh, your time cannot be thrown away in committing it to paper, both for the satisfaction of your friends, and the benefit of those who may be inclined to dispute the reality of such communications. In return, I can send nothing more agreeable to you than that I left our friends in Yorkshire well the beginning of last week. Mr. —— was there: he had lately been a progress with Mr. Venn into the northern parts of the county, where they saw nothing that gave them so much delight as did the company and conversation of Mr. Conyers, minister of Helmsley, of whose uncommon zeal and extraordinary love to the people who have been converted under him they give a wonderful account. 'You,' says Mr. Venn, 'who are a husband and a father, may know something of the love that he bears to his people by what you feel towards your wife and children.' Till these gentlemen came within his doors, he had never seen the face of a Gospel minister, nor heard a Gospel sermon but from a curate whom he has himself instructed, and to whom his instructions have been blessed. You may guess, then, what was his rapture at the sight of them. He accosted them in the most devout and serious manner, with 'Blessed be my God, who hath sent you to me: who am I, that I should be thus highly favoured?'" *

Whitefield revived the practice of open-air preaching. He began it, in 1777, in Islington Churchyard, where he preached outside the church, because the churchwarden refused to allow him to enter the building, although it had been previously promised to him.

On the eldest son of one of the noblest of England's families,—the Hills of Hawkstone,—becoming the subject of a personal change of heart and life, in 1759, he seized at once the true idea of duty, and became a soldier of the Cross. His own family, the servants, his father's tenantry, the neighbours rich and poor, in gatherings or alone, at all times, in season and out of season, not always with discretion, but always with one aim, suddenly became his opportunity for the proclamation of the glad tidings. A glorious harvest sprang up, with only the discouragements common to all manifestations of Christ's kingdom amongst men. We can read with lively plea-

* Sidney's Life of Sir R. Hill, p. 90.

sure the language in which Miss Hill writes to her brother Rowland, at college, concerning the work : " My dear brother, why should we doubt ? We can never have deserved so much as Christ has merited : justice can have no demand upon the believer. Jesus has discharged *all*. It is true, we have sinned, greatly sinned : but we are assured our iniquities are laid on Jesus ; and shall we suppose that God will demand payment of us also ? These are dishonourable fears. Cleave close to Jesus by faith, and lay hold on the everlasting promise of the Gospel."

The authorities of the University, the dignitaries of the Church, the family at home, all opposed, both by influence and direct authority, the wish of Rowland Hill to become an itinerant : but conviction of duty, and compassion for the souls of men, broke through all obstacles ; and he uttered, as Sheridan said, " red-hot from the heart," those vigorous, homely declarations of Gospel truth which, in all parts of England, soon made his name a household word.

The lapse of a century has consigned to merited oblivion the violent polemics of Toplady ; but the fervour of his exhibitions of personal saving faith in the work of Christ, still shines out in his hymns, to the delight of thousands. The ruling principle of his inner life, is readily ascertained by the aid of effusions such as the following :—

> " Supreme High Priest, the pilgrim's light,
>   My heart for Thee prepare,
> Thine image stamp, and deeply write
>   Thy superscription there.

> Oh, let my forehead bear Thy seal,
>   My arm Thy badge retain,
>   My heart the inward witness feel
>   That I am born again!
> "Into Thy humble mansion come,
>   Set up Thy dwelling here,
>   Possess my heart, and leave no room
>   For sin to harbour there.
>   Oh, give me, Lord, the single eye!
>   I fain would live; and yet not I,
>   But Jesus live in me."

The preaching of a homely peasant in a barn had been the means of Toplady's conversion, at the age of sixteen.

The latter half of the eighteenth century was in Ireland, as in England, the time of extensive religious awakening. Many men arose, like Averell, who, without orders, but with gifts, perseverance, purity, and zeal, went everywhere preaching the Gospel. They found additional joy in the discovery that the doctrines so novel to them, and methods so strange, into which they had been led, were really in accordance with the sentiments and actions of the English reformers. The excitement produced by open-air preaching, was unequalled in the social history of that excitable people. At such times men appear often to go beyond the urgency of the occasion; but it is only thus that the stagnant pools of indifferentism can be lashed into life.

Such instances disprove the modern heresy, that the Anglo-Saxon race alone, will receive and permanently retain the truths of the Gospel. From the day of Pentecost downwards, the Divine life has defied all the divisions of ethnology, and proved its paramount claim to be "the power of God unto salvation, unto *every one* that believeth;" as it proclaims to all the world, "God commandeth all men, everywhere, to repent." Whitefield was equally successful amidst the Danes of Northumberland, the Belgæ of Bristol, the Celts of Cornwall and Wales, or the mixed races of Colonial America. The drawing power of Christ crucified, is equal on all sides of Calvary.

At this time, too, arose a new branch of religious literature,—namely, periodical publications professing to give biographical sketches of individuals distinguished solely for evangelical piety. The "Arminian Magazine," and its more short-lived contemporary, the "Spiritual Magazine," abound in these narratives.

Some of the experiences thus detailed, are those of persons who had long known the happiness of true religion, but who had enjoyed it in secret. They now gladly threw off their reserve, proclaimed the source of their peace, and hailed the advent of Methodism with delight. Others, newly and suddenly converted, hastened to give some fresh aspect of the story of grace, as it affected their personal circumstances. Others had been so dazzled by the great marvel of divine love, that they attributed miracle to the commonest things in connexion with its development in their souls. Many of the accounts are deeply interesting, for the proofs they afford that obedience to the faith of the Gospel gives polish to the rustic, manners to the humble artisan, learning to the ignorant, and dignity to all. Who would have supposed, that society, at this time so apparently lost to all high-souled heroic purpose, contained within its bosom men such as the first Wesleyan local preachers, John Nelson, Thomas Walsh, Lee, Hopper, and many others, who sprang up at the call of their Divine Master, and exhibited powers, patience, and zeal worthy of everlasting remembrance?

Meanwhile, instruments of various kinds were being prepared in different manners, for the service of the Church of the future. Cowper's simple narrative of his own conversion, in 1764, is an instance of one of the thousand wonderful ways in which this was proceeding.

"But the happy period which was to shake off my fetters, and afford me a clear opening of the free mercy of God in Christ Jesus, was now arrived. I flung myself into a chair near the window. Seeing a Bible there, I ventured once more to apply to it for comfort and instruction. The first verse I saw was the 25th of the 3rd of Romans: 'Whom God hath set forth to be a propitiation through faith in His blood, to declare His righteousness for the remission of sins that are past, through the forbearance of God.'

"Immediately I received strength to believe it, and the full beams of the Sun of Righteousness shone upon me. I saw the sufficiency of the atonement He had made, my pardon sealed in His blood, and all the feelings of His justification. In a moment I believed and received the Gospel. Whatever my friend Madan had said to me long before, revived in all its clearness, with demonstration of the Spirit and with power. Unless the Almighty arm had been under me, I think I should have died with gratitude and joy. My eyes filled with tears, and my voice choked with transport. I could only look up to Heaven in silent fear, overwhelmed with love and wonder. But the work of the Holy Ghost is best described in His own words: 'It is joy unspeakable, and full of glory.'

"Thus was my heavenly Father in Christ Jesus pleased to give me the full assurance of faith, and out of a strong, stony, unbelieving heart to raise up a child unto Abraham. How glad should I now have been to have spent every moment in prayer and thanksgiving! I lost no opportunity of repairing to the throne of grace, but flew to it with an earnestness irresistible and never to be satisfied. Could I help it? Could I do otherwise than love and rejoice in my reconciled Father in Christ Jesus? The Lord had enlarged my heart, and I ran in the way of His commandments. For many succeeding weeks, tears were ready to flow if I did but speak of the Gospel or mention the name of Jesus. To rejoice day and night was all my employment. Too happy to sleep much, I thought it was but lost time that was spent in slumber. O that the ardour of my first love had continued! But I have known many a lifeless and unhallowed hour since; long intervals of darkness, interrupted by returns of peace and joy in believing." *

The jubilant, exulting character of the hymnology of this period, is in accordance with the hopeful symptoms of the Church. It is the privilege of poetry to be anticipatory of brighter things to come. The ground of confi-

* Grimshawe's Cowper, vol. v. p. 294.

dence was expressed in one of the hymns of 1760 thus :—

> "Paschal Lamb, by God appointed,
>   All our sins on Thee were laid;
> By Almighty love anointed,
>   Thou hast full atonement made:
> All Thy people are forgiven
>   Through the virtue of Thy blood;
> Opened is the gate of heaven;
>   Peace is made 'twixt man and God."

The clear perception of obligation, expressed by such beautiful hymns as Toplady's "A debtor to mercy alone," and by several others, composed by Doddridge and the Wesleys, current about this time, led to the expression of those high missionary expectations which were not fulfilled until the next generation. The poets were heralds, as they are ever wont to be. Such an announcement do we find made by Wesley in stirring stanzas, now well known:—

> "Blow ye the trumpet, blow
>   The gladly solemn sound;
> Let all the nations know,
>   In earth's remotest bound,
> The year of Jubilee is come;
> Return, ye ransomed sinners, home.
>
> "Jesus, our great High Priest,
>   Hath full atonement made:
> Ye weary spirits, rest;
>   Ye mournful souls, be glad;
> The year of Jubilee is come;
> Return, ye ransomed sinners, home.
>
> "Extol the Lamb of God,
>   The all-atoning Lamb;
> Redemption through His blood
>   Throughout the world proclaim.
> The year of Jubilee is come;
> Return, ye ransomed sinners, home."

And in 1768, by Michael Bruce, in strains that will continue to be appropriate until time 'shall be no more :—

> "Behold the mountain of the Lord
>   In latter days shall rise
> On mountain-tops, above the hills,
>   And draw the wondering eyes.
>
> "To this the joyful nations round,
>   All tribes and tongues shall flow :
> 'Up to the hill of God,' they'll say,
>   'And to His house we'll go.'
>
> "The beam that shines from Zion-hill
>   Shall lighten every land ;
> The King who reigns in Salem's towers
>   Shall all the world command.
>
> "Come, then, O come ! from every land,
>   To worship at His shrine ;
> And, walking in the light of God,
>   With holy beauties shine."

We can trace to its source, the revival of religion in the Established Church in London, which took place towards the end of the eighteenth century. Middleton, writing in 1786, says,—"It is an anecdote which deserves to be recorded, that, between thirty and forty years ago, when only one pulpit in or about the great Metropolis, and that only on a Sunday and Thursday afternoons during Term-time, was accessible for the pure doctrines of the Gospel and of the Church, a certain number of serious persons met at stated times for the sole purpose of praying that God would be pleased, in His mercy to the Establishment, to raise up faithful ministers in it, who should sound forth the Gospel of His grace as in the days of old, when the Establishment was adorned with gracious pastors in all parts of the land, and to give their ministry abundant success. Within a space it pleased God to answer these petitions." *

Writing of the last century, he says,—" In the former part of this century, the Established ministers, who thought themselves bound in conscience and duty to support their own articles by preaching and living, were but thinly scattered over the land. But nearer the middle of the century they became yet more scarce; and before the revival of religion which ensued about forty years ago, an evangelic ministry was hard to be found. Our pulpits sounded with morality deduced from the principles of nature and the fitness of things, with no relation to Christ or the Holy Spirit; all which the heathen philosophers have insisted upon, and perhaps with more than modern ingenuity; and, in consequence, our streets have resounded with heathen immorality. We had flowery language in the Church, and loose language out of it. There was no apparent spirit or grace in the public service; and the private life discovered none. Nay, the people were taught not to expect it, but to esteem everything of a sublime and spiritual influence as enthusiastic and delusive." †

In similar strains writes a contemporary: " All things, serious, solemn, and sacred, are wantonly thrown by, or treated only as proper subjects for ridicule. All that

* " Biographia Evangelica," vol. iv., p. 389.

† *Ibid*, vol. iv., p. 380.

the pert and polite sinner need do now to establish his reputation of wit, and be deemed the hero of all polite assemblies, is to get rid of religion as soon as possible, to set conscience at defiance, to deny the being or providence of God, to laugh at the Scriptures, deride God's ordinances, profane his name, and rally his ministry." *

There had been, however, some admirable exceptions. Mr. Thomas Jones, who died in 1762, after a well-spent life of thirty-three years, was an instance of a man who in private life, and as chaplain of Saint Saviour's, Southwark, sought with singleness of purpose to promote the glory of God in the extension of the kingdom of our Lord Jesus Christ among men. He felt the weight of his own personal indebtedness to his Divine Saviour, and under its pressure employed all his powers in personally and prayerfully commending to others His love and work. Amidst all the rebuffs which such close spiritual efforts is sure to encounter, it is remarkable to what a great extent it is ever ultimately "twice blessed." It is a source of satisfaction to the Christian observer to recollect how many there are who are thus humbly labouring, not under the approving view of men, but as "ever in the great Taskmaster's eye."

About the year 1760, a laborious young schoolmaster, living at Sutton Ashfield, in addition to daily labour in his calling for the support of his family, and to constant village preaching on the Sunday, wrote a treaties which he entitled "The Reign of Grace." He was an obscure and unfriended individual; but the MS. was sent to Mr.

* Monthly Review for 1765—Churchill's Sermons.

Venn, at Huddersfield, who was so much struck with its merit that he rode across the country to the author's residence, strongly urged its publication, wrote a recommendatory preface, and formed an attachment to the writer which endured during their joint lives, though separated in ecclesiastical and local station. The good rector invited Abraham Booth, the Baptist minister, to preach in his kitchen, promising to get him a congregation, which was duly effected.*

Mr. Vaughan, the biographer of the Rev. Thomas Robinson, writing of the state of things at Leicester about the year 1774, says,—"Leicester was at this time in the state exhibited by many other provincial towns, both previously and subsequently, in which pure Gospel light has for a long season been obscured. Religion was a feeble and sickly plant; it consisted for the most part in names and forms, and a sort of pharisaical attendance upon one service upon the Sunday. What little of vital religion there was, appeared principally among the Dissenters."†

About the year 1777, a young engraver of some note in London, being under the influence of strong religious impressions, caught the spirit of awakening Evangelism, and itinerated through the Southern and Midland Counties of England, proclaiming the glad tidings. He was mobbed and scorned, but crowds attended the proclamation; thus vindicating the true character of the Divine message, which, in spite of all that men or devils can do, is still the most popular of all themes. This itinerant was young George

* Life of Booth, prefixed to his Works, vol. i., p. 26.

† Life of the Rev. Thos. Robinson, p. 56.

Burder, who lived to see the flow of evangelical preaching gradually rise beyond it first irregular channels, and become diffused over the whole land.

The inequalities which may temporarily exist in a district as to its state of receptiveness for religion, are quite beyond our ken as to their causes. The fact is one constantly encountered in the history of the Gospel. Thus, Yorkshire and Cornwall received and retained Wesleyanism, more signally than other parts of the kingdom. Cheshire, Lancashire, and Yorkshire were anciently the strongholds of Presbyterianism; the eastern counties, the fortresses of Dissent. Puritanism was always strong in London; the halls of several of the City companies were used as meeting-houses for many years.

Although the foundation-facts and arguments of Christianity are unchangeable, and the identity of the Divine life in all ages and places unquestionable, yet there is no limit to the adaptations by which it becomes a new power, to the individual and to society. All its great organizations, have been successful by an outgrowth in connexion with the peculiar wants and circumstances of the age in which they were set on foot. They have not been struck out perfect at a heat, but welded piecemeal, as the occasion arose. The work of the Holy Spirit amongst men, depends upon the earnest faithfulness of the daily orison, "Thy kingdom come;" and it is given in accordance with the promise, "As thy day, *so* thy strength shall be."

In 1784, the low state of religion in general, affected the hearts of a few Baptist folk, who were holding an association meeting at Nottingham, inducing them to take the novel step of resolving to make common prayer for the bestowment of spiritual influence from on high, that God's cause might thereby be revived. The first Monday evening in every month was recommended for the purpose. The innovation was in accordance not only with the demand of the age, but with the high behests of our Heavenly Father. The practice has prevailed from that time. It was first afterwards adopted by the Midland Baptist Association, and soon became general. In 1789, Sutcliff, a Baptist minister at Olney, republished Jonathan Edwards's tract on the subject of united prayer, with a short preface ending thus:—

"In the present imperfect state, we may reasonably expect a diversity of sentiments upon religious matters. Each ought to think for himself; and every one has a right, on proper occasions, to show his opinion. Yet all should remember that there are but two parties in the world, each engaged in opposite causes: the cause of God and of Satan, of holiness and sin, of heaven and hell. The advancement of the one and the downfall of the other must appear exceedingly desirable to every real friend of God and man. If such in some respects entertain different sentiments, and practise distinguishing modes of worship, surely they may unite in the above business. O for thousands upon thousands, divided into small bands in their respective cities, towns, villages, and neighbourhoods, all met at the same time, and in pursuit of one end, offering up their united prayers, like so many ascending clouds of incense before the Most High!—May

He shower down blessings on all the scattered tribes of Zion! Grace, great grace be with all them that love the Lord Jesus Christ in sincerity! Amen!—JOHN SUTCLIFF. Olney, May 4th, 1789."

The practice of united specific prayer for the increase of Christ's kingdom, thus established, was adopted by the Dissenting Churches, and by the scattered societies of God's people throughout the land, not classing themselves in this category. A bystander, acquainted with the arrangements of the plan of salvation, would have said, "Now the day is at hand!"

It is always pleasant to recollect, that amidst the mazes of the great world, there are by-paths in which piety is flourishing. In the last year of the eighteenth century died one of the most eminent sculptors of his age, John Bacon. He was of a God-fearing lineage: his father seldom sat down to a meal without opening his Bible; he himself preserved, amidst the smiles of the gay world, unsullied personal piety; and his descendants have been blessed with the same characteristics. In rebuke, or rather rectification, of the vain-glorious epitaphs around, his in Westminster Abbey stands out, a testimony for "things unseen and eternal:"—

> "What I was as an Artist,
> Seemed to me of some importance
>   While I lived;
> But,
> What I really was as a believer
>   In Christ Jesus,
> Is the only thing of importance
>   To me now."

Cecil writes of him,—" Occupied with business, exalted by favour, and tempted with wealth, religion still was his grand concern. Animated by this, his family dwelt in a house of daily prayer and spiritual instruction. He even used to visit his workmen when sick, and discourse with them on the important subject that lay nearest his heart: in some instances, when he deemed it proper, he prayed with and for them at their bedside."*

Five years before Bacon's death (1795), Romaine had closed an evangelical ministry of fifty years' duration in the Metropolis, by testifying to his friends around his dying bed, that he then had the peace of God in his conscience, and the love of God in his heart. "I knew before, the doctrines I preached to be truths, but now I experience them to be blessings."

The lights now appearing, become so numerous, that it will be impossible to particularize. God's life in man's soul became a recognized power; one by one, and then many at once, instances of personal piety throughout all parts of the land emerged from the dreary wastes of formalism or indifference. Milner, Newton, Scott, Cecil, the Venns, and others, on the one hand,—and the Wesleys, Fletcher, Booth, Fuller, and a host of others, were the centres of long-continued evangelical influence, under which spiritual life grew and spread apace.

In the year 1793, good Mr. Venn was staying at Bath on a visit to young Wilberforce, who had then recently become the subject of personal religion. The friends visited Hannah More and her sisters, where they saw the

* Cecil, Life of Bacon, p. 42.

home-missionary operations which made the Mendips the scene of Gospel triumphs. They spent several days together in retirement at Perry's Mead. Wilberforce says, in his diary, "Venn with me here a fortnight: he is heavenly-minded and bent on His Master's work, affectionate to all around him, and, above all, to Christ's people, as such. How low are my attainments! Oh, let me labour with redoubled diligence to enter in at the strait gate! An indolent, soothing religion will never support the soul in the hour of death : then nothing will buoy us up but the testimony of our conscience that we have fought the good fight. Help me, O Jesus, and by Thy Spirit cleanse me from my pollutions; give me a deeper abhorrence of sin; let me press forward. A thousand gracious assurances stand forth in Christ's Gospel. I humbly pray to be enabled to attend more to my secret devotions; to pray over Scripture, to interlace thoughts of God and Christ, to be less volatile, more humble, and more bold for Christ." And then, soon afterwards,— "Saturday, August 3rd, I laid the first timbers of my tract."*

His meditation and prayer resulted in the formation of a powerful desire to address his countrymen on the inadequacy of their prevalent notions and practices concerning religion. He states that open and shameless disavowal of religion had then become common, and that, apart from this, few traces of it were to be found; that the public were becoming less and less acquainted with Christianity, whilst improving in every other branch of knowledge.

* Life of Wilberforce, by his Sons, vol. ii.

He discloses the root of the evil by ascribing this to the habit of ignoring the peculiar doctrines of the Gospel. Well did old John Newton pronounce the treatise, "the most valuable and important publication of the age," and say, with grateful fervour, "I accept it as a token for good—yea, the brightest token I can discover in this dark and perilous day."

Concurring with other causes working in other parts of the field, this work indicates the turning-point in the public religious history of our country.

The visits of children to their fathers have always an interest. Simeon, who was now as one of the former, in the course of his travels, went to see the venerable Fletcher of Madely, one of the latter. He introduced himself; the good old man took the hand of his visitor, led him into his house, and, kneeling down, poured forth for him the utterances of his inmost soul. It was Sunday: he asked Mr. Simeon to preach, and then went down into the village with his hand-bell, as was his wont, and proclaimed, "A gentleman from Cambridge will preach this afternoon: be sure you come, and bring everybody you can with you."

The prevalent feeling among the best men of the closing century, may be collected from the writings of Joseph Milner of Hull, one of the soundest promoters of the revival in high places. A tone of apology may still be traced in the composition.

"On a fair examination, we shall find that the principles which in this kingdom have been spreading for about forty years, and have been stigmatized with the opprobrious terms of Methodism or Enthusiasm, are in reality the religion of the apostles and primitive Christians. And a little candid examination will convince any reasonable man that they are no other than those which the Reformers in Germany and England professed, and on which the Church of England is founded. The decline has been so deep with us, and scepticism, profaneness, and an illegitimate and unscriptural charity have been propagated in so general a manner, that the revival of these principles subjects men to the censure of introducing some strange sectarian ideas, though they contain nothing new, nothing particular, nothing different from the creed of the wisest and most intelligent Christians of all ages, nor from the genuine doctrine of the Church. Much pains have been taken to suppress them; persecution has been tried, but the spirit of the times and the lenity of Government have ever rendered it ineffectual. The most indecent publications on the plan of wit and raillery have been attempted; nor has the more reasonable mode of argument been neglected. Yet these principles live and flourish; and every lover of truth will rejoice to find that many of the Established clergy are opening their eyes more and more, and entering into the spirit of the New Testament with increasing ardour. The hand of God also has evidently been with them. . . . Multitudes are reformed, and lead holy lives, wherever these principles prevail. I frankly avow that the recommendation of these principles was the design of this publication. Let it only be allowed that there is such a thing as a divinely revealed religion, that the knowledge and power of it are of infinite importance, and then if any one will still fastidiously refuse these principles a hearing, let him ask himself, where and among what sort of persons he can expect to find the real Christian religion ? If he is not quite buried in profaneness and pride, he will scarce look for it among Arians and Socinians. What! is the Spirit of God with those who degrade the essential dignity of the Saviour, or despise the operations of the Holy Ghost, or explain away the only hope of a sinner—the atonement of the Son of God? Will he look for the Christian religion among the common professors of orthodoxy ? This will, in our days, comprehend a very large part; about forty years ago, it comprehended almost the whole of the Established clergy. But what signature of divine life can be traced among them ? Is there not an evident want of zeal with respect to religion ? not to say among many, a want of any plan or system of ideas at all ? Is there the least spiritual good apparent among them ? Do any in hearing discourses from the pulpit ever obtain any benefit ? Can a single instance be produced, in the course of twenty or thirty years, of a single person reclaimed from vice in consequence of this religion ?

"He must then, if truly serious for his soul, look for the religion of Christ among those who, under God, have of late years been the instruments of the revival already mentioned. And may he look to good purpose! May the dawn of Gospel light, the very best symptom of Divine favour which this kingdom, amidst all its alarming evils, can boast, break out into open day! I would not despair but that even some of the dignitaries of the Church may not only view with more friendly eyes, as they lately have done, but themselves also, with honest zeal, espouse and support the precious peculiarities of Christianity. Devoutly should we pray, that that 'God, who alone worketh great marvels, would send down upon our bishops and curates, and all congregations committed to their charge, the healthful Spirit of His grace!'"*

On the 9th of March, 1796, a youth named Wilson, living at a silk salesman's in Milk-street, London, was engaged in the common congenial occupation of joining, with others, in the general ridicule of evangelical religion. One of the young men ventured an argument in favour of the despised tenets. Wilson denied all personal responsibility, on the ground that he was not elected to eternal life, and that he had no feelings towards God. His opponent merely said, "Then pray for the feelings!" The remark was parried by a jest, but the bolt had sped on its way. The same night, when alone in his chamber, he did pray for the feelings. God heard and answered. His eyes were opened: two days afterwards he sought further instruction from Mr. Eyre, a clergyman of judicious piety; then conferred with John Newton, found peace and joy in believing, became in the course of years vicar of Islington, and died bishop of Calcutta.

The great political gulf which until recently has separated Romanist from Protestant, has prevented justice being done by the latter, to those of the former, whose love and life for the truth have shone forth in spite of the grave

---

* "Reflections on the Life of William Howard," by Joseph Milner, A.M.

errors of their position. Yet such instances have never been wanting: Fisher in King Henry's time, poor Southwell in Elizabeth's days, Gother, Parsons, Leyburn, Godden, Challoner, and others, have continued the holy succession in their church, though scantily yet truly, down to our own times. There have always been persons professing Romanism, who have lived and died in simple reliance on the sacrifice of our Lord Jesus Christ alone, for acceptance with God. They have acquiesced in the existence of a thick veil of human fabrication, by which the precious truth has been all but totally concealed, and have even taken pride in the fancied advantages of their darkened position. They say that it is impossible, that the truths forming the quintessence of the Gospel, should in their church ever be forgotten, because they are inseparably interwoven in symbol with their service and ritual. They claim for the formula of their worship, the merit of embodying the entire substance of revealed truth concerning the atonement and teaching of Christ. Whilst deploring their most serious errors, let us not ignore the instances in which they have individually risen into real fellowship with all who love the Saviour. We, with spiritual advantages, higher because more in accordance, as we deem, with the simplicity that is in Christ, need not deny a welcome to those who, under disadvantages so great, have yet been our unknown companions in the pilgrimage to the better land.

Dr. Hook says that there is room, in the history of religion, for the large exercise of faith and charity. "The Christian believes that whatever may be the outward circumstances of the Church, the Spirit of the Holy God is ever comforting and elevating the unknown souls of thousands who, through the troubled sea of controversy, not unmoved, not without much of care and watchfulness, steer right onward, their compass being an honest heart and upright intentions. A great part of the effects of the Gospel must always remain hidden from the eyes of the majority of men, and can find no place in history. They are not made known to us by biographies of the present age, or the legends of ages past." *

At the close of the eighteenth century we are still rather amongst the germs of things than their expansions. At that time, amidst the turmoil abroad, and the fears at home,—with war raging from Syria to Spain, from Egypt to Ireland,—it would have been deemed fanatical to have predicated for the humble cause of Christ, a vitality and a growth more potent than that of any of the nationalities then conflicting throughout Europe. But amidst all the public alarms, God was silently pressing forward His own kingdom; enlarging its boundaries irrespective of all political partitions and revolutions of empire.

We must briefly retrace our steps to show the history of religious literature for the multitude.

In 1750, a society was formed on the principle of uniting all Christians in the promotion of the Gospel through the agency of the press. It was called "The Society for Promoting Religious Knowledge among the Poor." The labours of the Society were confined to a few districts. It was only one of the preparatives for better times. In 1756,

* "History of the Archbishops of Canterbury," vol. i., p. 335.

similar associations were formed in Edinburgh and Glasgow. It was not, however, until the last fifteen years of the century that successful efforts were made to enlist cheap literature in the diffusion of the Gospel. Miss Hannah More was the most assiduous and influential of the tract writers and distributors. The first of Miss More's tracts were rather moral and political than religious. Mr. Burder, a Dissenting minister at Lancaster, a scholar of Whitefield and Fletcher, conceived that publications more decidedly evangelical might be advantageously distributed. In 1781, he wrote and printed a small tract called "The Good Old Way," in which the fall and redemption of man were proved from Scripture, and stated from the Articles and Liturgy of the Church of England. This tract encountered opposition, which induced the writer to engage in the work with more zeal. He published a series of six, called "Village Tracts," exclusively religious. His bookseller failing, he laid before a meeting of ministers and others a plan for the formation of a publishing society, which was resolved upon at a meeting of forty persons, held on the 9th of May, 1799, at St. Paul's Coffee House, St. Paul's Churchyard.

By this time the editions and issues of the English Bible had become so numerous, that even industrious bibliographers have found it simply impossible to enumerate and distinguish them. The next step in the onward career was the formation of the British and Foreign Bible Society, which belongs to the succeeding century, though it had its origin in the last year of this. The decade of time commencing in 1800 witnessed the formation of great religious associations, and the public avowal of evangelical religion. The realities of the Christian life, which were previously classed with the vagaries of fanaticism, began to be considered as things possessing truth and importance. Henceforth, at least in England, spiritual life is openly treated as an actual feature of society, and as constituting an essential element in the glory which God has bestowed upon our land.

It is true that after the great evangelical revival which characterized the close of the eighteenth century, there was still in the aspect of things, much that was calculated to depress or moderate religious ardour : there were frequent temporary retrogressions. But in all reforms the ultimate wave-mark is below the temporary surf. Whilst watching the latter, we fain hope that it will never recede ; but unerring law requires that it should do so, and we must wait for the *average* of the effects, in order to count the permanent gain.

At the close of the century, an attentive observer would perceive signs that the good ship of the Church was about to sail on a bolder voyage than ever before : with all stores on board, her crew full of courage and hope, the elements propitious, the signal is sounded, "Stand-by!"— and all things are ready for the venture, towards a bright and brightening future.

> " 'Thank God !' the theologian said,
> 'The reign of violence is dead,
> Or dying surely from the world ;
> While Love triumphant reigns instead,
> And, in a brighter sky o'erhead
> His blessed banners are unfurled.

And most of all thank God for this:
The war and waste of clashing creeds
Now end in words, and not in deeds;
And no one suffers loss or bleeds
For thoughts that men call heresies.'"*

* Longfellow's "Tales of a Wayside Inn."

CHAPTER XIX.
Conclusion.

THERE are times in the history of every thoughtful Christian, when he is tempted to question the presidency of God in the affairs of the Church, and even to doubt the existence of a particular Providence. All things within and around us are so much opposed to faith, that the latter is frequently overcome by the current of adverse influences. In the heat of the battle of life, we lose sight of the Commander; the issue of the conflict seems to be doubtful: but we look again, and perceive unmistakeable proofs of His superintendence, and the victory which from the chaos around us, appeared to be lost, is already crowning the distant heights. So, the contemplation of the true history of God's cause on earth, is calculated to restore our fading confidence, and reassure our fainting hearts. If we analyze it, and first separate all that may be attributed to the working of natural laws, the residuum is the direct influence of God the Holy Spirit acting through revealed truth. There have ever been men, who, contrary to the tendencies of society, have truly professed to feel their own sinfulness and helplessness in the sight of God, who in this extremity have heartily sought pardon and aid on the ground of the Redeemer's merits, have realized spiritual communion with God, and have hence derived strength to resist evil and follow that which is good. These are the Christians, and their history is the history of Christianity. Those who blame the Gospel for the follies and vices displayed in ecclesiastical history, show their ignorance of the nature of true religion; for, as Joseph Milner said half a century ago, "the scenes which fill Mosheim's book have no more to do with Christianity than robbers and assassins have to do with good government."

It has been usual to class the religious revivals which have placed our country at the head of the evangelical action of the world, with the great events well known in its secular history, such as the Crusades, the invention of printing, the introduction of Greek literature, the discovery of America, the commencement of inductive philosophy, and the rise of the middle classes. But the origin and succession of spiritual life in England had a source paramount to all these occurrences. It was evidently the product of revealed truth, acting through the quickened consciences of men who sought and obtained Divine guidance. The Word of God and prayer, have been the beginning and continuance of the work throughout.

Formal scholastic theology has a history of its own. The Augustinism of the early converts here, was assailed by Pelagianism: the latter was vanquished, and the former compacted into an artificially complete system. Aristotelian methods prevailed from the time of Alcuin in 736; John Scotus taught it at Oxford in the ninth century, and the great Anselm instructed the whole world in the eleventh. John of Salisbury was a master of the logic current in the next century; and the renowned schoolman Duns Scotus, a Northumbrian, born in 1275, was his successor in the same line. After this, Roger Bacon vainly endeavoured to get rid of the obscurities which had become classical. William Ockham, about 1300, distinguished himself by similar efforts; and then Bradwardine, and his successor John Wycliffe, saw that the soul of theology was better than the body, and by unlocking the Bible opened the way for a flood of light.*

The Church, as a human institution, also has ample records of its own. The ponderous volumes of ecclesiastical history are full of its fierce political struggles.

Piety has a history of its own, written in the endowment-charters and stately fabrics of numberless institutions. The lawyer and the architect are its historians.

But, none or all of these constitute the history of true religious life.

We have attempted to show, that, independently of all surrounding circumstances, there have always been, in our country, persons who have lived in habitual realization of the Divine love through our Lord Jesus Christ; in earnest prosecution of Divine knowledge; in diligent endeavours for its diffusion; in newness of life towards God and man; in hearty enjoyment of Divine favour; in firm hope of the Divine inheritance. We leave to others the grateful task of demonstrating the secondary

* See Tennemann, "Manual of the History of Philosophy, Second Period."

blessings of spiritual life, in its effect on society. We claim for it, on the ground of recorded facts, the character of being true to its profession : *"To be spiritually-minded, is life and peace."*

The history of religion, too, bears internal proof of its relation to time. It had a beginning, and is developing a progress towards a consummation. Its earthly career is evidently limited to the partial accomplishment of its glorious mission. In its present phase it is not intended to be the perpetual condition of a permanent commonwealth : heaven is the home of its complete unfolding.

We see the direction in which things are tending, the constellation in the skies towards which the whole system is travelling. We can prove that the progress is not by natural selection, nor by the mere outworking of implanted properties.

But the rate of progress is not for us to know, the dial-plate of eternity is not legible from our present platform. Yet, there are some waymarks. We may usefully learn what stations we have left behind, and lawfully inquire what others are still to come. We ask with the prophet, "O Lord, what shall the end of these things be?" The coming voices announce to us the consolation vouchsafed in former days to the same question: "Go thou thy way till the end be; for thou shalt rest, and stand in thy lot at the end of the days."*

It is the known, and not the unknown, that is to guide our conduct and be the ground of our peace. Nor let the never-ending, still-beginning character of the work

* Daniel xii. 8.

appal us. So long as the field is the world, there will always be stony ground, and always an enemy to sow tares among the wheat. The condition of spiritual life, is the same as that of natural and commercial life, in so far as it is a competition for existence and progression. The struggle is necessitated by the present constitution of things. Doubtless, it is the best possible discipline for us, in both our degenerate and regenerate state on earth. We know that continuous powerful help is promised,—"Lo, I am with you always, even unto the end of the world,"—and, that ultimate success is guaranteed,—"Be of good cheer; I have overcome the world."

But will it always be, that the cry of the godly on earth, shall partake more of the plaintive than of the triumphant? This is, at least, the experience of the past. At first their complaint was, that the world would not receive the Divine message; next, that the people would not heed it; then, that the adversaries raged; afterwards, that unspiritualism prevailed. Yet the kingdom extends, spiritualism spreads more and more. The number of evangelical men is augmented every year. Each generation surpasses in some respects its predecessor. True it is, that sanguine Christians do not find their fond anticipations realized, and often retire from the scene at the end of their career with the air of defeat; but in other quarters the cause is advancing amidst songs of victory.

The fifteenth century was the age of the undergrowth of evangelical doctrine; the sixteenth, that of its manifestation: the seventeenth century witnessed a similar undergrowth of sentiment concerning the constitution and place of the Church; and the eighteenth, a corresponding manifestation. It may be that the nineteenth century will be characterized by the establishment of such relations between the inner truth and its outward forms, that the earthly variations of the latter shall no longer by their antagonism mar the heavenly beauty of the former; but everything, in and around the Church, shall proclaim to angels and men, "the manifold wisdom of God."

www.ingramcontent.com/pod-product-compliance
Lightning Source LLC
Chambersburg PA
CBHW030403230426
43664CB00007BB/718